Harvard Economic Studies

Volume 134

Awarded the David A. Wells Prize for the year 1968–69 and published from the income of the David A. Wells Fund.

The studies in this series are published by the Department of Economics of Harvard University. The Department does not assume responsibility for the views expressed.

Development Alternatives in Pakistan

A Multisectoral
and Regional
Analysis
of
Planning Problems

Arthur MacEwan

Harvard University Press
Cambridge, Massachusetts
1971

Preface

This book deals with development alternatives in the rather narrow sense of alternative sectoral and regional allocation programs. The book does not examine the more basic development alternatives that face Pakistan and other poor countries, namely, the alternative systems of social-political-economic organization.

The narrow scope of the book and the use of a formal planning model as the principle tool of analysis may lead the reader to infer incorrectly that the process of economic planning is essentially independent of social organization. That is, regardless of the social-political-economic system there are certain techniques that may be applied and rules of operation that may be developed which lead toward a socially optimal and efficient use of resources. The difference between systems, it might be concluded, lies only in the method by which a plan is implemented.

Such a view of planning and social organization seems to me to be implicit in much of the literature—especially the planning model and programming model literature—on development planning. This book does not provide an exception. Nonetheless, in my opinion, one cannot speak of planning as independent of social organization. For example, the very concepts of "socially optimal" and "efficient" cannot be defined independently of social forces. In a society divided by class barriers, groups stand in conflict with one another; their positions cannot be reconciled under some vague concept of "general welfare." Often, in work on development planning, economists obscure conflicts by using market prices to measure the relative welfare obtained by various programs. Such a procedure assumes that the market is somehow an impersonal arbiter of class differences. But, in fact, the market simply reflects the existing power relations of society.

Some aspects of social conflict can, of course, be examined in the context of development planning analysis. In this book one of the most prominent social conflicts in Pakistan, the issue of regional income distribution, is given paramount attention. Nonetheless, when considered in the context of conventional development planning analyses, solutions to such social problems are necessarily reduced to technical quantitative issues.

In Pakistan, as elsewhere, problems of determining regional distribution, of establishing sectoral priorities, of choosing production techniques are by no means simply technical problems. To treat them as such is not only incorrect in itself but may lead to further errors. It is misleading, for example, to assume that Pakistan planners wish to find a just solution to the problem of regional income disparity. Furthermore, it is misleading to imply that, in the face of the existing array of social and political forces, planners might be able to implement a technical solution to the problem. If such an approach leads people away from struggling to change the prevailing situation, then it must be viewed as having a pernicious effect.

Limiting an analysis of development planning only to issues that can be quantified might also have a pernicious effect. Such an analysis would obscure many social goals, some of which might be in conflict with the quantifiable goals. Examples readily come to mind: the goal of political and social sovereignty might be sacrificed to obtain sufficient foreign capital to attain the income growth goal; villages might be destroyed in the name of "progress" that comes with building a new dam; the values of local community might be forced to give way to institutions that "rationalize" the labor market. These biases cannot be viewed as mere oversights in the analysis; they are endemic to the approach.

Perhaps with these words of warning fewer readers of this book will be led astray by its hidden assumptions. Probably few persons would have been misled even without these comments unless they, like myself at the time this book was written, allow themselves to be channeled by the typical modern economics curriculum, away from basic questions of political economy. In any case, political developments in Pakistan have made it clear that social forces are what will resolve the major problems. Technical manipulations by planners and government will certainly not be decisive.

In light of these points, what might be the value of the present book? In it I have employed a multisectoral, regional linear programming planning model to analyze problems of resource allocation in Pakistan; thus I have approached a relatively narrow set of questions in a rather limited manner. As long as this is well understood, I think that the book may have two valuable functions.

First, I believe that it makes a methodological contribution. I have attempted to lay out a system of analysis in some detail, and if employed in the right circumstances, the approach should be of value. I would hope in addition that the approach will yield some general insights into the technical aspects of regional and sectoral resource allocation problems.

Second, the specific conclusions of the analysis seem to be of some value in understanding economic decision making in Pakistan, although in a rather negative manner. In general I have found that the pattern of decision making in Pakistan has run counter to what might be viewed as "socially optimal," even given the very limited worth of that term. Thus the study provides some very specific evidence for an indictment of past decisions and of the continuing power relations that determined those decisions.

This final point relates to the issue that is, for me, of

utmost importance. The problems of Pakistan are not problems of intellectual failing that can be solved by more and better research. Pakistan's problems are problems of power: those who hold power have interests that are in opposition to the welfare of the masses of the people. Thus, I would not urge those who are interested in the welfare of the Pakistani people to build more and better planning models or to refine my own work. Such efforts are of little use until control of the society is wrested from the hands of the present elite. Those who desire change should direct themselves toward that end.

In carrying out the study on which this book is based, I have received help from several people. I want to express my special thanks to Azizur Rahman Khan. During our year of collaboration at the Pakistan Institute of Development Economics, I gained immeasurably. To Wouter Tims I am also especially grateful. Throughout my stay in Pakistan he was generous with his help and advice. Although it is not possible for me to list each separately, I wish to express my appreciation to the many others who helped me at the Institute, at the Planning Commission, and in the other branches of the Pakistan government.

In Cambridge, my dissertation advisors, Wassily Leontief and Hollis Chenery, gave me many helpful comments. Also, I am grateful for help from Samuel Bowles and David Evans. During the last six months of the study Kathy Stone acted as my research assistant; in addition to the normal work of a research assistant, she read and helped to edit the entire manuscript. Also, simply her presence made cheerful many otherwise dreary days.

My wife, Phyllis, bore many of the costs of this study. Thanks and apologies which I extend are little compensation for playing the role of wife in our society.

Financial support for my research has come from several sources. A Ford Foundation Doctoral Dissertation Fellowship financed a year of preparatory work in Cambridge. The next eighteen months I spent as a Research Associate with the Yale University Pakistan Project at the Pakistan Institute of Development Economics. It was at the Institute that the data preparation for this study was undertaken and where the study itself began to take form. On my return to Cambridge, I received support and financing for computations from the Yale University Economic Growth Center, the Harvard Economic Research Project, and the Harvard Project for Quantitative Research in Economic Development.

None of the individuals or institutions mentioned above should be held responsible for any errors or disagreeable passages that the reader may find in the following pages.

Arthur MacEwan
Cambridge, Massachusetts
November 1970

Contents

Contents

Tables

Figures

Development Alternatives in Pakistan

1 | Setting Industrial Priorities: Problems, Background, and Method

1.1 Problems of Priority Setting

Formulating a proper development plan involves the consideration of many alternative sets of programs. The planning process is complicated by the fact that programs for different parts of the economy are interconnected by the demands they place upon one another and by their competition with one another for the use of scarce resources. Alternative development programs for the industrial sector of an economy are especially interesting because of the possibilities for international trade and national specialization.

In Pakistan, as elsewhere, the question of which sectors should lead the industrial development of the nation is a controversial one. Should Pakistan continue to rely heavily on textile industries as the basis of foreign exchange earning and import substitution? Should domestic production of manufactured consumer goods be curtailed? Which industries should be developed in which region? When should Pakistan develop its own capital goods industries?

The answers to those sorts of questions are dependent upon an empirical examination of the Pakistan economy —of the costs and benefits involved in the expansion of different sectors and of the existing resource limitations. The present study offers an empirical analysis of industrial priorities in Pakistan. The analysis should be of some direct use in Pakistan planning, and it should serve to demonstrate certain general propositions about industrial priorities. These general propositions should have relevance to the analysis of development problems in other poor countries as well as in Pakistan. The most important of these general propositions are introduced in the following paragraphs.

First, the desirable set of industrial priorities depends upon the expected availabilities of foreign exchange and capital. This proposition derives directly from the fact that different industries use (and generate) foreign exchange and capital in different proportions. For example, when export opportunities are expected to be meager and the outlook for capital availability is favorable, it will be desirable to give priority to industries that tend to use capital and save foreign exchange. On the other hand, when the outlook for capital availability is poor but foreign exchange earning possibilities are expected to rise, development emphasis should be placed upon those industries that save on capital while using foreign exchange (see, for example, McKinnon 1964; Chenery and Strout 1966; Chenery and MacEwan 1966). Under both sets of circumstances it may be possible to attain the same income or consumption targets or both, though with different industrial programs.

Because each different foreign exchange and capital program carries with it a separate industrial program, a variety of industrial development plans, each optimal under alternative conditions, is conceivable. Nonetheless, it seems unlikely that it would be desirable to maintain the set of industrial priorities which has characterized Pakistan's past growth. Several industries that have grown rapidly in the past, have done so under high levels of protection. Evaluation of the social costs and benefits of some of these industries would place them low on any list of priorities (For substantiation, see Lewis and Guisinger 1966; Soligo and Stern 1965). Furthermore, changes in industrial priorities will arise because of changes in domestic demand and changes in export possibilities.

In determining the industrial development program for a nation, it is useful to give explicit attention to the regional aspects of that program. While regional issues are important in many countries, they are especially acute in Pakistan.[1] Any economic question has its regional overtones. National planning should include the regional aspect, first, in order to uncover the benefits to be gained from regional specialization. By exploiting the comparative advantage of each region, the greatest national growth can be obtained. Second, the regional allocation of welfare is an important political issue, and the regional location of industry is interdependent with political decisions regarding the regional allocation of welfare. Because each region will have comparative advantage in different industries, the decision to emphasize the development of a region implies a decision to develop certain industries.

Decisions regarding which industries to develop and in which region to develop them are not internal problems of the industrial sector. Other branches of the economy place demands on the industrial sector, supply it with raw materials, and compete with it for the economy's resources. In this respect the interconnections between agriculture and industry are of particular importance in a country like Pakistan.

Much hope is being placed upon the adoption of new production techniques in Pakistan agriculture. The use of new varieties of wheat and rice could greatly increase yields and eliminate the need for imports of these staples. Import substitution through technical change in foodgrains production would thereby increase the foreign exchange available for the industrial sector and shift industrial priorities toward industries that are foreign exchange using. However, the direct foreign exchange saving would not be the only effect of agricultural change. The new technology, in addition to new seeds, involves a rise in the use of manufactured inputs, especially fertilizers and pesticides. The change would also lead to a higher income level and higher savings. Through changing demand for manufactured inputs and changing savings possibilities, introduction of new foodgrains production techniques would affect industrial priorities.

In addition to foodgrains production, other parts of the agricultural sector have important links to the industrial sector. In Pakistan progress in these other branches of agriculture, however, is not expected to be great in the next several years. If the economy is to grow rapidly, agriculture-based industrial sectors may be forced to rely heavily on imports for expansion. Such a reliance upon imports for raw materials would seriously affect the costs of these industries and alter their position in any industrial priorities scheme. For the industrial sector, the availability of agricultural raw materials is a problem analogous to foreign exchange and capital availability, and these matters should be considered simultaneously.

Foreign exchange and capital allocation, regional allocation of welfare, and progress of the agricultural sector necessarily dominate the problems of industrial priority determination.[2] The interrelationship of these issues and their effect upon industrial priorities, as well as more detailed problems of priority determination in Pakistan, are taken up in the following chapters with the aid of a multisectoral, regional linear programming model of the Pakistan economy. The model is of the comparative static type and distinguishes thirty-five producing sectors in each of Pakistan's two major regions. Decisions are made in terms of the increments in the values of variables between 1964–65 and 1974–75, the latter being the terminal year of Pakistan's Fourth Five Year Plan. Choice in the model exists with respect to which commodities will be produced in the country, in which region they will be produced, and what the level of production will be. The criterion of choice is the maximization of the national per capita consumption. The maximization is constrained by the ability of the economy to generate capital, by the availability of export possibilities, by the availability of foreign capital, by the possibilities for expansion of agriculture, and by the need to provide for future growth. (The model bears most similarity to those of Manne 1963, 1966; and Bruno 1966.)

In the remainder of this chapter, first, a brief description of the Pakistan economy in relation to major issues of Pakistan planning is presented. After a comment on the methods that have been employed to deal with these issues, the advantages and disadvantages of the method used in this study are pointed out.

Chapter 2 discusses the principles upon which a general equilibrium programming model for Pakistan should be based. It is argued that capital and foreign exchange are important growth-limiting factors. Furthermore, it is pointed out that the planning model should be designed to illustrate the interdependence between resource programs and industrial priority programs and between regional allocation programs and industrial priority programs.

In Chapter 3 the algebraic relationships of the model and the data employed in its implementation are presented. The model is laid out step by step with an explanation of each type of relationship. At the end of the chapter the entire model is brought together for the convenience of the reader.

A discussion of the general properties of the solution of the model—including the characteristics of the dual problem—is undertaken in Chapter 4. A complete "basic solution" to the model is presented, which serves as a reference point in analyzing the properties of alternative solutions.

Chapter 5 presents the principal empirical results of solutions to the model. The first half of the chapter serves to illustrate the interdependence between resource programs and industrial priority programs. In the second half, a priorities program is derived for Pakistan manufacturing industries. The properties of the program are analyzed in relation to past growth and the priority programs of other analysts of Pakistan development.

In Chapter 6 additional solutions to the model are presented to exhibit the effect of technical change in the production of foodgrains upon industrial development programs.

Throughout the discussion in Chapters 4, 5, and 6, regional issues are given emphasis. In Chapter 7 the particularly regional aspects of industrial priority problems are dealt with. The primary purpose is to illustrate the interconnection between regional allocation decisions and intersectoral allocation decisions.

Throughout, the emphasis is on the policy implications for Pakistan in particular and for developing countries in general. The final chapter, Chapter 8, serves to summarize and clarify those policy implications.

There are three appendices. Appendix A presents the complete set of data for 1964–65, the base year of the model. Appendix B presents some sensitivity analysis of the results obtained in the solution of the model. Appendix C discusses several limitations of the model.

1.2 The Pakistan Economy and Issues of Pakistan Planning

Poverty and Progress

Pakistan is an extremely poor country. Average per capita annual income is about US $100. The literacy rate is no more than 20 percent. Sixty-five percent of the labor force is engaged in agriculture. The unemployment rate, though difficult to define and measure, is probably around 20 percent.

In recent years, however, there has been significant economic growth in Pakistan. Between 1959–60 and 1966–67 real gross national product (GNP) rose at 5.4 percent per year. The rise in average per capita income over the seven years was about 20 percent.

It is not only the simple aggregate growth rate that makes Pakistan's recent development appear as a success. There are several favorable aspects to the growth. The manufacturing sector and the overhead sectors (electricity and gas, construction and transportation) have led the growth, their contribution to GNP rising from 18 percent in 1959 to 24 percent in 1966–67. Agriculture, although lagging behind the rest of the economy, has shown signs of change from the stagnation of the 1950s. In East Pakistan, where per capita income fell during the 1950s, the economy has begun to grow. In terms of financing its own growth, Pakistan has exhibited a trend growth rate of 7.5 percent for foreign exchange earnings in the 1960s.

Pakistan's development success during the 1960s can be partly explained by the economic policies which were effected in that period. The trend toward liberalizing import controls is often cited as a most important aspect of these policies (Tims 1968; Papanek 1967; Thomas 1966). From the direct controls of the 1950s there has been a steady movement toward a more "rational" allocation of foreign exchange. On the other side of the foreign exchange issue, a system of export bonuses has been developed to encourage nontraditional exports, and at least some of the export success of the period can be directly attributed to the export bonus scheme (Bruton and Bose 1963).

A complex of agricultural policies evolved during the period which seem to have had substantial payoff. The Planning Commission's own evaluation of the Second Five Year Plan (Pakistan 1966f) cites particularly the abandonment of foodgrain rationing, establishment of support prices for wheat, a 50 percent subsidy on fertilizer, and a more liberal policy toward the import of tubewells. Falcon and Gotsch (1968) in the most complete analysis of agricultural development during the Second Plan period give much credit to the government both for developing a set of incentives which encouraged private initiative in the use of modern inputs and for finding the appropriate mixture of private and public projects in the agricultural sector. Mason (1966), in his over-all comparison of the success of India and Pakistan during the 1960s, has singled out agricultural policies as among the most important in bringing about Pakistan's success. Considering the magnitude of the agricultural sector in Pakistan, it seems clear that any rapid growth of the economy requires at least moderate success in agriculture.

Aside from the direct economic policies, however, there are two factors that have contributed significantly to Pakistan's development: the high level of foreign aid and the general political stability and direction of government political policies. Mason (1966) emphasizes aid as the single most important explanation of Pakistan's success and presents figures showing that aid per capita rose from Rs (rupees) 10.8 in 1960–61 to Rs 25.8 in 1964–65.[3] The aid and political developments should not be viewed as independent phenomena: each supports the other. The advent of the Ayub regime in 1958 brought about a coalition of industrial, agrarian, and military elites which had been struggling among themselves since partition. The unity of these groups produced a set of policies favorable both to their own interests and, at least in the short run, to the growth of the Pakistan economy.

A Catalogue of Qualifications

Final judgment of the success of Pakistan's economic growth must wait until it can be seen whether the events of the early 1960s are short-run phenomena or the beginnings of long-run sustained growth. There are reasons to believe that the former may be the case.

Although Pakistan's trade policies seem to have led to a rationalization of foreign exchange allocation and a rise in foreign exchange earnings, it is not clear either that Pakistan is moving in the direction of less dependency upon imports or that Pakistan can maintain its high rate of growth of exports. A high level of aid and export earnings can make rapid growth possible, but at the same time the economy will adopt an industrial structure that is dependent upon a high import rate. Since aid is expected to diminish, Pakistan must necessarily reduce import dependency or expand exports more rapidly.

The progress of import substitution during the period of growth has been questionable. There is much evidence that Pakistan's trade policies are so structured as to create a bias against import substitution in capital goods industries (Soligo and Stern 1965; Lewis and Guisinger 1966; Radhu 1964; Naqvi 1966). Given the poor performance of agriculture and the need for agricultural imports which would be generated by high growth rates, it is doubtful that Pakistan can expect to become self-sufficient while failing to develop its own capital goods sectors. At least it is necessary that in formulating development decisions, priorities be determined for import substitution and policies be designed to effect these priorities.

The growth of exports may also develop into a serious problem. There has been no trend away from the dependence upon a few types of products in earning Pakistan's foreign exchange. Jute and jute textiles, cotton and cotton textiles, rice, and leather and hides have made up 80 to 85 percent of export earnings in almost every year since 1954–55 (Pakistan 1967c). The demand for these sorts of commodities cannot be expected to grow rapidly. Again, careful appraisal of priorities in the industrial sector is required (Glassburner 1965).[4]

In addition to problems relating to the earning and use of foreign exchange, capital allocation and generation problems loom large in any appraisal of Pakistan's growth success. The structure of protection in Pakistan seems to have led to a highly distorted system of investment incentives. It has been argued that for some sectors when inputs and output are measured at world prices, value added is negative (Soligo and Stern 1965; Lewis and Guisinger 1966). On that basis one can question the priorities that have been at the basis of Pakistan's development.

The strategy of capital mobilization which the Pakistan government has followed has been that of encouraging a highly unequal distribution of income in the (ostensible) hope of raising the level of savings (Haq 1963). The government seems to have failed, however, to develop a tax policy which captures the savings for use in high priority projects. Perhaps the negative distribution effects will be the most tangible result of the government's savings strategy.

Distribution problems appear in examination of rural-urban differences and in regional differences. In agriculture a real breakthrough is still "anticipated."[5] Even if there is a breakthrough, only rice and wheat production will be affected.

Very little effort has been devoted to other food crops.[6] With the progress that has been made in industry, the income differential between urban and rural areas is sizable. Bergan (1967) has estimated for 1963–64 that the rural average income was 60 percent and 70 percent of urban average income in East and West, respectively.[7] Studies by Khan (1967b) and Bose (1968) present the only intertemporal evidence on income distribution and concur in indicating that the income distribution is becoming more unequal.

The only improvement in income disparity between East and West Pakistan has been a decline in the rate at which the disparity has been rising. The problem between the regions is not simply one of unequal income; the distribution of development resources seems to be skewed highly in favor of the West. Capital inflow to West Pakistan has consistently been two to three times as high as the inflow to the East. During the First and Second Five Year Plans, respectively, public development expenditures were 80 percent and 25 percent higher in West than in East Pakistan. And while the Third Plan allocation for the East is 15 percent higher than for the West, in 1965–66 (the first year of the Third Plan) expenditures were 25 percent greater in the West than in the East (see Chapter 7 for the source of these data and for further discussion). Although no figures are published for regional disbursement of central government public administration and defense expenditures, the estimates of Stern (1967) for 1962–63 show central government current expenditures as two and one-half times higher in West than in East Pakistan. (There is no reason to think 1962–63 was not typical in that respect.) Correction of the regional disparity in per capita income will require dramatic changes in the nature of allocation decisions.[8]

The future growth of Pakistan will depend on the policies developed to cope with the many remaining problems. This book offers an approach to the development of these policies. Before discussing the approach used here, however, it will be useful to comment briefly upon the methods by which the Pakistan planners formulate their policies.

A Comment on Planning in Pakistan

The implementation of planning policy in Pakistan involves the use of a variety of instruments: direct government investment, import and export controls, direct price controls, and general fiscal and monetary policy. In principle the Planning Commission exercises a guiding influence over the use of these instruments (Tims 1968; Waterson 1963).

The Planning Commission is attempting to develop a macroeconomic framework for the more specific aspects of planning. In preparing the Third Five Year Plan, the commission developed a seven sector consistency model to derive over-all growth rates, export and import requirements, and savings and investment requirements. The aggregate model was supplemented with a fifty-four sector model, designed to determine the practical implications of the aggregate results (Pakistan 1965b; Tims 1968). Those models were used as guides in formulating the development programs and foreign exchange budgets.

The problem in Pakistan planning appears to come not so much in plan formulation as in plan implementation. In actual practice a great number of ministries and agencies have control over the instruments of planning, and the criteria of their decisions are difficult to discern. While the design of the system of export bonuses, for example, seems to be consistent with the Planning Commission's principles, the system of import regulations often seems to run counter to those principles. (The biases that exist in the import controls have been discussed in the previous section.) Indeed, import policies are probably the best example of the problem of devising a consistent set of incentives; and they have great importance in determining the pattern of trade and investment.

Even within the Planning Commission itself, the procedures followed by the technical sections are often at odds with the outlines set by the economic sections. For example, in the project planning of the technical sections there has been no systematic effort to incorporate the resource scarcity premiums implicit —and often explicit—in the work produced by the economic sections.[9] Under those circumstances it is not surprising to find that the liberalization of import controls is viewed as a positive step. Liberalization means a move away from administration by ad hoc judgments of many men in many places.

Despite the sophistication of the macroeconomic planning techniques of the Planning Commission, it does not seem unfair to characterize Pakistan planning as being inconsistent in many respects. The long-term economic planning of the commission remains to a great extent consistency planning. The problem of determining an optimal program, that is, the problem of priority setting, is dealt with in a decentralized and uncoordinated manner. The system of import controls, for example, remains in need of reform and constitutes a large barrier to the rationalization of investment and trade decisions. While the difficulty appears to lie in the realm of plan implementation, improvements might be made by bringing implementation closer to formulation by coordination of consistency planning and priority setting.

1.3 A General Equilibrium Programming Approach to Industrial Priorities

There are, of course, systematic alternatives to the current ad hoc priority setting procedures followed in Pakistan. Some of these alternatives have been experimented with in the Planning Commission, but their impact upon policy has been slight. There are at least three ways by which such analysis can be undertaken: project and industry studies, a deterministic input-output approach, and a general equilibrium programming approach.

The principal advantages of the industry study approach are that it allows consideration of special characteristics of each industry, it is computationally and conceptually simple, and it requires a minimum of data. What is involved is a standard cost-benefit study for the sector in question (Marglin 1967; Manne 1967). The important aspect that differentiates such analysis by a planning authority from the cost calculation of a private firm is that the planning authority makes a measure of social costs and benefits, that is, the planning authority uses shadow prices rather than market prices. The drawbacks of a sector-by-sector approach or "micro" approach are the standard difficulties of any partial equilibrium analysis. First, it obscures the need for simultaneous decisions regarding events in different sectors of the economy. In an analysis of the cotton textile industry, for example, an assumption must be made about the source of supply—domestic or foreign—of processing chemicals; whatever decision is made, however, might be contradicted by an analysis of the chemical industries. Second, industry studies tend to ignore indirect effects. To build on the previous example, expansion of the cotton textile sector has the effect of requiring expansion of the chemical sector which in turn requires expansion of other industries. These secondary expansions have costs and benefits of their own which must be taken into account. Finally, if undertaken outside the context of an over-all study of the economy, there is no a priori way to know where to begin. And, of course, it is not feasible to employ a careful analysis for every sector.

A deterministic input-output approach to sectoral priorities overcomes some of those difficulties, but not without cost. Essentially, what must be used are the inverse elements of an input-output matrix to take into account both direct and indirect effects of the expansion of a sector. Shadow prices, as in the case of industry studies, are employed where appropriate (Tims 1967; Lewis and Guisinger 1966; Soligo and Stern 1965). This approach, however, also ignores certain problems of simultaneous choice, since the structure of imported inputs is taken as given (usually, but not necessarily, that of a base year). In that it eliminates consideration of choices regarding source of supply, it must be viewed as a very short-run approach. Furthermore, an input-output approach to sectoral priorities embodies the practical difficulties of any input-output approach: many problems are obscured by aggregation, special problems of certain sectors are overlooked, and everything is assumed to be linear.

A general equilibrium programming approach to industrial priorities includes some of these input-output type problems. Nonetheless, the programming approach has certain important advantages for dealing with the particular problems and general issue taken up in this study. First, as well as taking account of indirect effects of an industry's expansion, the programming approach allows simultaneous consideration of interrelated decisions in different parts of the economy. Second, this approach embodies an over-all description of the economy so that the relationship between industrial priorities and certain macroeconomic variables can be analyzed.

It should be emphasized that the programming approach does not stand alone as a means of setting specific industrial priorities. It is a multisectoral method, and it is, in practice, impossible to take account of special details for each sector. Furthermore, the sectors are necessarily aggregates, and any one may contain several industries about which separate policy decisions will be made. It is desirable, perhaps essential, that a programming model such as the one used here be complemented by selected industry studies. What is important is that the programming study should provide a basis for the industry studies. The rankings of industries which the programming approach yields show where important questions arise. While some faith can be placed in the general ranking of industries, marginal decisions must be backed up by more careful, detailed appraisal.

It should be useful at this point to give a brief general description of the model to clarify its relationship to the problems at hand. Full details are given in Chapter 3. Section 1.1 emphasized three sets of problems which the Pakistan economy faces and with which planners must deal in setting industrial priorities: (1) the availability of foreign exchange and savings, (2) the regional allocation of welfare, and (3) the progress of the agricultural sector. In designing the model, it was necessary to define relationships so that these issues could be quantitatively and explicitly specified, thus allowing analysis of the relationship between priority setting and different assumptions about these problems. Also, it was necessary to work at a sufficient level of disaggregation so that rankings of industries would have some operational significance (for a list of sectors see Table 3.2).

11

Several models have been used by others which can easily be adapted to meet these criteria (Bruno 1966; Manne 1963, 1966; Chenery and Kretschmer 1956; Clark 1966; Weisskopf 1967; Tendulkar 1968). The basis of the model is a comparative static input-output framework (Leontief 1953; Dorfman, Samuelson, and Solow 1958; Chenery and Clark 1959).* In such a model, growth is constrained by the availability of foreign exchange earning possibilities, foreign capital, and the rate at which the economy can generate its own capital, that is, save. Foreign exchange earning possibilities are specified by perfectly elastic export demand functions with fixed upper limits. Foreign capital inflow is exogenously specified. Beside foreign capital, the economy can generate its own capital, increments to savings being proportional to increments in output. Tradable commodities can be obtained through production in one of the regions or through imports. Production of any commodity requires capital and foreign exchange to the extent any inputs (capital or current) are imported. Importing requires foreign exchange and capital to the extent that the foreign exchange is earned by exporting. Any consumption expansion plan can be met by a variety of programs involving the—direct and indirect—use of foreign exchange and capital in various amounts. By varying export earning possibilities, foreign capital availability, and domestic savings rates, it is possible to study different expansion programs each with a different set of goods being produced and imported. The different programs can be translated into sets of industrial priorities which are optimal under different foreign exchange and savings circumstances.

Consideration of regional problems requires that production and trade activities be specified separately for the two regions and that interregional trade activities be included. Adjustment of consumption allocation between the regions is possible when resources are allowed to flow freely between them. Foreign

---

* While the model used in this study draws heavily for its design on these other studies, it can be distinguished in several ways. In addition to the fact that this model is regional, the following aspects of its design should be pointed out. (1) Special account is taken of the changing technology in foodgrains production; in the foodgrains sectors, nonlinear production functions (step functions) are used. (2) In other agriculture sectors, production is constrained by "agriculture-specific factors" as well as by the availability of capital and foreign exchange. (3) In all sectors, cost coefficients are incremental. (4) Working capital requirements of each product are charged against the users rather than against the producers. (5) The relationship between total consumption and its components is determined by linear functions rather than by proportional functions. (6) Some choice is allowed in the determination of the export program. (7) Savings rates on value added are specified separately for agriculture. (8) Government savings is taken account of endogenously.

exchange earned by production in one region, for example, can be used to finance imports for the other. Capital is likewise transferable. Different regional allocation solutions can be obtained by valuing welfare (consumption) differently in the two regions. Each solution will produce a different interregional foreign exchange and savings transfer program, and a different set of priorities will be obtained.

To take into account technological changes in rice and wheat production, separate production functions are specified for crop area under modern cultivation techniques and crop area under traditional methods. The production function for modern cultivation is a linear step function that incorporates the diminishing returns that occur when the intensity of application of modern inputs is increased. Solutions to the model can be obtained under different assumptions about the division of the crop area between modern and traditional cultivation, thus simulating different degrees of success in the introduction of the new techniques. In a particular solution the modern-traditional split of acreage is predetermined; however, the solution determines the degree of intensity of operation with the modern techniques. In each alternative solution the foodgrains sectors will place different demands upon the economy's supply of foreign exchange and capital and thus effect the optimal industrial development program.

For nonfoodgrain agricultural sectors, some exogenous productivity changes and input structure changes are assumed, but no special production functions are employed, that is, proportional input-output relations are assumed. Because the growth potential of these parts of agriculture is limited by factors other than the availability of physical inputs, upper limits on their outputs have been included in the model. The availability of these agriculture expansion possibilities will have a direct impact upon the cost of industrial inputs and thereby upon industrial priorities.

Each solution to the model begins with a set of assumptions regarding capital and foreign exchange availability, regional welfare allocation, and the progress of the agricultural sectors. From the alternative solutions a general picture of industrial priorities emerges.

2 | Foreign Exchange, Capital, and the Setting of Priorities

2.1 Foreign Exchange and Capital as the Scarce Factors

It is now common in the analysis of problems of development planning to treat foreign exchange and capital as the scarce factors of production. This departure from the more traditional dichotomy of labor and capital is based on two observations about development problems of many poor countries: first, (unskilled) labor is available in surplus; and second, imported commodities are required in the development process and foreign exchange earning opportunities are limited.

Extremely high levels of unemployment and "disguised unemployment" in underdeveloped economies have given rise to the argument that labor per se is not a scarce resource and therefore not a constraint to economic development. The supply of labor relative to complementary resources is so great that the marginal productivity of labor is zero or near zero (Lewis 1954; Eckaus 1955; Sen 1960).[1]

The surplus labor model is usually formulated in terms of a dual economy with a relatively large and backward sector, peasant agriculture; and a small, modern industrial sector. Labor in the backward sector is in large part nonwage labor, that is, peasant family labor. The remuneration of labor in the traditional sector will effectively be the average product of labor rather than the marginal product (Sen 1966). Furthermore, withdrawal of labor from the traditional sector will involve no loss in production. The cost of labor to the industrial sector, the industrial wage, is determined as the excess over the average remuneration in the backward sector which is necessary to induce labor to give up the traditional life style. Given the small size of the industrial sector, at that fixed wage labor is virtually unlimited in supply.[2]

Underlying the argument that the removal of labor from the backward sector results in no loss of production is the assumption that when marginal labor is removed to the modern sector a costless reorganization of production in the traditional sector takes place. In other words, the removal of labor from the backward sector induces labor-augmenting technical change in the traditional production processes. Furthermore, the withdrawal of labor is assumed to be a withdrawal of the marginal laborer, that is, the laborer who has the least effect upon total production.[3]

Pakistan, with its large traditional agricultural sector and small industrial sector, provides a caricature of the labor surplus economy. The rapidly growing population—the growth rate is at least 3 percent per annum—continually replenishes the oversupplied labor market.[4] What little statistical evidence there is tends to support the proposition that Pakistan is a labor surplus economy. Khan (1967b) has shown that the real wage in manufacturing industries of both regions did not rise in the decade prior to 1962–63; and Bose (1968), in a study confined to East Pakistan, concluded that in the period 1948–1966 there is no evidence of any upward trend in rural wages.

The present study begins with the assumption that Pakistan is a labor surplus economy. The model presented in Chapter 3 does not include labor as a constraint to development; that is, in comparing the desirability of alternative development programs from the point of view of social costs and benefits, labor costs are not considered.[5]

The exclusion of labor, however, does not leave capital as the only scarce factor. Since underdeveloped countries are often dependent upon imports to provide certain types of goods and since the foreign exchange required to finance these imports is limited, it is useful in formulating a development program to treat foreign exchange as a scarce resource.

The need for imports in the development process is a result of the primitive nature of the industrial sector. Certain types of goods cannot be produced domestically because of technological limitations. These goods would include, for example, complex capital goods and spare parts, automobile and truck tires, and special high-quality agricultural raw materials. In the short run, Pakistan will not be able to substitute domestic production for the import of these goods. The source of the limitation to the domestic production can best be described

15

as lack of "technical know-how" or lack of labor skills, but it has its expression in forcing a dependency on imports (see Section 3.7 for more discussion of the types of "necessary" imports).

A dependency upon imports in itself, however, is not sufficient to justify the treatment of foreign exchange as a scarce resource. Were there no direct limits to earning foreign exchange by exporting, domestic resources could be transformed to foreign exchange. It would then be necessary to specify as development constraints only the domestic resource limits that constrain the production of exportable commodities.

For a country like Pakistan, however, it does seem that there are foreign exchange earning limits other than the domestic production limits. The creation of markets is probably the most important limit to export expansion. The trade barriers established by possible customer countries must be broken through, and the traditional trade practices must be overcome. The process of market creation requires time and administrative resources. If the problem is trade barriers of customer countries, negotiations by the Pakistan government will usually be required to expand markets. If the problem is traditional trade practices, private exporters must expend their own administrative and managerial personnel in foreign selling operations. In an underdeveloped country the scarcity of both the government and private personnel that are required to carry out these functions provides a limit to export expansion.

Marketing limitations can provide a constraint to the expansion of old markets as well as to the creation of new ones. Expanding the sales of jute and jute textiles, of cotton and cotton textiles, and of other agriculture-based exports would require a market effort similar to that for new products. In fact, it could be argued that the marketing effort would have an even lower payoff for the traditional agricultural and agriculture-based exports because of the very limited scope of the market.[6] However, unless there are significant productivity changes throughout the agricultural sector, it seems likely that domestic resource limitations will become active before the market expansion limitations.

The view of the limits to foreign exchange earning expressed here leads to a rather complex formulation of export limits in the formal planning model of Chapter 3. The constraint to foreign exchange earning—marketing ability— should not be viewed as entirely industry specific. Especially to the extent that the government has a role in the process of market expansion, the marketing ability could be used to favor some products while little if any attention is given to other products. On the other hand, some of the marketing ability should be treated as sector specific, and there are probably diminishing returns to marketing effort in any one sector. All of these considerations lead to the specification of a set of regional and sectoral constraints for "modern" exports in a way that allows some choice about the appropriate export program (see Section 3.9).[7]

It should be pointed out that capital and foreign exchange are not completely independent resources. Foreign exchange must either be earned by exporting or obtained in the form of foreign grants (aid, loans, and so on). In the former case, capital is required to produce the exports with which foreign exchange is earned. In the latter case, foreign funds contribute to capital supply as well as to foreign exchange supply, as long as the propensity to consume increments to supply is less than unity. If foreign funds are channeled through the government and if, from the point of view of the government, the supply of capital is too low, then the entire inflow of foreign funds may be a contribution to capital.[8]

Because the economy cannot obtain foreign exchange without simultaneously changing the supply of capital, the foreign exchange supply is not an independent constraint to development. The basic and independent limits to development are provided by the supply of capital and the availability of foreign exchange earning possibilities. Nonetheless, it is in providing foreign exchange that the foreign exchange earning opportunities contribute to growth, and it is useful to treat foreign exchange per se as the resource. So long as it is kept in mind that the foreign exchange limit is one step away from the basic resource limit, no incorrect analysis should result.

Behind the discussion of surplus labor and the discussion of foreign exchange scarcity that have been undertaken in the preceding paragraphs lies the specter of skilled labor. The argument that labor in underdeveloped countries is in surplus applies only to unskilled labor. Various kinds of skilled labor provide very serious bottlenecks to economic development. Indeed, the limitation on export expansion is based on the argument that the skilled personnel needed to carry out marketing are in short supply, and the argument that imports are needed for development is ultimately based on the assumption that certain skills are lacking.

The model presented in Chapter 3, however, only indirectly embodies any specification of skilled labor requirements. Noncompetitive import requirements, export limits, and agricultural growth limits are all based on a general notion of skilled labor scarcity. But insofar as skilled labor plays other roles in the development process—and it surely does—the model is in error. The results of the model will tend to be biased in favor of activity intensive in the use of skilled labor.

The exclusion of skilled labor from the model is necessitated by the complete lack of relevant data, and the resulting shortcomings of the model cannot be easily dismissed. Nonetheless, the model remains a useful tool for the analysis of general problems of foreign exchange and capital allocation, and so long as the qualifications are understood, the specific results can be an aid in industrial priority setting in Pakistan.

2.2 Substitutability between Capital and Foreign Exchange

Opportunities for substitution between capital and foreign exchange arise because tradable commodities may be supplied either by domestic production or by importing. Domestic production requires the direct use of capital, while importing requires the direct use of foreign exchange. Switching from domestic to foreign supply can be viewed as a substitution of foreign exchange for capital.

Because production requires intermediate inputs as well as the direct use of capital, there are also possibilities for substitution within domestic production activity. A particular production activity will be capital intensive to the extent that the current inputs that it uses are domestically produced, and it will be foreign exchange intensive to the extent that it relies upon imported intermediate inputs. But these opportunities for substitution are directly dependent upon the decisions made in other sectors—sectors in which intermediate inputs are classified—regarding whether to produce or import. Therefore, all decisions regarding capital and foreign exchange substitutability can be reduced to the decisions in each sector of whether to produce or import.[9]

The opportunity for alternative sources of supply at the sectoral level implies the possibility of substitution between capital and foreign exchange in the production (supply) of aggregate consumption or income. Under conditions of scarce capital and plentiful foreign exchange, the highest level of consumption and income can be attained by operating domestically those production activities that are foreign exchange intensive and by importing commodities the production of which is capital intensive. When foreign exchange is relatively scarce, the economy moves toward a production program that saves foreign exchange and uses capital. Since the degree of capital or foreign exchange intensity of production activity in one sector depends upon the source of supply of the products of other sectors, a set of simultaneous decisions is involved in determining the course of the economy.[10]

An analogy may be made to the microeconomic production theory. The analogy is a rough one, however, because in the macroeconomic problem the availability of capital and foreign exchange cannot be specified as such. Only a savings rate and a foreign exchange earning limit may be specified; the level of savings and the level of exports are determined in the solution. In Figure 2.1

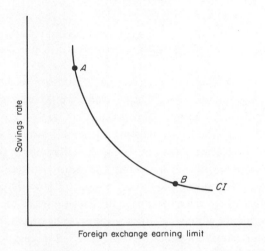

Figure 2.1   Capital and Foreign Exchange Substitutibility

the savings rate (the ability of the economy to generate capital) is measured along the vertical axis, and the foreign exchange earning limit is measured along the horizontal axis. It is then possible to conceive of an isoconsumption line (*CI*) along which the aggregate consumption is constant. The consumption level *CI* can be attained with a high savings rate and a low foreign exchange earning limit by concentrating domestic production in capital intensive sectors and choosing to import a set of products which would, if produced domestically, require relatively intensive use of foreign exchange. Such a situation might be depicted in the figure by point *A* on *CI*. Alternatively, at point *B*, when the savings rate is low and the foreign exchange earning opportunities are high, the same level of aggregate consumption can be obtained. At point *B*, the development program would call for the import of goods, the domestic production of which would be capital intensive; production would be concentrated in sectors that were relatively capital saving and foreign exchange using.[11]

For the purposes of this study, the important point is that there exists an interconnection between the different resource programs and the optimal industrial development program. Different industries will be given priority under different resource programs. The model in Chapter 3 is designed to illustrate the interconnection between resource programs and industrial priority programs which arises from the possibilities for substitution between capital and foreign exchange in the production of aggregate consumption.

2.3 Regional Allocation

Planning problems in Pakistan are complicated—and made more interesting—by the need to consider regional allocation issues. Industrial development decisions involve the choice of region in which to produce as well as the choice of whether to produce or import. The location of production, however, determines the location of income generation and consumption. Therefore, production decisions and regional income and consumption allocation decisions are mutually dependent. That is, the comparative advantage of any region is not independent of the emphasis placed upon welfare in that region. If, for whatever political reasons, development of one of Pakistan's two regions is given high priority, capital and foreign exchange can be shifted to that region, and the development program will be affected accordingly.

It is useful to conceive of the problem in terms of a regional consumption frontier as in Figure 2.2. The plan period increment to consumption in one region is measured along the horizontal axis, and the increment to consumption in the other region is measured along the vertical axis. The convex space OCC' includes all the possible combinations of increments to consumption in the two regions. Movements along CC' involve a shift of resources from one region to the other. The consumption frontier will be concave to the origin, as in Figure 2.2, rather than a straight line if some resources are region specific and if there are diminishing returns to scale in production or both if both existed. In this study no scale problems are considered, but certain resources are region specific. Most important, the foreign exchange earning limits and agricultural production limits are region specific.

The position of the regional consumption frontier will depend on the availabilities of the basic resources of the system and on the relative costs (in terms of those resources) of providing consumption in the two regions. For example, a decline in foreign exchange earning possibilities would cause the consumption

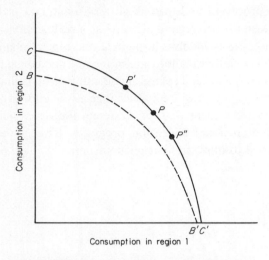

Figure 2.2   Regional Consumption Frontier

frontier to move inward toward the origin. If consumption in region 2 were relatively more foreign exchange intensive, the consumption possibilities for region 2 would be reduced more. Such a situation is illustrated in Figure 2.2 by the curve *BB'*.

The choice of a point on the consumption frontier is a function of the political goals regarding the relative desirability of generating consumption in the two regions. Various points on *CC'*—for example, *P*, *P'*, *P''*—will correspond to alternative political preferences. What is more, each such point involves a different industrial development and trade program.

A movement along the consumption frontier can be accomplished through one of two forms of resource transfer and industrial program adjustment. First, capital and foreign exchange can be reallocated between the regions by a net redistribution of foreign funds. The consequence of that form of resource transfer will be a relatively balanced expansion of one region and contraction of the other.[12] However, region specific resource limits prevent a completely balanced change. Second, foreign exchange can be transferred between regions without an equal transfer of capital if the trade patterns are adjusted so that the favored region runs a regional trade surplus in order to finance a foreign trade deficit. The region that is discriminated against is forced to produce certain goods domestically which it would otherwise import or it is forced to import certain goods from the favored region that it would otherwise produce or it must do both. The process of trade pattern adjustment and the process of shifting foreign funds between the two regions accomplish a reallocation of consumption and income and necessarily involves an unbalanced type of change.[13]

Another way of saying that reallocation of income and consumption between the regions involves unbalanced expansion and contraction is that the industrial development programs in the two regions change as the allocation of consumption and income between them changes. Different industries will be given priority under different regional allocation programs. The model presented in Chapter 3 is designed to illustrate that phenomenon.

3 | A Multisectoral Regional Planning Model for the Pakistan Economy

3.1 Introduction

The structure of a general equilibrium planning model is determined by the purpose for which it is designed and by the availability of relevant data. In the previous chapters the purposes of the model have been explained. Briefly, the problem is to determine the relationship between industrial priorities and certain macroeconomic variables, namely, the level of foreign exchange earnings, the rate of saving, the amount of foreign capital inflow, the degree of progress in the agricultural sector, and regional welfare distribution. Both the particular results that are obtained and the general nature of the results should be of interest.

The principal obstacle to the development of a model to deal with these issues is the paucity of statistical information. It should be evident from this chapter that it is sometimes necessary to revert to less desirable theoretical forms in order to remain in the realm of realistic statistics; for discussion of problems relating to the empirical basis of the model, see MacEwan (1968) and Khan and MacEwan (1967a, 1967b).

3.2 General Properties of the Model

The model is comparative-static. Variables are defined as the changes that take place between 1964–65—the base year of Pakistan's Third Five Year Plan—and

1974–75—the terminal year of Pakistan's Fourth Five Year Plan. The model yields a comparison of 1974–75 with 1964–65, but it does not reveal anything about the time pattern of change between those two years.[1] The 1964–65 values of relevant variables are presented for the two regions of Pakistan on a multi-sectoral basis in Tables A.3 and A.4. National and regional accounts for 1964–65 are shown in Table 3.1.

Table 3.1. Pakistan Regional and National Accounts for 1964–65[a]
(million rupees)

	East Pakistan	West Pakistan	All Pakistan
Consumption	19,447.4	23,530.6	42,978.0
Private	18,724.2	21,872.9	40,597.1
Government	723.2	1,657.7	2,380.9
Gross investment, fixed capital	3,183.3	5,839.8	9,023.1
Net investment	2,345.8	4,021.0	6,366.8
Replacement investment	837.5	1,818.8	2,656.3
Net inventory change	980.5	1,224.6	2,205.1
Foreign exports	1,268.1	1,139.6	2,407.7
Foreign Imports	1,743.5	3,726.9	5,470.4
Net foreign trade surplus	−475.4	−2,587.3	−3,062.7
Regional exports	536.1	856.4	
Regional imports	856.4	536.1	
Net regional trade surplus	−320.3	320.3	
Net capital inflow	795.7	2,267.0	3,062.7
Gross domestic product	23,611.2	30,595.0	54,206.2
Gross national product	22,815.5	28,328.0	51,143.5
Net national product	21,978.0	26,509.2	48,487.2

[a]See Appendix A for complete details on the data used.

Variables of the model are measured in 1964–65 prices. This year is chosen as a base year to facilitate comparison of the results with work of the Pakistan Planning Commission. Prices are not endogenous variables of the system, and price substitution in production and final demand is not considered. Empirical and computational difficulties are so formidable, they necessitate this, although it is an unfortunate departure from reality.

The model is regional. Production processes and demand in the two major regions of Pakistan are considered separately, while tied together by tariff free trade and a common supply of certain resources. All parameters are estimated separately for the two regions.

The model is a multisectoral or an input-output type. Explicit account is taken of the deliveries of goods and services between sectors as well as to final demand categories. The thirty-five producing sectors that are distinguished for each of the two regions are listed below. Appropriate abbreviations of the sector names are used throughout the book and appear in parentheses in the list.

1. Rice growing and processing   (rice)
2. Wheat growing and processing   (wheat)
3. Jute growing and baling   (jute)
4. Cotton growing and ginning   (cotton)
5. Tea growing and processing   (tea)
6. All other agriculture   (other agriculture)
7. Sugar refining   (sugar)
8. Edible oils
9. Tobacco products   (tobacco)
10. Other food and drink   (other food)
11. Cotton textiles
12. Jute textiles
13. Other textiles
14. Paper and printing   (paper)
15. Leather and leather products   (leather)
16. Rubber and rubber products   (rubber)
17. Fertilizer
18. Other chemicals
19. Cement, concrete, and bricks   (cement)
20. Basic metals
21. Metal products
22. Machinery
23. Transport equipment
24. Wood, cork, and furniture
25. Construction of residential houses   (construction of houses)
26. Construction of nonresidential buildings   (construction of buildings)
27. All other construction   (other construction)
28. Miscellaneous manufacture
29. Coal and petroleum products
30. Electricity and gas
31. Transport
32. Trade
33. Ownership of dwellings   (housing)
34. Government*
35. Services n.e.s.†

* Public administration and defense.
† Not elsewhere specified.

The basis of the sector classifications is explained in Section 3.5.

While the model falls into the input-output class, it departs from the procedure of using unadjusted base year technical coefficients for projection. Rather than assuming that the base year relationships hold for 1974–75, attempt has been made to anticipate the important structural and technical changes that will take place. In manufacturing sectors, technical coefficients have been adjusted to take into account the changing relative importance of small- and large-scale activity. In agricultural sectors, especially in foodgrains production, coefficients have been adjusted to take into account the large technical changes that are expected. In the foodgrains sectors, explicit account has been taken of the nonlinear nature of the production function and of the simultaneous existence of modern and traditional techniques (see Section 3.11).

The model excludes consideration of cottage manufacturing activity. Though this is an important part of the Pakistan economy in terms of absolute size, it is best excluded from the analysis primarily because cottage activity is not directly affected by the policy tools that are used to affect the general direction of economic activity. Also, though the cottage sector is large, its incremental share will be of questionable significance. Finally, data for the cottage sector is of very poor quality.[2]

The mathematical technique of linear programming is used to obtain solutions to the model. Choice exists in the model concerning the source of supply for each tradable commodity—production in one of the regions or importing from abroad. Each solution yields an "optimal" set of choices. Criteria for optimality are explained in Section 3.3. The basic constraints to the optimizing process are the supply of domestic savings, the supply of foreign exchange, and the ability of the economy to expand production in agricultural sectors.

In this chapter the model is presented in terms of a "basic form" or "basic solution." That is, a single complete set of relationships and parameter values is presented and explained. In later chapters solutions to the model will be obtained based on alternative forms of relationships and alternative parameter values. However, the basic solution will provide a point of departure and a basis for comparison.

The formal problem with which the model deals is to find a set of production and trade variables which meet

1. limitations on the structure of final demand
2. limitations on over-all demand in each sector
3. limitations imposed by the structure of production

4. limitations on what must be provided for the future
5. limitations on the availability of savings and foreign exchange
6. limitations imposed by special policy

and which maximize national "welfare."

3.3 The Welfare Function and the Structure of Consumption

Welfare is defined in terms of the increment to national per capita consumption; that is, the goal is to find a program to maximize

$$W = \frac{c}{N} + Q$$

where c is the increment to aggregate consumption over the plan; N is national population for 1974–75; and Q, a negative constant, is the decline in per capita income which would take place due to population growth if incremental aggregate consumption were zero. This welfare function may be rewritten as a weighted average of the increments to per capita income in the two regions where the weights are population shares:

$$W = \frac{N^e}{N^e + N^w}\left(\frac{c^e}{N^e} + Q^e\right) + \frac{N^w}{N^e + N^w}\left(\frac{c^w}{N^w} + Q^w\right)$$

where the superscripts e and w denote regions. It is more desirable to think of the welfare function in this second form, for it will facilitate consideration of regional allocation questions.[3]

The advantage of defining welfare in terms of per capita consumption is that the most unambiguous end of economic planning is (or ostensibly is) to raise per capita consumption. Of course, that the goal of planning is to raise per capita consumption does not necessarily mean that a maximum should be obtained in the year 1974–75. The concept of consumption maximization is a multiperiod problem (perhaps an infinite time problem), and it is necessary to make provision for other years. Such provision is included by requiring sufficient investment in 1974–75 to insure continued growth at the 1964–65 to 1974–75 rate (see Section 3.6). With this terminal condition, the model operates not to maximize 1974–75 consumption but to maximize the level of the consumption path the economy is on in 1974–75.

The level of the increment to aggregate consumption in each of the regions is related to the increment to consumption of each category of goods by a linear function of the form

$$c_i = \gamma_i + \beta_i c$$

where c_i is the increment to consumption of the output of sector i. These functions are linear approximations of Engel's functions.

The parameters of the expenditure functions for the two regions are shown in Tables 3.2 and 3.3. Also shown are the shares of each type of good in total consumption in the base year and elasticity of expenditure on each product with respect to total expenditure at the 1974–75 expenditure levels of the basic solution.

Table 3.2. East Pakistan Expenditure Function Parameters, Expenditure Elasticities, and Base Year Consumption Proportions

Sector[a]	γ[b]	β	Expenditure elasticity[c]	Base year share of private consumption
1. Rice	1,200.0	.2050	.6143	.3944
2. Wheat	6.0	.0001	.0534	.0033
5. Tea	−20.0	.0056	1.7584	.0018
6. Other agric.	270.0	.2090	.8624	.2584
7. Sugar	−57.9	.0200	1.7589	.0057
8. Edible oils	79.1	.0277	.8037	.0366
9. Tobacco		.0143	1.0301	.0133
10. Other food	−138.0	.0300	1.6464	.0136
11. Cotton text.	−23.3	.0376	.8904	.0476
13. Other text.	−37.2	.0232	1.1884	.0176
14. Paper	−110.0	.0200	1.9374	.0064
15. Leather	−55.0	.0100	1.9759	.0030
16. Rubber	−25.0	.0050	1.9628	.0014
18. Other chem.		.0250	1.1614	.0178
21. Metal prod.	−42.0	.0126	1.3797	.0078
22. Machinery	−55.0	.0164	1.3839	.0101
23. Transport eq.	−6.0	.0020	1.4306	.0011
24. Wood, etc.	−45.0	.0119	1.4086	.0073
28. Misc. manuf.	−75.0	.0219	1.3870	.0135
29. Coal, etc.	−30.0	.0138	1.5504	.0055
30. Elec. and gas	−15.0	.0093	1.5942	.0031
31. Transport	−120.0	.0450	1.6066	.0171
33. Housing	100.0	.1030	1.2158	.0601
35. Services	−800.7	.1316	1.8396	.0534

[a]Full sector names are given in Table A.1.
[b]Million rupees.
[c]At the 1974–75 expenditure level of the basic solution.

Table 3.3.   West Pakistan Expenditure Function Parameters, Expenditure Elasticities, and Base Year Consumption Proportions

Sector[a]	γ[b]	β	Expenditure elasticity[c]	Base year share of private consumption
1. Rice		.0350	.8085	.0412
2. Wheat	650.0	.0450	.3890	.1289
5. Tea	24.2	.0110	.7360	.0142
6. Other agric.	238.8	.2300	.7424	.3044
7. Sugar	50.6	.0345	.9284	.0286
8. Edible oils	195.0	.0375	.6297	.0584
9. Tobacco	65.0	.0275	.7304	.0358
10. Other food	−24.0	.0110	1.0408	.0087
11. Cotton text.	−10.0	.0469	.7988	.0569
13. Other text.	−33.9	.0350	1.0124	.0274
14. Paper	−63.8	.0155	1.3255	.0080
15. Leather	22.8	.0125	.8751	.0116
16. Rubber	−20.0	.0080	1.3825	.0031
18. Other chem.		.0325	.9680	.0266
21. Metal prod.	−24.2	.0076	1.1741	.0049
22. Machinery	−36.2	.0114	1.1773	.0073
23. Transport eq.	−27.5	.0085	1.1741	.0055
24. Wood, etc.	−24.2	.0076	1.1741	.0049
28. Misc. manuf.	−71.1	.0222	1.1753	.0143
29. Coal, etc.	−20.0	.0130	1.3393	.0050
30. Elec. and gas	−30.0	.0148	1.3691	.0056
31. Transport	−236.5	.0736	1.1854	.0465
33. Housing	75.0	.0957	1.1001	.0540
35. Services	−700.0	.1637	1.2534	.0982

[a]Full sector names are given in Table A.1.
[b]Millions of rupees.
[c]At the 1974–75 expenditure level of the Basic Solution.

3.4 Supply and Demand Balances: Commodities and Resources

For each type of commodity in each region, total increases of deliveries to demand categories cannot exceed increases in supply. For each region, there are three sources of supply—production, foreign imports, and regional imports— and eight demand categories—consumption, intermediate demand, net investment in fixed capital, replacement of fixed capital, investment in working capital, foreign exports, regional exports, and government consumption. The balance constraint for the ith sector in one of the regions is

$$x_i + m_i + r_i^1 \geq c_i + \sum_j x_{ij} + \sum_j h_{ij} + \text{rep}_i + w_i + e_i + r_i^2 + \text{gov}_i$$

where

x_i = the increment to production of the ith good (or service)

m_i = the increment to imports from abroad

r_i^1 = the increment to imports from the other region

c_i = the increment to consumption

x_{ij} = the increase of current deliveries from sector i to sector j

h_{ij} = the increment to net fixed investment deliveries from sector i to sector j

rep_i = the increment to the amount of i needed for replacement investment

w_i = the increment of working capital of type i

e_i = the increment to foreign exports

r_i^2 = the increment to exports to the other region

gov_i = the increment to government consumption expenditures (zero except for $i = 34$)

An adjustment must be made to the balance equations for trade and transport to allow for the port-to-user costs of importing commodities.[4] This is accomplished by inserting on the demand side of the balance equation for each trade and transport sector the term

$$\sum_j (\tau_j m_j + \tau_j' r_j^1)$$

where τ_j and τ_j' are the port-to-user trade or transport costs (whichever the case may be) on the jth foreign import and the jth regional import, respectively.

In addition to the commodity balances, a similar balance exists for each of the basic resources of the system—foreign exchange and savings. In the cases of the resources, however, the balances are specified as equalities, for they actually represent accounting identities.[5]

For each region the increment to export earnings plus the increment to net foreign capital inflow are equal to the increment to import costs:

$$\sum_i p_i e_i + \sum_i p_i' r_i^2 + f = \sum_i q_i m_i + \sum_i q_i' r_i^1$$

where

p_i = the foreign exchange earning of a unit of export of the ith good abroad

p_i' = the foreign exchange earning of a unit of export of the ith good to the other region

q_i = the foreign exchange cost of a unit of import of the ith good from abroad

q'_i = the foreign exchange cost of a unit of import of the ith good from the other region

f = the net inflow of funds to the region.

and for each region, regional savings plus foreign capital inflow plus tariffs on imports are equal to investment plus government consumption expenditures:

$$S + f + \sum_i \text{tar}_i = \sum_i \sum_j h_{ij} + \sum_i w_i + \sum_i \text{rep}_i + \sum_i \text{gov}_i$$

where tar_i is the total tariff earned on the import of the ith commodity. This is, of course, not quite the usual savings-investment relationship, since tariffs and government consumption are included. For the central planner, trying to determine how to raise a surplus and how to allocate it, those terms should enter into the savings-investment relationship. The tariffs necessarily enter the system as the difference between CIF (cost, insurance, and freight) price and domestic producers' price and represent a source of revenue, and government consumption as well as investment is an item which must be covered by the total revenue (other taxes—sales taxes, income taxes—are included in savings; see Section 3.10.)

In addition to those balances for each region, there is a national limit on the supply of foreign capital:

$$f^e + f^w = F$$

while f^e and f^w are variables of the model, the increment to total capital inflow to Pakistan, F, is exogenously set. This equation will hereafter be referred to as the national supply of funds constraint.

3.5 Intermediate Demand and Sector Classification

Demands for current inputs to production processes are determined by Leontief-type fixed coefficient relationships:

$$x_{ij} = a_{ij} x_j$$

where a_{ij} is the incremental input-output coefficient; that is, the amount of the ith good required as current input to expand the output of the jth sector by one unit. This relationship holds for all producing sectors except rice production in both regions and wheat production in West Pakistan; production relationships for these special foodgrain sectors are explained in Section 3.11.

The incremental input-output coefficients are shown in Tables 3.4 and 3.5.

Table 3.4. East Pakistan Incremental Input-Output Matrix
(requirements per 100,000 rupees increase of output)

Sector[a]	1[b]	2	3	4	5	6	7	8	9	10	11
1. Rice	0	0	0	0	0	9205	0	0	0	0	0
2. Wheat		3463				20				11567	
3. Jute		0	655			0				0	
4. Cotton			0	4929							28250
5. Tea			0		868						0
6. Other agric.		25481	2543	11500	1138	1164	54828	36503	26485	12415	79
7. Sugar		0	0	0	0	0	0	0	0	8654	0
8. Edible oils								10382		3042	
9. Tobacco									0	0	
10. Other food										738	
11. Cotton text.										0	10963
12. Jute text.										3621	135
13. Other text.										0	2581
14. Paper							149	674	1035	3036	202
15. Leather							0	0	0	0	0
16. Rubber											
17. Fertilizer		4457	569	5530	1677	238					
18. Other chem.		957	150	150	534	60	281	80	878	2542	1338
19. Cement		0	0	0	0	0	0	0	0	0	0
20. Basic metals									909		
21. Metal prod.								1595	0	2660	
22. Machinery		1375	179		52	91		0		0	241
23. Transport eq.		0	0		0	0					0
24. Wood, etc.										491	289
25. Const., houses										0	0
26. Const., buildings											
27. Other const.											
28. Misc. manuf.									102		3073
29. Coal, etc.								425	295	798	1138
30. Elec. and gas							1161	373	70	422	2987
31. Transport		477	3044	3156	2454	3503	6618	2134	2375	1591	2567
32. Trade		460	8782	7607	9489	7049	5221	8678	13071	7029	9119
33. Housing		0	0	0	0	0	0	0	0	0	0
34. Government					52		72	47		628	207
35. Services			143		1085	15	1317	283	191	210	1250
Total		36670	16065	32873	17342	21343	69647	61175	45410	59445	64417

12	13	14	15	16	17	18	19	20	21	22	23	24
0	0	0	0	0	0	0	0	0	0	0	0	0
34519												
0												
	69	9500	48173		1121	2849	1504		626		307	36408
	0	0	0		0	117	0		0		0	0
						2273						
						0						
			1145									
	19851		285	1355					792			
	1315		0	0	5342		6033		0		493	
	31098		343	0			0				0	
207	133	21062	0			1709		248	156			
0	0	0	6454			0		0	0			
	26		256	20391					1133		4371	
	0		0	0					0		0	
953	3384	9545	11134	6025	1737	11582		261	3054	1309	777	3004
0	0	0	0	0	0	0	8806	0	0	0	0	0
							0	42689	39302	17447	3421	1256
		642	178	3274		191		1533	2660	851	798	3718
848	272	158				284	601	250	546	5580	8912	193
0	0	0				0	0	0	0	0	18882	0
47						3055		123			656	7235
0						0		0			0	0
		880	309	15825	2545	1600	4645		121	2028		
794	4987	5083	559	2840	4584	1289	5373	2020	1223	4623	821	277
1933	242	12050	641	1633	10393	323	5605	1170	540	661	913	1125
2082	738	4215	2858	5085	4809	1929	13368	5199	3251	4364	4302	5222
6922	7451	10411	15319	12248	10758	12452	7189	9273	9458	13823	14421	4469
0	0	0	0	0	0	0	0	0	0	0	0	0
48	134	783				237	302	251	303	286	275	
874	406	1089	576	2157	2991	954	911	1515	913	1438	553	341
49226	70106	75418	88231	70834	44280	40844	54335	64531	64077	52410	59903	63249

Table 3.4. (*continued*)

Sector[a]	25	26	27	28	29	30	31	32	33	34	35
1. Rice	9000	0	0	0	0	0	0	0	0	0	0
2. Wheat	15										
3. Jute	0										
4. Cotton											
5. Tea											
6. Other agric.	12132	7853	3129	133			600			267	
7. Sugar	0	0	0	0			0			0	
8. Edible oils											
9. Tobacco											
10. Other food				813							
11. Cotton text.				5948							
12. Jute text.				0			441				
13. Other text.				5479			0			17	
14. Paper				699		403	209	48		661	448
15. Leather				0		0	0	0		0	0
16. Rubber							575				
17. Fertilizer							0				
18. Other chem.	2168	2171	2153	8917						243	78
19. Cement	204	10597	21693	0						0	0
20. Base metals	94	10250	8780	1863							
21. Metal prod.	849	4634	573	3445			524	232		87	10
22. Machinery	559	5167	0	6342		1626	0	0		31	97
23. Transport eq.	0	0		0		0	670			0	0
24. Wood, etc.				812			0				
25. Const., houses				0					29392		
26. Const., buildings									0		
27. Other const.											
28. Misc. manuf.	95	1022	1015	2133			311	108		153	159
29. Coal, etc.	0	0	686	2641		16658	3471	0		1052	0
30. Elec. and gas			0	990		5588	209	188		2403	246
31. Transport				2503		0	0	0		8784	0
32. Trade				18887						0	
33. Housing				0							
34. Government	450	435	442	1112		327	414	11		5652	573
35. Services	16	146	92	1119		0	184	503	724	2381	130
Total	35981	42275	38563	63837		24602	7609	1090	30117	21731	1741

[a]Full sector names are given in Table A.1.
[b]Rice in East Pakistan is produced according to a nonlinear production function (see Section 3.11).

The sector classification is that of Khan and MacEwan (1967a) and MacEwan (1968) and will be only briefly discussed here.[6]

Each of the first five sectors includes growing, harvesting, and processing of a principal crop. The vertical integration of the processing activity with the growing and harvesting of crops is not the usual practice. But, since all of each of these crops does undergo processing and since much of the processing is done by the agriculturalists themselves, little if any substance is lost by the aggregation.*

Other agriculture (6) is a rather heterogeneous sector of residual category. It includes growing of sugar cane, tobacco, oil seeds, fruits, and vegetables; the growing and processing of nonwheat, nonrice, and nontea food crops; livestock products, forestry, and fishing. The reason important subsectors such as livestock are not shown separately is the lack of information.

The agricultural activities include such ancillary activities as trading and transporting crops to rural processing units (farmers themselves in many cases) and to rural consumers. The services delivered to agriculture from the trade (32) and transport (31) sectors include only the margins on crops sold to urban processors and on cash crops sold to large-scale manufacturing. By including much of the trade and transport activity in the agricultural system it is not necessary to estimate imputed value and input structure of self-provided service and the realism of the system remains unaffected.

The next four sectors, (7) to (10), are food-processing industries. In each case there are special reasons for not vertically integrating these with the growing of corresponding agricultural inputs; for example, sugar refining, unlike grain processing, adds a large amount of value to the crop. For each of these industries, unlike grain processing, there are important policy questions to consider regarding the alternatives of domestic production and importing.

Sectors (11) to (20), (28), and (29) produce manufactured consumption and intermediate goods. Titles explain the contents of these sectors reasonably well. Mining and quarrying activities, small in the West and all but nil in the East, have been vertically integrated with the manufacturing sectors to which they deliver.

Several sectors, (21)–(27), supply fixed capital. Four sectors (21)–(24) produce manufactured capital goods while the other three are construction sectors. The disaggregation of construction is especially useful in view of the considerable differences in input structures and sources of demand for output. Construction of houses (25) supplies capital to only one sector, housing (33). Construction of

---

* Actually, in West Pakistan, tea (5) includes no growing or harvesting but is simply processing of imported tea.

Table 3.5. West Pakistan Incremental Input-Output Matrix
(requirements per 100,000 rupees increase of output)

Sector[a]	1[b]	2[b]	3[c]	4	5	6	7	8	9	10	11
1. Rice	0	0	0	0	0	632	0	0	0	0	0
2. Wheat						4465					
3. Jute						0					
4. Cotton				4613		1099		15384			26598
5. Tea				0	79387	0		0		0	0
6. Other agric.				7341	0	5316	34836	4551	32148	2544	209
7. Sugar				0		0	0	0	0	6694	0
8. Edible oils						1		20841		3564	
9. Tobacco						0		0		0	
10. Other food						172		18			
11. Cotton text.				34		0	47	1252			27116
12. Jute text.				213		196	998	57	104	700	47
13. Other text.				0		51	0	0	0	0	1595
14. Paper				9	4384	0			3563	3081	123
15. Leather				0	0			0	0	0	
16. Rubber											
17. Fertilizer				3418		1434					
18. Other chem.				150	102	278	5124	654	650	3758	6540
19. Cement				0	0	0	0	0	0	0	0
20. Basic metals											
21. Metal prod.						244		190			
22. Machinery				1244		131	70	175	602	1344	657
23. Transport eq.				0		0	0	0	0	0	0
24. Wood, etc.									124		
25. Const., houses									0		
26. Const., buildings											
27. Other const.											
28. Misc. manuf.									1492		
29. Coal, etc.				664		24	664	823	103	628	1090
30. Elec. and gas				562	115	266	148	999	335	810	2088
31. Transport				2329	576	1632	863	980	1739	4521	674
32. Trade				2262	5221	9923	261	10362	9286	19972	11284
33. Housing				0	0	0	0	0	0	0	0
34. Government				60	111	5	24	143	97	326	107
35. Services				520	896	71	742	683	942	852	786
Total				23420	90792	25941	43778	57113	49568	50410	78914

12c	13	14	15	16	17	18	19	20	21	22	23	24
0	0	0	0	0	0	0	0	0	0	0	0	0
						4466						
						0						
	1174	2982	15128			1654			74	486	207	45209
	0	0	0			240			0	0	0	0
						591						
						0						
	8310		649	1582						117		
	808	71	0	430		29	6026			0		
	34159	0		0		0	0					
	326	21248	842	394		738	2179		547			434
	0	0	14520	0		0	0		0			0
			734	19919							3184	
				0							0	
	1376	6521	4372	7702		20173	321	545	1130	1112	132	1613
	0	0	0	0		0	14894	0	0	0	0	0
							0	51926	25962		4082	
			623					0	6347	21013	2805	3826
	561	2332	634	2360	1110	763	2014	1032	851	19866	2866	0
	0	0	0	0	0	0	0	1993	0	0	31048	
							129	0			0	
							0					
							0					
			313			1404	1557			85		
	741	1201	563	1287	9416	832	6063	1837	3686	2475	1404	
	1432	1503	1362	1660	19516	1035	2253	2031	2915	1412	836	513
	1401	1707	1974	2488	18207	1867	11728	9062	5606	6717	658	2736
	13566	20218	8007	18796	10409	12108	1499	14364	14150	1390	2742	0
	0	0	0	0	0	0	0	0	0	0	0	
	150	264	66	400		333	150	210	159	296	347	440
	786	2256	264	1612	127	1256	2376	1091	493	1460	2529	609
	64791	60303	50052	58631	66616	47488	51189	84090	61920	56428	52840	55380

37

Table 3.5. (*continued*)

Sectors[a]	25	26	27	28	29	30	31	32	33	34	35
1. Rice	819	0	0	0	0	0	0	0	0	0	0
2. Wheat	5759										
3. Jute	0										
4. Cotton				173							
5. Tea											
6. Other agric.	3846	3429	773	1366						277	
7. Sugar	0	0	0	0						0	
8. Edible oils											
9. Tobacco											
10. Other food				81							
11. Cotton text.				154			6				
12. Jute text.				84			288				
13. Other text.				0			0			14	
14. Paper				7936			869	53		679	598
15. Leather				74			0	0		0	0
16. Rubber				0			3125				
17. Fertilizer							0				
18. Other chem.	2730	3668	569	19837	891		108			222	65
19. Cement	11587	16182	19859	0	0		0			0	0
20. Basic metals	4817	11124	24617								
21. Metal prod.	6972	12329	4091	3774	2448					91	10
22. Machinery	2579	2070	1105	0	0	1458				33	90
23. Transport eq.	0	0	0			0	13145			0	0
24. Wood, etc.					33		0				
25. Const., houses					0				14549		
26. Const., buildings									0		
27. Other const.											
28. Misc. manuf.	502	754		7090						155	164
29. Coal, etc.	0	0	772	2765	12988	1851	19742			1084	0
30. Elec. and gas	27	911	1416	3241	288	25538	11	298		1748	362
31. Transport	0	0	0	2348	7844	0	0	1359		9041	1573
32. Trade				8356	10269			0		0	0
33. Housing				0	0						
34. Government	14	53	50	861	35	27	64	432		5825	790
35. Services	53	248	125	2439	1992	163	307	2616	944	285	703
Total	39704	50768	53377	60579	36788	29037	37663	4557	15493	19453	4355

[a]Full sector names are given in Table A.1.
[b]Rice and wheat in West Pakistan are produced according to nonlinear production functions (see Section 3.11).
[c]There is no jute or jute textiles production in West Pakistan.

buildings (26) supplies capital to all other sectors. Other construction (27) furnishes supplies to agriculture (1)–(6)—water control systems—electricity and gas (30)—hydroelectric plants—and transport (31)—road, railways, airports, and ports.

The remaining sectors—electricity and gas (30), transport (31), and the service sectors (32)–(35)—are sufficiently explained by their titles. It need only be noted that, contrary to the Pakistan national accounting procedure, postal and tele-communications are included in government services rather than in transport.

3.6 Fixed Capital Requirements

Investment plays a dual role in the growth of an economy as it is both a source of demand and a creator of supply capacity.[7] On the one hand, in the model, investment enters into the commodity supply-demand balance equations as an element of demand—as a reason for output expansion. On the other hand, investment enters in the savings constraint as the cost of output expansion. And output expansion to meet a priori demand creates a requirement for capital, that is, for capacity. This requirement is in itself a demand that creates the need for more expansion, and so on.

The relationship between output expansion in a given sector and the expansion of the stock of fixed capital in that sector is assumed to be proportional:

$$k_j = b_j x_j$$

where

k_j = the amount of capital required in sector j to allow output expansion of x_j

b_j = the capital required per unit of output expansion (the incremental capital-output ratio)

To determine the relationship between the increase of the capital stock over the plan period and the increase of the flow of investment over the period, it is assumed that investment in each sector grows in some smooth pattern over the plan period. The assumption adopted here (see Manne 1963; Bruno 1966; Sandee 1960) is that investment in each sector, if it grows at all, grows exponentially during the plan period. Then investment in sector j in year t of the plan is given by

$$H_{tj} = (1 + \rho)^t H_{1j}$$

where

H_{1j} = the level of investment in the first year of the plan in sector j
ρ = the rate of growth of investment

By definition (assuming replacement)

$$k_j = \sum_{t=1}^{T} H_{tj}$$

where T is the length of the time interval covered by the plan. Then

$$H_{Tj} = \alpha k_j$$

where

$$\alpha = \frac{(1 + \rho)^T}{\sum_{t=1}^{T} (1 + \rho)^t}$$

from which

$$H_{tj} = \alpha b_j x_j$$

and the change in investment over the period is given by

$$h_j = \alpha b_j x_j - H_{0j}$$

The term "α"—the stock-flow conversion factor—is determined by an a priori specification of the growth rate ρ. It must be emphasized that the prespecified ρ is the growth rate from year one of the plan through the terminal year. Solution of the model implicitly yields a growth rate for each sector from the base year zero through the terminal year. A difference between these two growth rates implies a discontinuity in the investment path between year zero and year one, but such a difference does *not* mean a misspecification of investment in the model. Furthermore, for a ten-year plan period if α is taken as 0.15, implying ρ is about 0.08, then α is relatively insensitive to small variation of the rate of growth. Solutions to the model do in fact have growth rates of investment of about 8 percent per annum from year zero through the terminal year, so no serious discontinuity is implied. While some sectors do grow much faster than 8 percent during the period, they are industries that are small in the base year; a discontinuity in their investment paths is not so unreasonable.[8]

As already pointed out, investment enters the model in both the commodity and the savings constraints. For commodity constraints, total investment in any sector must be specified by sector of origin,

$$h_{ij} = \alpha b_{ij} x_j - H_{0ij}$$

where i is one of the capital goods-producing sectors. Conveniently, the model does not require specification of base year investment by sector of destination; for each type of capital good only total investment deliveries of the base year must be specified.[9]

The assumption that the relationship between output expansion and capital requirements is proportional involves a considerable simplification of reality.[10] The important problems of choosing among alternative techniques and structures of production are eliminated. Nonetheless, with proper qualification of results, the proportionality assumption is probably not an unreasonable way to approximate the costs of output expansion in different sectors.

A more serious problem arises, however, because of the likelihood of an unstable relationship between output and capacity. The capital coefficients used here are based upon observations of capital-output ratios for 1962–63 and have been adjusted for any abnormal rates of capacity utilization in that year. The concept of "abnormal rate of capacity utilization" is based upon output trends for the period 1959–60 to 1964–65. No allowance is made for the possibility that normal capacity utilization rates in this period were significantly different from what they will be in the period 1964–65 to 1974–75. In addition to the capacity adjustment, the original observations have been adjusted to obtain incremental coefficients. The incremental capital-output ratios are shown in Tables 3.6 and 3.7 (see MacEwan 1968; Khan and MacEwan 1967b).

3.7 Working Capital Requirements

In addition to the increases of fixed capital which are required when production expands, increases in the stocks of working capital (or inventories) are also required. This need arises, first, from the natural delay in getting products transferred from producers to users, and second, from the need of users to assure against any uncertainty of supply. Stocks of working capital also arise because the production process is not instantaneous; that is, work in progress necessarily exists.[11]

It is important to recognize that inventories of a particular commodity are not required by the producers but by the users of that commodity. For example, it is not the process of producing wheat flour or metal products that requires

Table 3.6. East Pakistan Incremental Fixed Capital-Output Matrix
(requirements per 100,000 rupees increase of output)

Sector[a]	1[b]	2	3	4	5	6	7	8	9	10	11
21. Metal prod.	0	1599	584	1728	2753	0	1470	134	347	467	416
22. Machinery		82019	22026	50058	68632	16020	77239	10110	13416	22052	54668
23. Transport eq.		0	0	0	1126	0	2388	202	607	840	729
24. Wood, etc.		1041	304	1165	1955	0	1053	70	271	389	217
25. Const., houses		0	0	0	0	0	0	0	0	0	0
26. Const., buildings		16381	13308	51341	37299	2009	20327	5234	11734	16167	21005
27. Other const.		27028	11663	13226	1923	12341	0	0	0	0	0
		128069	47885	117518	113687	30369	102477	15750	26375	39916	77035

	12	13	14	15	16	17	18	19	20	21
21. Metal prod.	529	173	3806	354	928	544	633	291	1000	400
22. Machinery	86688	32484	75579	12997	35490	174540	16750	61208	40452	24991
23. Transport eq.	529	260	5519	472	1578	854	1085	485	1600	800
24. Wood, etc.	459	90	1982	123	677	405	471	202	625	312
25. Const., houses	0	0	0	0	0	0	0	0	0	0
26. Const., buildings	36057	9942	32170	14507	12554	19734	20568	14902	26635	20284
27. Other const.	0	0	0	0	0	0	0	0	0	0
	124263	42949	119057	28453	51227	196077	39518	77088	70312	46787

	22	23	24	25	26	27	28	29	30	31
21. Metal prod.	850	1700	1344	5000	5000	5000	960	0	0	272
22. Machinery	46600	24568	35277	5000	7000	5000	45240		407028	3747
23. Transport eq.	1322	2600	2112	0	2000	8000	1440		0	86110
24. Wood, etc.	492	937	900		0	0	500			189
25. Const., houses	0	0	0				0			0
26. Const., buildings	34633	46304	28226		1000	2000	31766			5577
27. Other const.	0	0	0		0	0	0		451269	106524
	83897	76109	67859	10000	15000	20000	79906		858297	135887

	32	33	34	35
21. Metal prod.	2447	0	1879	2428
22. Machinery	19831		15815	19582
23. Transport eq.	4046		3194	3922
24. Wood, etc.	1666		1370	1654
25. Const., houses	0	1000000	0	0
26. Const., buildings	109609	0	87273	108301
27. Other const.	0		0	0
	137600	1000000	109529	135887

[a]Full sector names are given in Table A.1.
[b]Rice in East Pakistan is produced according to a nonlinear production function (see Section 3.11).

Table 3.7. West Pakistan Incremental Fixed Capital-Output Matrix
(requirements per 100,000 rupees increase of output)

Sector[a]	1[b]	2[b]	3[c]	4	5	6	7	8	9	10	11	12[c]	13
21. Metal prod.	0	0	0	174	116	0	446	127	2029	1503	684	0	623
22. Machinery				19377	588	7456	44311	19133	17547	34698	64448		48543
23. Transport eq.				88	0	0	726	129	1501	1912	696		543
24. Wood, etc.				0			265	63	1276	1022	387		440
25. Const., houses							0	0	0	0	0		0
26. Const., buildings				7892	4152		11570	9820	15452	23798	44453		18553
27. Other const.				151073	0	122832	0	0	0	0	0		0
				178604	4856	130288	57318	29273	37806	62933	110669		68702

	14	15	16	17	18	19	20	21
21. Metal prod.	882	308	761	1423	949	498	300	400
22. Machinery	42565	11487	57474	180417	58773	88527	23503	30523
23. Transport eq.	897	104	774	1671	1073	1519	305	305
24. Wood, etc.	581	101	564	866	625	295	99	198
25. Const., houses	0	0	0	0	0	0	0	0
26. Const., buildings	20910	13716	22192	55890	24074	33359	11169	13762
27. Other const.	0	0	0	0	0	0	0	0
	65835	25717	81765	240266	85493	124199	35376	45188

	22	23	24	25	26	27	28	29	30	31
21. Metal prod.	1081	1966	303	5000	5000	5000	809	1532	0	746
22. Machinery	48300	56700	20172	5000	7000	5000	48680	79033	223704	15647
23. Transport eq.	1300	13100	515	0	2000	8000	823	1650	0	133999
24. Wood, etc.	680	1360	200		0	0	500	980		461
25. Const., houses	0	0	0				0	0		0
26. Const., buildings	29111	49695	25219		1000	2000	34702	27769	260615	7529
27. Other const.	0	0	0		0	0	0	0	0	84216
	80473	122821	46409	10000	15000	20000	85514	110965	484319	242597

	32	33	34	35
21. Metal prod.	2417	0	2573	2398
22. Machinery	19080		16001	18838
23. Transport eq.	4032		3436	4002
24. Wood, etc.	1529		1335	1517
25. Const., houses	0	1000000	0	0
26. Const., buildings	106525	0	89774	105431
27. Other const.	0		0	0
	133583	1000000	112573	132187

[a]Full sector names are given in Table A.1.
[b]Rice and wheat in West Pakistan are produced according to nonlinear production functions (see Section 3.11).
[c]There is no jute or jute textiles production in West Pakistan.

working capital stocks of these commodities to be held. It is the use of them, whether by other producing sectors or by final demand sectors, that requires they be held as inventories. This is true despite the fact that stocks of finished products are observed as being held by producers of those products. In holding stocks of finished products, the producer is performing a service (distinct from the production service) for the user.

To recognize that inventory stocks are held for users regardless of who actually holds them is important in the context of the programming model being developed here. Primary concern is with the comparison of costs of production and costs of importing. Were the cost of holding finished products to be charged against the producer of the commodity and were no equivalent charge recorded against the import of the commodity, a bias would be created in favor of importing, for imported commodities must be stocked in (at least) as great a quantity as are domestically produced commodities. The problem may be avoided through a parallel treatment of imported and domestically-produced stocks of working capital. All stocks of finished products, regardless of origin, are charged against the using sector (including final demand sectors), since it is the expansion of the using sector which requires that these stocks be held.[12]

Once the principle of allocating working capital stocks to the using sector is established, the treatment of working capital stocks in the model is straightforward and parallel to the treatment of fixed capital. Increase in the change of working capital of each commodity over the plan period is linearly related to the uses of that commodity:[13]

$$w_i = \sum_j w_{ij} + w_{ic} + w_{ih} + w_{ir} + w_{ie}$$

where w_i is the increase over the plan of the change in inventories of the ith type of commodity. The terms on the right side of the equal sign represent the share of the increase accounted for, respectively, by increases in producing sectors, increases of consumption, increases of investment, increases of regional exports, and increases of foreign exports. (The second order effect—increases of working capital due to increases in the change of working capital—are ignored.) Each of these components is determined as follows:

$$w_{ij} = \alpha\omega_{ij}x_j - W^0_{ij}$$
$$w_{ic} = \alpha\omega_{ic}c_i - W^0_{ic}$$
$$w_{ih} = \alpha\omega_{ih}h_i - W^0_{ih}$$
$$w_{ir} = \alpha\omega_{ir}r_i^2 - W^0_{ir}$$
$$w_{ie} = \alpha\omega_{ie}e_i - W^0_{ie}$$

Where α is the stock-flow conversion factor explained above, the ω are working stock coefficients, and the W^0 are base year values. Substituting in the original equation:

$$w_i = \alpha\sum\omega_{ij}x_j + \alpha\omega_{ic}c_i + \alpha\omega_{ih}h_i + \alpha\omega_{ir}r_i^2 + \alpha\omega_{ie}e_i - W_i^0$$

As with fixed capital, the only base year variable required is the total change of working stock of the ith type. The value of these base year variables for 1964–65 are shown in Tables A.1 and A.2.

The working capital output ratios themselves (the ω_{ij}'s) are shown in Tables 3.8, 3.9, and 3.10. Their derivation is explained in MacEwan (1968).

3.8 Foreign Imports and Regional Trade

The basic element of choice in the programming model being developed here is among sources of supply. Any tradable commodity can be produced within a region, imported from the other region, or imported from abroad. The function of the model is to simultaneously determine sources of supply for all tradable commodities in both regions in order to maximize the welfare function.

Were sectors of the model defined in terms of homogenous commodities and were all cost elements completely specified, it would not be necessary to consider further limits to the choice of source of supply. However, since in a model of this sort sectors are defined in terms of groups of commodities and since not all cost elements can be specified, it is necessary on a priori grounds to identify some imports—foreign or regional or both—as complementary to, rather than competitive with, production within a region.

It is useful to distinguish two broad classes of complementary, or noncompetitive imports. One such class is specified because a particular kind of import classified under a domestic producing sector either is technologically impossible to produce within the region or has a potential cost of production known to be much more than that for the aggregate domestic sector. Frequently such imports will be use-specific. Their pattern of distribution among users will be dissimilar to the pattern of the distribution of products of the aggregate sectors under which they are classified. For example, (a) superior quality cotton imports cannot be produced in Pakistan due to technological considerations and are used up entirely by the cotton textiles sector, while domestic cotton delivers to many sectors; (b) superior quality tobacco imports (classified under other agriculture) are also technologically difficult to produce in Pakistan and are used up entirely by cigarette manufacturing, while all other agriculture delivers to many sectors;

12	13	14	15	16	17	18	19	20	21	22	23	24
0	0	0	0	0	0	0	0	0	0	0	0	0
13215												
0												
	24	4891	15694		878	1547	1123		458		307	13359
	0	0	0		0	78	0		0		0	0
						1007						
						0						
			430									
	7040		96	677					588			
	564		0	0	4631		5014		0		534	
	8168		84		0		0				0	
84	49	11370	0			970		230	118			
0	0	0	2540			0		0	0			
	6		58	7993					719		3940	
	0		0	0					0		0	
335	1062	4618	3282	2765	1306	5928		227	2143	1311	753	1009
0	0	0	0	0	0	0	6712	0	0	0	0	0
							0	51108	40423	23180	4432	833
		315	54	1526		99		1345	1884	859	779	1275
329	95	82	0	0		156	452	226	403	5790	8952	72
0	0	0				0	0	0	0	0	22591	0
20						1762		115			678	2901
0						0		0			0	0
		467	106	8007	2033	894	3545		90	2126		
343	1968	2871	210	1534	3817	764	4283	1921	957	5004	862	115
0	0	0	0	0	0	0	0	0	0	0	0	0
14326	18976	24615	22561	22502	12664	13204	21129	55172	47783	38270	43826	19564

Table 3.8. (continued)

Sector[a]	25	26	27	28	29	30	31	32	33	34	35
1. Rice	14021	0	0	0	0	0	0	0	0	0	0
2. Wheat	23										
3. Jute	0										
4. Cotton											
5. Tea											
6. Other agric.	18900	15304	8696	54			90			40	
7. Sugar	0	0	0	0			0			0	
8. Edible oils											
9. Tobacco											
10. Other food				372							
11. Cotton text.				2483							
12. Jute text.				0			103				
13. Other text.				1783			0			1	
14. Paper				302		150	37	8		116	78
15. Leather				0		0	0	0		0	0
16. Rubber											
17. Fertilizer											
18. Other chem.	3311	4163	5918	3357						29	9
19. Cement	5039	20811	60623	0						0	0
20. Basic metals	2769	23009	27002	1311							
21. Metal prod.	10505	8920	1579	1321			66	29		11	1
22. Machinery	874	10097	0	2616		574	0	0		5	15
23. Transport eq.	0	0		0		0	232			0	0
24. Wood, etc.				359			0				
25. Const., houses				0							
26. Const., buildings											
27. Other const.											
28. Misc. manuf.	149	2008	2837	903			52	18		25	26
29. Coal, etc.	0	0	1942	1208		6630	694	0		210	0
30. Elec. and gas			0	0		0	0			0	
31. Transport											
32. Trade											
33. Housing											
34. Government											
35. Services											
Total	55590	84310	108599	16070		7354	1304	56		437	130

[a]Full sector names are given in Table A.1.
[b]Rice in East Pakistan is produced according to a nonlinear production function (see Section 3.10).

(c) automobile and truck tires could be produced in Pakistan, but only at costs far exceeding those of the aggregate rubber products sector, and are delivered to the transportation sector, while rubber products are delivered to many sectors. This class of imports will be referred to as use-specific noncompetitive imports.

Though there are no specific technological considerations the second class of noncompetitive imports is specified because it would be unreasonable to allow complete substitution of imported goods of that type during the subsequent ten years. Expansion of domestic production in the sector could not take place at a sufficiently rapid rate without incurring a considerable rise in costs. Machinery imports into Pakistan is an example. While it would be possible before 1974–75 to substitute domestic production for any single kind of imported machine— textile or milling equipment for example—it would be impossible to eliminate all incremental imports of machinery. This is primarily a result of skill limita-tions—administrative, managerial, and productive—that are specific to the industry. It would be arbitrary and misleading to select a few categories of ma-chinery and designate them as complementary, but some limit must be placed on the degree of import substitution for the sector as a whole. Other examples are the petroleum and coal sectors, basic metals, and transport equipment. This second class of complementary imports will be designated as nonuse-specific noncompetitive imports.

The essential difference between the two classes is that the destination of the use-specific import is known and can be charged against a receiving sector, while the receiver of the nonuse-specific import is not known. In the latter case, the limit must be in terms of the share of supply which must originate from foreign sources. It is possible, of course, that a given sector will be the recipient of a use-specific noncompetitive import and will have its expansion limited by the need for nonuse-specific noncompetitive imports. Basic metals and coal and petroleum products are good examples.

Total foreign imports (m_i) of any type include both the competitive $(\hat{m}_i)$ im-ports, explicit variables of the model, and the noncompetitive imports $(\overline{m}_i)$

$$m_i = \hat{m}_i + \overline{m}_i$$

Noncompetitive imports are determined by the equation

$$\overline{m}_i = \sum_j \mu_{ij} x_j + \mu_{ic} c$$

For $i \neq j$, the μ_{ij} is the use-specific noncompetitive import of i required per unit of expansion of sector j. The μ_{jj} is the incremental ratio of nonuse-specific

Table 3.9. West Pakistan Incremental Working Capital-Output Matrix
(requirements per 100,000 rupees increase of output)

Sector[a]	1[b]	2[b]	3[c]	4	5	6	7	8	9	10	11
1. Rice	0	0	0	0	0	134	0	0	0	0	0
2. Wheat						946					
3. Jute						0					
4. Cotton				2341		233		9309			15257
5. Tea				0	19859	0		0			0
6. Other agric.					0	1126	13655	2754	13471	1392	120
7. Sugar						0	0	0	0	4713	0
8. Edible oils								10527		1593	
9. Tobacco								0		0	
10. Other food						28		10			
11. Cotton text.				11		0	22	857			17696
12. Jute text.				65		51	441	38	49	418	29
13. Other text.				0		11	0	0	0	0	920
14. Paper				2	1136	0			1525	1713	71
15. Leather				0	0				0	0	0
16. Rubber											
17. Fertilizer				239		80					
18. Other chem.				0	26	30	2024	398	274	2067	3771
19. Cement						0	0	0	0	0	0
20. Basic metals											
21. Metal prod.						43		108			
22. Machinery				339		30	29	109	264	761	389
23. Transport eq.				0		0	0	0	0	0	0
24. Wood, etc.										74	
25. Const., houses										0	
26. Const., buildings											
27. Other const.											
28. Misc. manuf.										865	
29. Coal, etc.				202		6	293	539	48	375	680
30. Elec. and gas				0		0	0	0	0	0	0
31. Transport											
32. Trade											
33. Housing											
34. Government											
35. Services											
Total				3200	21021	2718	16464	24648	15631	13970	38933

12c	13	14	15	16	17	18	19	20	21	22	23	24
0	0	0	0	0	0	0	0	0	0	0	0	0
						4487						
						0						
	500	2035	7906			1662			61	404	187	17225
	0	0	0			279			0	0	0	0
						534						
						0						
	4197		390	1053						106		
	385	52	0	274	5277	31	4747			0		
	14656	0		0	0	0	0					
	142	14697	448	235		748	1627		457			169
	0	0	9708	0		0	0		0			0
			325	10090							2618	
			0	0								
	591	4471	2298	4540		20328	238	396	937	926	119	619
	0	0	0			0	11284	0	0	0	0	0
							0	51243	28279		4756	
			304					0	5022	16703	2433	1324
	249	1636	343	1429	714	781	1524	766	719	16864	2641	0
	0	0	0	0	0	0	0	1636	0	0	31025	
							101	0			0	
							0					
			174			1457	1200			73		
	353	880	323	820	6346	877	4775	1421	3230	2178	1337	
	0	0	0	0	0	0	0	0	0	0	0	
	21072	23772	22219	18440	12337	31183	25496	55463	38704	37254	45116	19337

Table 3.9. (*continued*)

Sector[a]	25	26	27	28	29	30	31	32	33	34	35
1. Rice	1157	0	0	0	0	0	0	0	0	0	0
2. Wheat	8134										
3. Jute	0										
4. Cotton				71							
5. Tea				0							
6. Other agric.	5431	5704	1608	558						42	
7. Sugar	0	0	0	0						0	
8. Edible oils											
9. Tobacco											
10. Other food				29							
11. Cotton text.				75			2				
12. Jute text.				39			97				
13. Other text.				0			0			2	
14. Paper				3313			257			108	95
15. Leather				41			0			0	0
16. Rubber				0			646				
17. Fertilizer							0				
18. Other chem.	3864	6112	1186	8162	316		31			34	10
19. Cement	16596	27241	41724	0	0		0			0	0
20. Basic metals	8070	21430	57704								
21. Metal prod.	9602	20076	8371	1409	775					10	1
22. Machinery	3691	3483	2320	0	0	555				6	15
23. Transport eq.	0	0	0			0	5045			0	0
24. Wood, etc.					13		0				
25. Const., houses					0						
26. Const., buildings											
27. Other const.				3130							
28. Misc. manuf.	725	1280	1646	1267	5217	762	6649			28	30
29. Coal, etc.	0	0	0	0	0	0	0			217	0
30. Elec. and gas										0	
31. Transport											
32. Trade											
33. Housing											
34. Government											
35. Services											
Total	57270	85327	114557	18094	6322	1317	12727			447	151

[a]Full sector names are given in Table A.1.
[b]Rice and wheat in West Pakistan are produced according to nonlinear production functions (see Section 3.11).
[c]There is no jute or jute textiles production in West Pakistan.

Table 3.10.   Working Capital Requirements Per Unit Increase of Final Demand

Sector[a]	East Pakistan	West Pakistan
1. Rice	0.150	0.150
2. Wheat	.150	.150
3. Jute	.150	
4. Cotton	.150	.150
5. Tea	.150	.150
6. Other agric.	.150	.150
7. Sugar	.277	.307
8. Edible oils	.050	.050
9. Tobacco	.014	.014
10. Other food	.200	.100
11. Cotton text.	.160	.229
12. Jute text.	.234	.234
13. Other text.	.068	.153
14. Paper	.175	.159
15. Leather	.219	.296
16. Rubber	.052	.070
17. Fertilizer	.118	.106
18. Other chem.	.119	.153
19. Cement	.165	.170
20. Basic metals	.446	.413
21. Metal prod.	.126	.115
22. Machinery	.155	.169
23. Transport eq.	.347	.247
24. Wood, etc.	.184	.194
28. Misc. manuf.	.166	.183
29. Coal, etc.	.200	.200

[a]Full sector names are given in Table A.1.

import of type j to regional production of type j plus use-specific noncompetitive import of type j required per unit of expansion of the output of sector j. The term μ_{ic} is the noncompetitive requirement of imports of type i per unit of expansion of consumption. There is no conceptual reason why deliveries of use-specific noncompetitive imports are not required to other demand categories. Primarily, since noncompetitive capital goods imports are classed as nonuse-specific, it was not necessary to show use-specific requirements for demand categories other than intermediate and consumption.

The formulation of the regional trade equations is parallel to the foreign import equations:

$$r_i^1 = \hat{r}_i^1 + \bar{r}_i^1$$

and

$$\bar{r}^1 = \sum \mu'_{ij} x_{ij} + \mu'_{ic} c$$

where the notation is as in the case of foreign imports and the prime notation indicates a regional parameter.

The noncompetitive import requirements are shown in Tables 3.11, 3.12, and 3.13. Note that diagonal coefficients for sectors where nonuse-specific coefficients are specified include, in some cases, use-specific requirements (note particularly the basic metals and coal and petroleum products industries). In Table 3.14 foreign import cost data are broken down into foreign exchange cost (CIF), tariff, trade margin, and transport margin per unit of product measured at domestic purchasers' prices. Regional trade cost data are shown in Tables 3.15 and 3.16.[14]

3.9 Exogenous Demand Elements

Two elements of final demand are exogenously determined: replacement of fixed capital and government expenditures on public administration and defense. Exogenous specification of these items is justified on the grounds that given the general level of the economy, these items are not sensitive to other elements of the model. Furthermore, even though there is some degree of dependence of these variables upon others of the model, knowledge of this relationship is too poor to allow meaningful specification. The estimates employed are shown in Table 3.17, and their derivation is explained in MacEwan (1968).

3.10 Exports, Savings, and Foreign Funds

The model considers those basic limits to the expansion of the economy that are imposed by the availability of foreign exchange for importing and the availability of capital for producing commodities. Both these resources can be created within the system—foreign exchange through exporting, and capital through saving. Further, the internally created resources can be augmented from abroad by the inflow of foreign funds.

Table 3.11. Noncompetitive Foreign Import Coefficients, East Pakistan[a]

Import	Receiving sector	Purchasers' price coefficient	Foreign exchange coefficient
5. Tea	Private consumption	0.00040	0.00030
6. Other agric.		.00090	.00060
13. Other text.		.00040	.00020
14. Paper		.00110	.00060
16. Rubber		.00070	.00030
4. Cotton	11. Cotton text.	.03390	.02825
11. Cotton text.		.00908	.00547
13. Other text.	13. Other text.	.03998	.01212
14. Paper	14. Paper	.08808	.04541
16. Rubber	16. Rubber	.20391	.08061
18. Other chem.	18. Other chem.	.20000	.10990
20. Basic metals	20. Basic metals	1.00000	.56810
21. Metal prod.	21. Metal prod.	0.10000	.05128
22. Machinery	22. Machinery	.66500	.35185
23. Transport eq.	23. Transport eq.	.50000	.26455
6. Other agric.	24. Wood, etc.	.08336	.05955
24. Wood, etc.		.06000	.02554
29. Coal, etc.	29. Coal, etc.	.50000	.24150
16. Rubber	31. Transport	.00575	.00228
31. Transport		.03000	.03000
35. Services	35. Services	.00500	.00500

[a]Each entry is shown at purchasers' price and at foreign exchange price.

Table 3.12. Noncompetitive Foreign Import Coefficients, West Pakistan[a]

Import	Receiving sector	Purchasers' price coefficient	Foreign exchange coefficient
5. Tea	Private consumption	0.00010	0.00010
6. Other agric.		.00110	.00080
9. Tobacco		.00010	.00010
14. Paper		.00150	.00080
15. Leather		.00060	.00010
6. Other agric.	9. Tobacco	.07923	.05660
6. Other agric.	10. Other food	.00201	.00144
4. Cotton	11. Cotton text.	.00296	.00247
11. Cotton text.		.00116	.00070
13. Other text.		.00156	.00048
6. Other agric.	13. Other text.	.00827	.00596
11. Cotton text.		.00504	.00304
13. Other text.		.06845	.02074
6. Other agric.	14. Paper	.02779	.01985
11. Cotton text.	15. Leather	.00130	.00078
15. Leather		.00062	.00037
16. Rubber	16. Rubber	.19919	.12450
6. Other agric.	18. Other chem.	.00114	.00081
18. Other chem.		.20000	.10990
20. Basic metals	20. Basic metals	1.00000	.56810
21. Metal prod.	21. Metal prod.	0.10000	.05128
22. Machinery	22. Machinery	.66500	.35185
23. Transport eq.	23. Transport eq.	.50000	.26455
6. Other agric.	24. Wood, etc.	.05882	.04202
6. Other agric.	28. Misc. manuf.	.00241	.00172
11. Cotton text.		.00154	.00093
29. Coal, etc.	29. Coal, etc.	.50000	.24150
16. Rubber	31. Transport	.03125	.01236
31. Transport		.02400	.02400
35. Services	35. Services	.00200	.00200

[a]Each entry is shown at purchasers' price and foreign exchange price.

Table 3.13. Noncompetitive Regional Trade Coefficients[a]

Supplying sector	Receiving sector	Purchasers' price coefficient	Coefficient exclusive of margins[b]
		East to West	
6. Other agric.	Private consumption	0.0038	0.0023
15. Leather		.0005	.0003
18. Other chem.		.0041	.0031
5. Tea	5. Tea	.79387	.54642
15. Leather	15. Leather	.02350	.01382
		West to East	
6. Other agric.	Private consumption	0.0007	0.0005
13. Other text.		.0005	.0005
14. Paper		.0005	.0004
6. Other agric.	9. Tobacco	.13242	.09129
4. Cotton	11. Cotton text.	.22035	.15628

[a]Does not include jute trade.
[b]Margins are the trade and transport costs.

In this section the limits to export earning and generation of savings and inflow of funds are presented. While the accuracy of the specific variable limits and parameter values chosen for the basic solution may be subject to serious doubt, it is precisely these limits and parameters that will be varied in subsequent chapters in order to learn their relationship to industrial priorities.

Exports

Regional exports from one region are, of course, the regional imports of the other region. Therefore, regional exports have been implicitly dealt with in Section 3.8. Accordingly, here only foreign exports will be dealt with.

While almost all of Pakistan's foreign exports are an insignificant part of world supply—jute and jute textiles are the exceptions—this study has argued that, nonetheless, limits to export expansion other than the ability to produce exist. Perhaps the most serious such limit at any one time is the marketing

Table 3.14. **Foreign Import Costs**
(in percent of market value)

Sector	CIF	Tariff	Trade	Transports
1. Rice	0.6666	0	0.3084	0.0250
2. Wheat	.7585		.0923	.0585
4. Cotton	.8333	.0833	.0584	.0250
5. Tea	.7194	.1007	.1699	.0100
6. Other agric.	.7143	.0857	.1800	.0200
7. Sugar	.2344	.1450	.6006	.0200
8. Edible oils	.4854	.2282	.2664	.0200
9. Tobacco	.2336	.6425	.1039	.0200
10. Other food	.3832	.4137	.1831	.0200
11. Cotton text.	.6024	.3233	.0602	.0141
13. Other text.	.3030	.5455	.1415	.0100
14. Paper	.5155	.3968	.0677	.0200
15. Leather	.5882	.3295	.0588	.0235
16. Rubber	.3953	.1621	.4056	.0370
17. Fertilizer	.8696		.0248	.1056
18. Other chem.	.5495	.2253	.2052	.0200
19. Cement	.5405	.2918	.0542	.1135
20. Basic metals	.5681	.0966	.2703	.0650
21. Metal prod.	.5128	.3385	.1087	.0400
22. Machinery	.5291	.0661	.3548	.0500
23. Transport eq.	.5291	.0661	.3848	.0200
24. Wood, etc.	.4255	.4085	.1210	.0450
28. Misc. manuf.	.3985	.2430	.3385	.0200
29. Coal, etc.	.4830	.2755	.1615	.0800
Special paper	.5155	.3968	.0677	.0200

problem. Commodities cannot simply be sold on the world market per se. Expansion of exports requires the creation of new markets or the expansion of old markets or both. That often requires breaking through trade barriers and established trade practices by either government trade treaties or special marketing efforts. Though such limits should ideally be specified in terms of falling returns to exporting (or rising costs), they are specified in the model in terms of absolute upper limits.

For each region an over-all export limit is specified, and for each sector in each region, with the exception of nonfoodgrain agricultural sectors, sector specific limits are specified, with the sum of the sector specific limits exceeding

Table 3.15. **Regional Trade Costs, East to West**
(in percent of market value)

Sector	CIF	Trade	Transports
5. Tea	0.6883	0.3067	0.0050
6. Other agric.	.5896	.3942	.0162
7. Sugar	.9410	.0500	.0090
8. Edible oils	.8344	.1356	.0300
9. Tobacco	.8406	.1418	.0176
10. Other food	.6956	.2844	.0200
12. Jute text.	.0351	.0363	.0100
13. Other text.	.6111	.3742	.0147
14. Paper	.7758	.2134	.0108
15. Leather	.5391	.4348	.0261
16. Rubber	.8513	.0987	.0500
17. Fertilizer	.8696	.0258	.1056
18. Other chem.	.7494	.2341	.0165
19. Cement	.7977	.0823	.1200
20. Basic metals	.8656	.0884	.0500
21. Metal prod.	.8666	.1034	.0300
22. Machinery	.9107	.0493	.0400
23. Transport eq.	.9107	.0493	.0400
24. Wood, etc.	.8760	.1024	.0216
28. Misc. manuf.	.8760	.1024	.0216
29. Coal, etc.	.8307	.0893	.0800
Special paper	.7758	.2134	.0108

the over-all limit for the region. The model, then, is presented with a limited choice in expanding exports.[15] The limits for a region are:

$$p_i e_i \leq \bar{e}_i$$

where $\bar{e}_i$ is the limit on the increment to exports from sector i;

$$\sum_i p_i e_i \leq \bar{E}$$

where $\bar{E}$ is the over-all limit on the increment to exports for the region; and

$$\bar{E} < \sum_i \bar{e}_i$$

As well as being desirable because it allows the model some choice in determining exports, this method seems reasonable on the basis of the export limits. While

Table 3.16. Regional Trade Costs, West to East
(in percent of market value)

Sector	CIF	Trade	Transports
2. Wheat	0.6447	0.3411	0.0043
4. Cotton	.7092	.2626	.0282
6. Other agric.	.6894	.2806	.0300
7. Sugar	.8888	.0812	.0300
8. Edible oils	.8344	.1356	.0300
9. Tobacco	.8562	.1188	.0250
10. Other food	.6956	.2844	.0200
11. Cotton text.	.9151	.0649	.0200
13. Other text.	.9152	.0748	.0100
14. Paper	.8750	.0750	.0500
15. Leather	.8461	.1289	.0250
16. Rubber	.8513	.0987	.0500
17. Fertilizer	.8696	.0258	.1056
18. Other chem.	.8816	.0984	.0200
19. Cement	.7977	.0823	.1200
20. Basic metals	.8656	.0884	.0500
21. Metal prod.	.8666	.1034	.0300
22. Machinery	.9107	.0493	.0400
23. Transport eq.	.9107	.0493	.0400
24. Wood, etc.	.8849	.0851	.0300
28. Misc. manuf.	.8849	.0851	.0300
29. Coal, etc.	.8307	.0893	.0800

Table 3.17. Estimates of Increments to Government Expenditures and Replacement Investment, 1964–65 to 1974–75
(in million rupees)

	East Pakistan	West Pakistan
Government expenditures	361.6	828.9
Replacement investment by type of asset		
21. Metal prod.	4.0	7.2
22. Machinery	281.2	578.5
23. Transport eq.	224.7	336.8
24. Wood, etc.	3.0	5.3
26. Const., buildings	103.4	108.3
27. Other const.	340.1	558.7
Total	956.4	1,594.8

Table 3.18. **Sector Specific Limits on Increments to Foreign Exports and
1964–65 Exports from Those Sectors**
(in million rupees of foreign exchange)

	East Pakistan		West Pakistan	
Sector	1964–65 exports	Limit on increment	1964–65 exports	Limit on increment
1. Rice		150	123	500
2. Wheat			2	100
7. Sugar		5	5	10
8. Edible oils		5		10
10. Other food		5	4	10
11. Cotton text.	5	10	275	275
12. Jute text.	282	400		
13. Other text.	19	50	33	100
14. Paper	6	10		10
15. Leather	12	50	56	100
16. Rubber		5	2	10
18. Other chem.	1	10	17	50
21. Metal prod.		5	7	10
22. Machinery		5	14	40
23. Transport eq.		5	4	10
24. Wood, etc.		5		5
28. Misc. manuf.	1	10	54	50
29. Coal, etc.		5	32	10

market limitations apply to the products of individual sectors, there is a degree
to which the export of one product can be promoted at the expense of another.
Especially with regard to government barter agreements, but also with regard
to private export marketing, it is not possible to push everywhere at the same
time. The model is forced to choose where to push. No sector specific limits have
been set for nonfoodgrain agricultural products since these are, in general,
traditional, that is, well-established, exports and since the agricultural growth
limits (see Section 3.11) implicitly provide export limits.

The export limits were estimated by first choosing an over-all growth rate for
exports and then specifying limits for each sector in line with the over-all limits
and with past experience. The over-all rate of growth of exports for the basic
solution is 7.5 percent per annum, based on the Third Plan estimates. That is,
the value of $\bar{E}$, the limit to the increment to total foreign exchange earnings, is
Rs1345 million for East Pakistan and Rs1209 million for West Pakistan. The
export limits for specific sectors and the 1964–65 actual export levels are shown
in Table 3.18. The limit of Rs5 million is set on the increment to exports in those

sectors where there was no export prior to the plan period. The limit of Rs10 million is set for sectors where there has been some very, very small exporting in the past. By specifying these small limits, it is possible to learn where export expansion might prove profitable without allowing any unreasonable results to occur. Other limits have been estimated on the basis of a consideration of past performance and examination of Third Plan expectations. Only exports of cigarettes, fertilizer, basic metals, and cement and concrete products have been completely excluded on a priori grounds.

The limits so far have been specified in terms of foreign exchange earnings. However, exports are measured in terms of domestic prices. The unit foreign exchange earning of exports in the model is equal to the unit foreign exchange cost of imports (see Tables 3.14, 3.15, and 3.16). That involves a slight conceptual error, since CIF prices should exceed FOB (free on board) prices; but as a practical matter, this should be of no consequence, since other costs are what make the big difference.

Savings

Domestic savings is defined to include all forms of saving out of domestic income, whether "voluntary" personal savings or savings "forced" by one or another form of fiscal or monetary policy. The basic assumption is that there are certain limits to what the public will be willing to save, but exactly how that saving is brought about is not within the scope of this study. The savings limits imposed upon the model are simply assumptions about what can be done.

There is no empirical information available that allows any rigorous estimation of marginal savings rates for various parts of the economy. Ideally, value added in each sector would be broken into component parts—profits, wages, rents—and a separate savings rate would be estimated for each component. Differences between sectors would be explained by different shares of the components. In the absence of pertinent information, only two marginal savings rates are distinguished in any solution to the model: a savings rate for value added in agricultural sectors and a savings rate for value added in all other sectors. That is, in a region

$$S = \sum_{i=1}^{6} s_1 v_i + \sum_{i=7}^{35} s_2 v_i$$

where

s_1 = the marginal savings rate on value added in agricultural sectors
s_2 = the marginal savings rate on value added in other sectors
v_i = increment to value added in the ith sector.

For sectors other than special foodgrain sectors

$$v_i = \nu_i x_i$$

where

$$\nu_i = 1 - \sum_j a_{ji}$$

that is, ν_i is the incremental ratio of value added to output. In special foodgrains sectors value added is specified separately for each part of the production activity (see Section 3.11).

In the basic solution, the savings rates are taken as 14 percent of value added for agricultural sectors and 24 percent for nonagricultural sectors. Those rates were chosen to obtain an aggregate marginal savings rate of about 22 percent, the rate assumed for the Third Plan (Pakistan 1965a). Those rates are the same for both regions, but it should be noted that since agriculture provides a larger share of value added in East Pakistan, the aggregate savings rate will tend to be lower in East Pakistan.

There is one exception to the specification of a uniform savings rate on value added for the nonagricultural sectors. Because of the extremely high tax rates on tobacco products (9), the savings rate for that sector is specified 62 percent, that is, 50 percent plus 24 percent of the remainder.

Foreign Funds

All inflow of funds from abroad not earned by exports is subsumed under the heading of foreign funds—foreign aid, foreign private investment, remittances from Pakistanis working abroad. However, the model is formulated on the assumption that the central planning authority controls all of this inflow as though it were aid given directly to the government. It should be emphasized that the inflow of funds is a net concept and the model takes no explicit account of the repayment obligations that may be incurred.

In the basic solution it is assumed that there will be no net change in the inflow of foreign funds between 1964–65 and 1974–75, that is, F is zero. This assumption is roughly equivalent to that of the Third Plan document (Pakistan 1965a). This limit is a national limit only. Solution of the model determines the flow of funds between the regions.

3.11 Production in Agriculture

Some special attention must be given to specifying production possibilities in the agricultural sectors. The traditional input-output approach used for the other sectors cannot be adopted in agriculture without modification for three reasons:

1. Technological changes are expected to be quite significant in some agricultural sectors during the period 1964–65 to 1974–75. Because of their disembodied nature, these changes can affect the entire production structure of the sectors.

2. Traditional and modern methods of cultivation exist simultaneously in Pakistan agriculture, although in terms of resource constraints explicitly specified in the present model, there is no economic reason for this dualism.

3. Because the availability of land is fixed, output cannot increase proportionally to inputs without limit; that is, diminishing returns exist.

For the major foodgrain sectors—rice in both regions and wheat in West Pakistan—in which technical change will be of most importance, separate production functions have been specified for traditional and modern cultivation. In any single solution of the model it is necessary to prespecify the acreage division of the land between modern and traditional cultivation. By obtaining alternative solutions to the model, it is possible to investigate the implications of various degrees of success of the introduction of the new techniques in foodgrains production (see Chapter 6).

Although modern techniques of cultivation are economically superior,[16] there are several limitations to the rate of adoption, and these limitations cannot be explicitly specified in the model. First, the old technology is embodied in agricultural human capital, and to change the human capital requires education and dissemination of information.[17] Second, there is the problem of the physical supply of new seeds. And for the new seeds to have their full value, the complementary imports of fertilizer and water control must be available. Third, there is a certain amount of uncertainty involved both with respect to the actual success of the new varieties and with respect to market conditions that will encourage their adoption. All those factors lead to a good deal of uncertainty about the degree of adoption of new cultivation practices by 1974–75.

In the basic solution to the model a "medium" level assumption is made with regard to adoption of new practices in each of the foodgrain sectors; in Chapter 6, the implications of alternative assumptions are investigated. In all solutions to the model the acreage allocated to the entire crop and the acreage yield on land under traditional cultivation are the same. The division in the basic solution between modern and traditional and the yield on traditional for each of the sectors are shown in Table 3.19 (Alim et al. 1966; Narvaez 1966).

For modern cultivation, while the degree of adoption in acreage is specified, solution to the model determines the intensity of operation. The production

Table 3.19. Foodgrain Acreage and Yield Assumptions
(in millions of acres)

Foodgrain	Total acreage	Modern area	Traditional area	Traditional area yield per acre
East Rice	23.0	6.0	17.0	966 lbs.[a]
West Rice	3.5	2.0	1.5	834[a]
West Wheat	13.0	6.0	7.0	701

[a]Cleaned rice

functions for the modern part of foodgrains production are constructed upon two principal assumptions:

1. Inputs of the modern physical inputs—fertilizer, pesticides, (increments to) capital, spare parts and fuel—are in fixed proportion to one another. Therefore part of the optimizing process, the choice of input proportions, is prespecified. (It should be pointed out that the primary use of capital is for water control. That fact makes the fixed relationship between fertilizer and capital less unreasonable.)

2. There are diminishing returns with respect to this bundle of inputs (recall that land is fixed).

The diminishing returns production function is approximated by a linear step function. In fact, it is the step function which is directly estimated.[18] For each of the foodgrain sectors a step function has been defined in terms of fertilizer and capital (other inputs are specified in relation to these). The parameters of these step functions are shown for the three foodgrain sectors in Table 3.20. For West Pakistan wheat, the total modern output function as defined in the table is illustrated in Figure 3.1. Without the application of any modern fertilizer, a yield of 900 pounds per acre can be obtained.[19] As fertilizer is applied, each nutrient pound of fertilizer combined with Rs1.13 additional capital yields 18 pounds of wheat. However, once 90 pounds of fertilizer has been applied and a total yield of 2520 pounds of wheat obtained, the fertilizer response rate drops to 14. Beyond 180 pounds of fertilizer and a yield of 3780 pounds of wheat, the response rate drops to 10. Additions of fertilizer-capital bundles beyond 210 pounds of fertilizer yield no output increase.

Notes to Tables 3.21, 3.22, 3.23

In Tables 3.21, 3.22, and 3.23, the complete set of numerical relationships for the foodgrains sectors is presented.

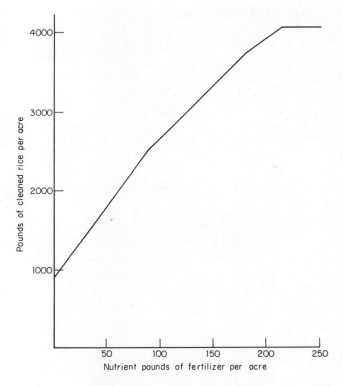

Figure 3.1 Output-Fertilizer Relationship for Modern Cultivation of West Pakistan Wheat

The tables present in tableau form complete numerical specifications of the foodgrains sectors for the basic solution. Following are details of estimation.[20]

1. All inputs recorded as proportional to the change in output (x) are inputs to grain processing and service inputs. They are taken at the base year rate.

2. Inputs of pesticide (sector 18) are taken at a base level of Rs1 per acre for wheat and Rs2 per acre for rice. This is charged against traditional activity (X^T) and the basic level of the modern activity (X_0^M). Increases in output by the modern activity require increases in pesticide application proportional to the increase of fertilizer—Rs0.5 of pesticide with 90 pounds of fertilizer for wheat and Rs0.6 per 100 pounds of fertilizer for rice.

3. Inputs to the nonprocessing part of each sector of spare parts (sector 22) and of fuel (sectors 29 and 30) are proportional to the amount of machinery capital embodied in each activity. Thus, though activity (X_0^M) requires no addi-

Table 3.20. Basic Input-Output Relations for Modern Cultivation of Foodgrains[a]
(values in 1964–65 rupees)

Value of output per acre	Pounds of cleaned rice per acre	Fertilizer response rate	Nutrient pounds of fertilizer per acre	Value of fertilizer per acre	Value of capital stock per acre
		East Pakistan Rice			
426.7	1066.7		0	0	281.5
1093.3	2733.3	16.67	100	85.0	351.9
1360.0	3400.0	13.33	150	127.5	387.1
1560.0	3900.0	10.00	200	170.0	422.3
		West Pakistan Rice			
426.7	1066.7		0	0	563.0
1093.3	2733.3	16.67	100	85.0	703.8
1360.0	3400.0	13.33	150	127.5	774.1
1560.0	3900.0	10.00	200	170.0	844.5
		West Pakistan Wheat			
270.0[b]	900.0		0	0	406.0
756.0	2520.0	18.00	90	76.5	507.5
1134.0	3780.0	14.00	180	153.0	609.0
1224.0	4080.0	10.00	210	178.5	642.8

[a]Note that in terms of 1964–65 prices, incremental returns exceed incremental cost at all levels for each crop. However, in solution of the model these relative prices will change, that is, relative shadow prices will vary.

[b]The price used for wheat is the value of wheat flour obtained per pound of wheat, since the output of the wheat sector in the model is actually wheat flour. The physical output, however, is expressed in terms of pounds of wheat, not wheat flour.

tion to capital stock, it requires these current inputs. Fuel inputs for East Pakistan rice are zero in the base year input-output table; incremental rates are based on the West Pakistan relationships.

4. While base level capital requirements are the per-acre requirements of the base year, the proportions between machinery and construction capital have been altered in the increments associated with activities X_1^M, X_2^M, X_3^M. The alteration is designed to reflect the rising importance of tubewells and low-life pumps in water control.

5. No direct observation on the base year investment of each type in agriculture (the H_{ij}^0's) are required (see Section 3.6).

6. The α's in the capital input equations are the stock-flow conversion factors explained in Section 3.6.

Table 3.21. Tableau for East Pakistan Rice

	Increment to output	Total output T	Total output M	Steps in process of modern cultivation					Million rupees
	x	X^T	X^M	X_0^M	X_1^M	X_2^M	X_3^M		
	1.0	−1.0	−1.0					=	−8,229.0
		1.0						=	6,568.8
			1.0	−1.0	−1.0	−1.0	−1.0	=	0
				1.0				≤	2,560.2
					1.0			≤	3,999.6
						1.0		≤	1,600.2
							1.0	≤	1,200.0

Incremental current inputs from

1. Rice (seed)	0	0		0	0	0	0	=	99.8
6. Other agric.								=	0
12. Jute text.	.00281								
14. Paper	.00033								
17. Fertilizer		.00727			.12751	.15936	.21250		−59.8
18. Other chem.		.00518		.00469	.00090	.00112	.00150		−15.0
22. Machinery		.00452		.00532	.00232	.00290	.00387		−37.2
28. Misc. manuf.	.00009								
29. Coal, etc.	.00112			.00069	.00028	.00035	.00047		
30. Elec. and gas	.00008			.00075	.00033	.00041	.00054		
31. Transport	.03003								
32. Trade	.03760								
34. Government	.00009								
35. Services	.00046								

Incremental capital inputs from

21. Metal prod.	.00216α							−	
22. Machinery	.06526α				.02112α	.02639α	.03520α	−	
24. Wood, etc.	.00011α							− H_{i1}^0	
26. Const., buildings	.02326α							−	
27. Other const.					.08449α	.10544α	.14080α	−	

Table 3.22.   Tableau for West Pakistan Rice

	Increment to output	Total output T	M	Steps in process of modern cultivation					
	x	X^T	X^M	X_0^M	X_1^M	X_2^M	X_3^M		Million rupees
	1.0	−1.0	−1.0					=	−1,101.9
		1.0						=	500.4
			1.0	−1.0	−1.0	−1.0	−1.0	=	0
				1.0				≤	853.4
					1.0			≤	1,333.2
						1.0		≤	533.4
							1.0	≤	400.0
Incremental current inputs from									
1. Rice (seed)	0	0		0	0	0	0	=	20.3
6. Other agric.								=	0
12. Jute text.	.00704								
17. Fertilizer		.01621			.12751	.15936	.21250		−17.9
18. Other chem.		.00600		.00469	.00090	.00112	.00150		−3.2
22. Machinery		.01064		.01064	.00464	.00580	.00774		−11.7
29. Coal, etc.	.01032	.00128		.00128	.00056	.00070	.00093		−1.4
30. Elec. and gas	.00233	.00149		.00149	.00065	.00081	.00108		−1.6
31. Transport	.12902								
32. Trade	.03208								
34. Government	.00048								
35. Services	.00347								
Incremental capital inputs from									
21. Metal prod.	.00192α								−
22. Machinery	.11619α				.04224α	.05227α	.07040α		−
23. Transport eq.	.00195α								$-H_{i1}^0$
24. Wood, etc.	.00094α								−
26. Const., buildings	.10531α								−
27. Other const.					.16898α	.21108α	.28160α		−

Table 3.23. Tableau for West Pakistan Wheat

	Increment to output	Total output T	M	Steps in process of modern cultivation				
	x	X^T	X^M	X_0^M	X_1^M	X_2^M	X_3^M	Million rupees
	1.0	−1.0	−1.0					$=$ −2,580.5
		1.0						$=$ 1,472.1
			1.0	−1.0	−1.0	−1.0	−1.0	$=$ 0
				1.0				$\leq$ 1,620.0
					1.0			$\leq$ 2,916.0
						1.0		$\leq$ 2,268.0
							1.0	$\leq$ 540.0

Incremental current inputs from

2. Wheat (seed)	0	0		0	0	0	0	$=$ 74.5
6. Other agric.								$=$ 0
12. Jute text.	.00279							
17. Fertilizer		.01616			.15741	.20238	.28333	−41.7
18. Other chem.		.00476		.00370	.00103	.00132	.00186	
22. Machinery		.00784		.00784	.00273	.00352	.00492	−20.2
29. Coal, etc.	.00099	.00042		.00042	.00015	.00019	.00026	−1.1
30. Elec. and gas	.00385	.00149		.00149	.00052	.00067	.00093	−3.8
31. Transport	.00893							
32. Trade	.02786							
34. Government	.00012							
35. Services	.00121							

Incremental capital inputs from

21. Metal prod.	$.00127\alpha$							$-$
22. Machinery	$.03755\alpha$				$.04177\alpha$	$.05371\alpha$	$.07510\alpha$	$-$
23. Transport eq.	$.00086\alpha$							$-H_{i2}^{0}$
24. Wood, etc.	$.00042\alpha$							$-$
26. Const., buildings	$.01864\alpha$							$-$
27. Other const.					$.16709\alpha$	$.21482\alpha$	$.30042\alpha$	$-$

7. Seed requirements for both rice and wheat are most accurately determined as functions of acreage under each type of cultivation, with the optimal seed rate for modern cultivation about twice that of traditional cultivation (see reports of Alim et al. 1966; Abbasi et al. 1966; and Qureshi and Narvaez 1967). Incremental requirements of seed-input for each foodgrain crop are determined according to:

$$x_{jj} = PAs^1 + (1 - P)As - X_{jj}^0$$

where s and s^1 are the per acre seed rates for traditional and modern cultivation. The numbers used are shown in Tables 3.21–3.23. Per acre requirements of bullock power and dung are taken at the 1964–65 level, that is, incremental requirements are zero. Without significant change in acreage, the requirements of these inputs will not rise. Increased yield will not be due to increased application of these inputs; in fact, it is likely that modern inputs will tend to replace these inputs rather than complement them.

So that the numerical relationships will be understood, the algebraic relationships for these sectors will be laid out. For any one of the foodgrain sectors, the increment to output over the plan period is given by:

$$x = X^T + X^M - X^0$$

where

$$X^T = \text{1974–75 output by traditional methods}$$
$$X^M = \text{1974–75 output by modern methods}$$
$$X^0 = \text{1964–65 output}$$

Total acreage (A), the share of acreage allocated to modern cultivation (P), and the per acre (value) yield of traditional cultivation (Y^T) are prespecified. Therefore X^T is predetermined as:

$$X^T = (1 - P)AY^T$$

Inputs to traditional cultivation (except bullock power, dung, and seed) are proportional to output and therefore predetermined. Output by modern cultivation practices is the sum of output attained by operation of each activity of the step function. That is,

$$X^M = X_0^M + X_1^M + X_2^M + X_3^M$$

and

$$X_i^M \le PAY_i^M$$

where Y_i^M is the maximum yield attainable by the ith activity of the step func-

71

tion described in Table 3.20. Each X_i^M defines the level of operation of a step in the process of raising the intensity of modern cultivation. Service inputs and inputs to processing are proportional to total output. Seed, bullock power, and dung inputs are determined as a function of acreage (see notes to Tables 3.21, 22, and 23). Modern inputs—inputs of fertilizer, pesticides, capital, spare parts, oil fuel—to each step in the process are proportional to that step. That is, for an input from sector i to modern cultivation in the foodgrains sector:

$$X_{ij} = a_{ij}^1 X_1^M + a_{ij}^2 X_2^M + a_{ij}^3 X_3^M$$

where

$$a_{ij}^1 < a_{ij}^2 < a_{ij}^3$$

because of increasing cost. (Recall that X_0^M requires no input of fertilizer or increased capital; however, X_0^M does require spare parts, fuel and pesticides inputs.

For the nonfoodgrains agricultural sectors, large changes in technology are not expected prior to 1974–75. Nonetheless, it would be unreasonable to assume output growth in these other sectors without technological change; even with technological change, some limits must be placed on output in addition to those imposed by the supply of physical inputs, capital, and foreign exchange.[21]

Although only a single fixed coefficients production function has been employed for each of the nonfoodgrain sectors, the incremental current and capital input coefficients (see Tables 3.4, 3.5, 3.6, and 3.7) have been estimated to take into account expected technical changes. In particular, incremental use of fertilizer, pesticides, and capital has been estimated as much higher than average.

In spite of these adjustments, there are certain limits to agricultural growth which must be taken into account. Without the sort of changes that are being undertaken in the foodgrains sectors, without changes in human capital, without changes in overhead capital systems, without the development of agricultural financing, without general changes in the social and institutional system, there is no reason to expect rapid growth of Pakistan agriculture. Therefore, in the model absolute upper limits have been specified for the growth of nonfoodgrain sectors (and wheat in East Pakistan) of 63 percent over the peak output obtained up to 1964–65, that is, a limit of 5 percent per annum over the plan period.[22] This limit, however, was modified for East Pakistan tea when it was found to play an unreasonably important role in early solutions. For East Pakistan tea a limit of 6.5 percent per annum was used.

3.12 Special Constraints

In addition to the constraints presented and explained in the preceding sections, certain limits or boundary conditions must be specified which will insure the "realistic" operation of the system. Some of these play an important role in determining the solution of the model.

Imports of Raw Cotton to West Pakistan

In addition to the growth rate limits on the output of nonfoodgrain agricultural sectors, limits were placed on the import of goods classified under other agriculture (6). This limit was 20 percent of production. The imposition of such a limit is justified by the perishable or nontradable character, or combination of both, of a large portion of the output of sector (6). The same limit, 20 percent of production, is placed on the imports of raw cotton to West Pakistan. This limit is imposed on the a priori grounds that whatever the model shows, it would not be reasonable for West Pakistan to have a cotton textile industry largely based upon imported cotton. (The reasoning is similar to that used in specifying noncompetitive imports.)

Importing in Order to Export

Because prices of regional exports may exceed prices of regional imports, it can prove profitable for one region to import from the other to reexport to the other. Also, because the international export limits are region specific, it might prove profitable for one region to import from the other simply to export abroad. Both these complications can be viewed as aggregation problems. They can be dealt with simultaneously by specifying constraints that require production in a region not to be less than regional and foreign export deliveries. This constraint for each tradable commodity eliminates the unrealistic importing-to-export phenomenon. The same constraint is used to insure that noncompetitive regional exports from one region will be produced within that region.[23]

Excessive Imports to Earn Tariff Revenue

Because of the very high tariff revenue earned from certain categories of imports, it can prove optimal to import excessive quantities of the item to earn the tariff revenue. That occurs when investment funds are scarce relative to foreign exchange. Such behavior is prevented by specifying as equalities, rather than as inequalities, the balance relationships for sectors where it could occur— tobacco products (9), other food (10), and other textiles (13).

Absolute Import Substitution

Choices in the model concern increments to output and imports between 1964–65 and 1974–75. That is, there is no absolute import substitution; only substitution at the margin is considered. That approach is justified, since the model is intended only to deal with questions regarding patterns and directions of change; in most cases, significant absolute import substitution can be ruled out on a priori grounds.[24] There are, however, two departures from this procedure. First, to take into account the full potential of the foodgrain production programs, absolute import substitution for these commodities must be considered. Import activities for foodgrain sectors are therefore formulated in terms of absolute amounts. Second, because of the abnormally large amounts of imports of basic metals in the base year, supply in that year was unusually high.[25] Without allowing some absolute import substitution in the basic metal sectors, there would be very little growth of supply in those sectors. Therefore, absolute import substitution activities for the basic metals sectors are included, and more about the proper program for those sectors can be learned. Those activities are simply negative import activities with upper limits of Rs100 million of import substitution.[26]

Special Paper Imports

In estimating noncompetitive import requirements, regional and foreign imports have been considered separately. That is, a noncompetitive import has been specified as being of origin either abroad or in the other region. In one case, however, the model chooses the origin of a noncompetitive import into West Pakistan. West Pakistan cannot produce certain kinds of paper that must therefore be imported. These items can be imported from either East Pakistan or abroad. In the model, a special row is specified for those kinds of paper, and special import activities to West Pakistan can create that supply of them. The requirements for these noncompetitive imports of paper are shown in Table 3.24.

Jute Textile Imports

Jute textile imports to West Pakistan are also somewhat of a special case. No foreign import of jute to either East or West is allowed in the model, and West must obtain jute textiles from East. The requirements of West Pakistan are simply specified as a row in the input-output table, and the only source of supply is the East-to-West trade activity.

Table 3.24.   Requirements of Noncompetitive Paper Imports for West Pakistan[a]

Receiving sector	Coefficient[b]
5. Tea	0.029604
9. Tobacco	.028059
10. Other food	.025702
11. Cotton text.	.000574
13. Other text.	.001563
14. Paper	.168858
15. Leather	.000727
16. Rubber	.004293
18. Other chem.	.001275
19. Cement	.016474
21. Metal prod.	.003571
28. Misc. manuf.	.048913
31. Transport	.005352
32. Trade	.000185
34. Government	.002709
35. Services	.002573

[a]Does not include noncompetitive import of printed matter.
[b]Quantity divided by output of the using large-scale sector; includes inventories.

Interregional Paper Trade

Because of the very different product mixes of the paper industries in the two regions of Pakistan, it would not be reasonable to allow one region's supply to be produced entirely in the other region. Therefore, competitive regional imports of paper are limited to 33 percent of supply for each region.[27]

West Pakistan Cottonseed Oils

In West Pakistan edible oils production is significantly dependent upon cottonseeds. However, since cottonseeds are only a by-product of the cotton sector, the delivery from the cotton sector to the edible oils sector in West Pakistan is limited as a percentage of the output of the cotton sector. That limit is specified by preventing the value of output of the edible oils sector from exceeding that of the cotton sector.

Appendix
to
Chapter 3:
The Complete
Model

Throughout Chapter 3, the complete linear programming model was laid out. The system is brought together here for the convenience of the reader. However, here the special relationships for foodgrains production have not been shown. Regional relationships—those that enter the system separately for each region— are shown here only once and without superscript. National relationships— those including variables of both regions—are shown here with superscripts denoting the region to which each variable belongs. Variable and parameter definitions follow the complete model. Unless otherwise specified, sectoral subscripts run from 1–35.

Definitions

Maximize:

$$W = \frac{N^e}{N^e + N^w}\left(\frac{c^e}{N^e} + Q^e\right) + \frac{N^w}{N^e + N^w}\left(\frac{c^w}{N^w} + Q^w\right)$$

Subject to:

Structure of Consumption

$$c_i = \gamma_i + \beta_i c$$

Supply and Demand Balances

Goods and Services*

$$x_i + m_i + r_i^1 \geq c_i + \sum_j x_{ij} + \sum_j h_{ij} + \mathrm{rep}_i + w_i + e_i + r_i^2 + \mathrm{gov}_i$$

Foreign Exchange

$$\sum_i p_i e_i + \sum_i p_i' r_i^2 + f = \sum_i q_i m_i + \sum_i q_i' r_i^1$$

* Note the modification in the trade and transport rows for margins on imports and in the basic metals rows for import substitution (see pages 30 and 74, respectively). Also, note that the relationship is specified as a strict equality for $i = 09, 10, 13$ (see page 73).

Capital

$$S + f + \sum_i \text{tar}_i = \sum_i \sum_j h_{ij} + \sum_i w_i + \sum_i \text{rep}_i + \sum_i \text{gov}_i$$

Over-all Supply of Funds

$$f^e + f^w = F$$

Intermediate Demand

$$x_{ij} = a_{ij}x_j$$

Fixed Capital Requirements

$$h_{ij} = \alpha b_{ij}x_j - H_{0ij}$$

Working Capital Requirements

$$w_i = \alpha \sum_j \omega_{ij}x_j + \alpha\omega_{ic}c + \alpha\omega_{ih}h_i + \alpha\omega_{ir}r_i^2 + \alpha\omega_{ie}e_i - W_i^0$$

Foreign Imports

$$m_i = \hat{m}_i + \overline{m}_i$$

and

$$\overline{m}_i = \sum_j \mu_{ij}x_j + \mu_{ic}c$$

Regional Imports

$$r_i^1 = \hat{r}_i^1 + \overline{r}_i^1$$

and

$$r^1 = \sum_j \mu'_{ij}x_{ij} + \mu'_{ic}c$$

Exogenous Demand Elements

$$\text{rep}_i = \overline{\text{rep}}_i$$
$$\text{gov}_i = \overline{\text{gov}}_i$$

Export Limits

$$p_ie_i \leq \overline{e}_i$$
$$\sum_i p_ie_i \leq \overline{E}$$

where

$$\overline{E} < \sum_i \overline{e}_i$$

Savings Limits

$$S = \sum_{i=1}^{6} s_1 v_i + \sum_{i=7}^{35} s_2 v_i$$
$$v_i = \nu_i x_i$$

where

$$\nu_i = 1 - \sum_j a_{ji}$$

Availability of Foreign Funds

$$F = \overline{F}$$

Agricultural Growth Limits

$$x_i \le X_i^*[(1.05)^{10} - 1] \quad \begin{matrix} i = 02, 03, 04, 06 \text{ in East} \\ i = 04, 06 \text{ in West} \end{matrix}$$

$$x_i < X_i^*[(1.065)^{10} - 1] \quad i = 05 \text{ in East}$$

Limits on Importing in Order to Export

$$x_i \ge r_i^2 + e_i$$

Interregional Paper Trade

$$r_{14}^1 \le 0.33 \, (x_{14} + m_{14} + r_{14}^1)$$

West Pakistan Cottonseed Oil

$$x_{08} \le x_{04}, \quad \text{for West only}$$

The symbols for variables of the system, predetermined and base year variables, and parameters are listed below in the order they appear in the preceding relationships. Variables and parameters are listed without superscript denoting region. Except in the case of national variables and parameters specifically noted, all variables and parameters have separate values for the two regions.

Variables

Increments Over the Plan Period

c aggregate regional consumption

c_i regional consumption of the products of sector i

x_i regional gross output of sector i

m_i imports to the region from abroad of goods classified under sector i

r_i^1 imports to the region from the other region of goods classified under sector i

x_{ij} current deliveries to sector j of goods classified under sector i

h_{ij} net fixed capital deliveries to sector j of goods classified under sector i

rep_i deliveries of goods classified under sector i for replacement investment

w_i working capital deliveries of goods classified under sector i

e_i exports of goods of sector i from the region to abroad

r_i^2 export of goods of sector i from the region to the other region

gov_i government public administration and defense expenditure on the products of the ith sector (zero except for $i = 34$)

f net regional inflow of funds

s aggregate regional savings

tar_i total tariff earned on imports of goods classified under sector i

F net inflow of funds to the nation from abroad

v_i value added in sector i

Predetermined Base Year Variables and Exogenous Variables

N population in 1974–75

Q a negative constant, the decline in per capita consumption which would take place due to population growth were there no growth of consumption

H_{0ij} deliveries of net fixed investment to sector j of goods classified under sector i in the base year

W_{0ij} deliveries of working capital investment to sector j of goods classified under sector i in the base year

$\overline{\text{rep}}_i$ exogenously specified increment over the plan of replacement-investment of type i

$\overline{\text{gov}}_i$ exogenously specified increment over the plan of government expenditures on public administration and defense

$\bar{e}_i$ upper limit on foreign exchange earned from exports abroad of type i

$\overline{E}_i$ upper limit on foreign exchange earned from total exports abroad

$\overline{F}$ exogenously specified increment over the plan to net inflow of funds to other nations from abroad

x_i^* peak output attained up to 1964–65 in nonfoodgrain agricultural sectors

Parameters

γ_i intercept term in ith consumption function

β_i the marginal change in consumption of the ith product with a change in total consumption

p_i FOB price of foreign exports of type i

p_i' FOB price of regional exports of type i

q_i CIF price of foreign imports of type i

q_i' CIF price of regional imports of type i

a_{ij} marginal input-output coefficient

α stock-flow conversion factor

b_{ij} incremental capital output ratio

$\left\{\begin{array}{l} w_{ij} \\ w_{ii} \\ w_{ih} \\ w_{ir} \\ w_{ie} \end{array}\right.$ incremental working capital required per unit of product delivered to the jth sector, consumption, investment, and regional and foreign exports

μ_{ij} increment of noncompetitive foreign imports of type i required per unit of production in sector j

μ_{ic} increment of noncompetitive foreign import of type i required per unit of consumption

μ_{ij}' increment of noncompetitive regional imports of type i required per unit of production in sector j

μ_{ic}' increment of noncompetitive regional imports of type i required per unit of consumption

ν ratio of value added to output

4 | Solution, Dual, and Reference Point

4.1 Solution

The model presented in Chapter 3 should be viewed as a "development planning model" in which trade and output expansion variables are the planners' instruments. The solution of the model is a set of values for the instruments which yield the maximum increment to national per capita consumption, the planners' assumed goal.[1] This chapter describes the general characteristics of the solution to the model and points out the aspects of the solution which are especially important for industrial planning. The nature of the dual programming problem is discussed; certain variables of the dual are as important to an understanding of the industrial priority issues as are the variables of the primal solution. The complete basic solution—primal and dual—is presented and will serve as a reference point in analyzing the relationship between the important macroeconomic variables and industrial priorities. With a reference point established, other solutions can be described in terms of how they differ from the basic solution.

The tendency of the model is to choose in the solution a single source of supply for each tradable commodity. Either a tradable good will be produced in one region and traded to the other or it will be imported to both from abroad; with linear production and import cost functions, one source of supply will be "cheapest" at all levels of supply.[2]

The specialization tendency is the reflection of the nation's, and of each region's, comparative advantage. The specialization of the solution—when qualified in the ways discussed in this chapter—is the basis of the specification of industrial priorities. A sector that would produce a tradable product falls into one of two classes: either domestically producing or importing. The domestic producers are the priority sectors, the ones in which expansion should take place. Among these the model further dictates in which region each industry should operate. In this way the basic solution yields a set of industrial priorities. Among producing sectors, it is possible to distinguish degrees of priority by determining the marginal costs of importing rather than producing (see Section 4.2).

The specialization tendency of the solution is, however, qualified in several ways, and the priority results of the solution must take the following qualifications into account.

1. Some noncompetitive trade is specified in the model. If it is desirable to expand a sector within a region and if noncompetitive imports of that type of product are somewhere specified, then there will be two sources of supply. Similarly, where noncompetitive regional exports are specified and it is not desirable to expand the sector in general, the sector will be expanded only to meet the noncompetitive regional export requirement. Other demand will be met by imports, regional or foreign.

2. The cost of trading goods between regions may outweigh the benefits of regional specialization. In such cases there may be only one source of supply for each region, but the source of supply will not be the same for the two regions.

3. Though domestic production of an agricultural product may be "cheaper" than importing the product, the upper limits on agricultural expansion may make it necessary to import as well as to produce. These limits can also have their effect on industries outside of, but closely tied to, agriculture. That is, it may be the product of the agriculture using industry which is both domestically produced and imported, for example, sugar or cotton textiles. The constraints that limit imports of all other agriculture and of cotton, the constraint that ties the output of the edible oils sector (in West Pakistan) to the output of the cotton sector, and the constraints limiting interregional paper trade will have similar effects.

4. While it may be desirable to produce within a region for foreign export, other types of demand may be met, first, by regional or, second, by foreign imports. In the first case, where other demand is met by regional import, the phenomenon is explained by the specification of export possibilities as region

specific. In order to exploit the export opportunity of a region, it is explicitly required in the model that production in that region be at least as great as exports. Then it can be the case that the products of a particular sector in region one are most cheaply provided by importing from region two. Nonetheless, production of the product for export may take place in region one and all other demand will be met by regional imports. In the second case, where demand is met by foreign imports, the explanation lies in the tariff earned on imports and on the requirement that exports be supplied by domestic production. If the foreign exchange value of a product is greater than the cost of domestic production, it will be desirable to produce it for export. However, the foreign exchange cost of importing is partly offset by the tariff benefit of importing (the tariff revenue is a source of financing investment and government expenditures). Therefore, importing may be preferable to producing and production will take place only to meet export demand.

5. Finally, there are the cases of the "marginal" sectors. As pointed out in Chapter 2, the model effectively has three over-all basic resource constraints: the supply of funds and each region's ability to earn foreign exchange. In the use of each of these resources there is necessarily a marginal sector, which has more intense use of that resource than other sectors and is the last to use it. Except in the singular case where supply requirements of the marginal sector are fulfilled precisely at the point the resource is exhausted, the products of the marginal sector will be obtained from two sources of supply. With three basic resources, three marginal sectors can be expected.

While these factors greatly affect the appearance of a solution to the model, they make it only slightly more difficult to derive a priority set from the solution. A sector that expands even though some of its product is noncompetitively imported is a priority sector; one that expands only to meet the noncompetitive regional export demand is not. Sectors that expand simultaneously in both regions can be classed as priorities for both regions. Sectors expanding domestically and then importing to obtain supply beyond some upper bound on their production would also be priority industries. The priority classification of industries producing only for export represents a problem; and when important foreign exchange earners are concerned, they should be given some special attention. Finally, the marginal sectors must be classed as just that— marginal. Thus the priority set is contained in the solution: the qualifications of specialization only make it somewhat difficult to discern.

In addition to determining production and import patterns for each region, the solution of the model yields the optimal set of export activities, the regional allocation of consumption, and the interregional flow of resources. The values of these variables are, of course, determined simultaneously with the values of production and trade variables.[3]

The limited choice exercised among alternative export programs is based on comparison of the benefits of exporting a product with the costs of supplying that product for export. This comparison will tend to prove most favorable for the high priority industries within a region. Therefore, the choice of an export program in a solution offers some basis for distinguishing degrees of priority among those sectors that are domestically active.[4]

It is an important feature of the model that no direct limits have been placed on either the regional allocation of consumption or the interregional flow of resources—and a limit placed upon one would indirectly act to limit the other. If, for a moment, the expansion of national consumption is viewed as a step-by-step process, then the model can be seen as operating at each step to expand consumption in the region where the consumption bundle is more cheaply provided. At subsequent steps, however, as the economy expands and different constraints become active, the relative costs of providing consumption in the two regions may reverse. Then consumption expansion will take place in the other region. There is no reason why such conceptual reversals should not take place several times in the process of expansion. Similarly, at each step, resources are allocated where they make the greatest contribution to consumption expansion—either direct or indirect. The regional distribution of increments to income will tend to correspond to the regional distribution of consumption. Income and consumption distribution can, however, differ to the extent that one region transfers resources to the other. Such transfer is rather limited because one region can transfer resources to the other only to the degree that the savings from income generation exceeds the capital required by that income generation.

In addition to the values of production, trade, consumption, and resource flow variables, solution of the model will implicitly yield values of certain macroeconomic variables. Most important are, by region, value added, aggregate capital-output ratios, and aggregate savings ratios. The values of those variables; the consumption and flow of resource variables; and the prespecified values for foreign funds inflow, sectoral savings rates, and export growth rates provide a general macroeconomic description of the Pakistan economy. It is the interrelationship between the macroeconomic situation and the industrial priorities —as represented by the production and trade variables—which is what this book is all about.

4.2 The Dual

The dual programming problem associated with the linear programming problem that constitutes the planning model can be interpreted in the following manner. Find a set of resource prices—shadow prices—which will minimize the cost (value) of the resources available for plan-period expansion and which satisfy a set of constraints specifying that no resource has a unit value exceeding the unit cost of supplying that resource. The term "resources" as used here includes:

1. foreign funds, capital, and foreign exchange
2. commodities
3. the ability to earn foreign exchange as embodied in the export limits
4. the ability to expand agriculture as specified by the agriculture growth limits
5. the ability to expand each type of foodgrains production as specified by the limits on the various methods of expansion
6. the capability to expand exports, a resource having zero value when production expansion is zero

The constraints of the dual fall into six groups, each associated with a type of activity in the primal:

1. Those constraints associated with the consumption variable for each region: the cost of supplying a unit of consumption cannot be less than unity.

2. Those associated with a regional inflow of funds variable: the value of foreign funds in its uses, that is, as capital and foreign exchange, cannot exceed the cost of supplying foreign funds. And those associated with a regional outflow of funds variable: the value of supplying funds cannot exceed the cost of withdrawing funds from its uses. These combine to insure that the value of foreign funds will equal the combined value of its uses as capital and foreign exchange.

3. Those associated with each production activity: the value of a product plus the value of the export expansion capability created by producing that product cannot exceed the cost of the resources required to produce the commodity. In agricultural sectors, resource costs include the cost of the ability to expand the sector (of the ability to expand the activity, in the case of foodgrain sectors).[5]

4. Those associated with each regional competitive trade activity: the value of a commodity in the receiving region cannot exceed the cost of releasing that commodity from the other region plus the cost of transferring the commodity between the regions.

5. Those associated with each foreign competitive import activity: the value of a commodity plus the value of the tariff earned on importing that commodity cannot exceed the cost of importing it.

6. Those associated with each foreign export activity: the value of the foreign exchange earned by exporting a product cannot exceed the cost of supplying that product for export plus the cost of the export ability (sector specific and regional) used in exporting that product plus the cost of creating export expansion capability.

The constraints of the dual insure an efficiently operating system. If an activity is nonzero in the primal, the associated dual constraint will be met with equality (see Dorfman, Samuelson, and Solow 1958). That property of the programming system insures that marginal products of foreign funds, capital, foreign exchange, and commodities will be equal to their marginal costs. Therefore, the solution to the model fulfills the primary condition of Pareto optimality, and in that sense resources will be efficiently allocated among alternative uses.[6]

Dual variables are most useful in the analysis of industrial priority issues as indicators of the relative scarcities of resources. Of primary importance are the shadow prices of capital and of foreign exchange. The ratio of these two prices obtained in any solution indicates the resource position of the economy. Therefore, the ratio is a convenient way to compare different solutions of the model to see how the relative resource position changes between solutions. Another price of the dual which is particularly useful in analyzing the differences between solutions is the shadow price of foreign funds. The relationship among that price, the ratio of the foreign exchange and capital prices, and the set of industrial priorities will aid in determining when and how—through augmenting savings or foreign exchange earnings—foreign funds are of most use.

Shadow prices associated with agricultural growth limits are also of special use because they are indicators of the importance of the agricultural limits. Since industrial priorities can be affected by those limits in the same way they can be affected by the capital and foreign exchange limits, it is necessary to examine industrial priorities in relation to those prices.

Shadow prices associated with commodity balance constraints of the primal are not of direct value in dealing with the industrial priority issues here. Such prices would, however, have an important use were a model such as this to be used in actual plan formulation. If multisectoral models are to be practically employed in national planning, they must be complemented by more detailed sectoral studies. Sectoral studies commonly use shadow prices for evaluating direct use of basic resources, for example, foreign exchange, capital, labor. If, however, the sectoral studies are carried out in the framework of a multisectoral model, the indirect costs of resources can be taken into account; that is, shadow prices from the model may be used to evaluate commodity inputs.[7] Though it may not be realistic to assume that planning commissions actually will follow this practice, the commodity shadow prices of the model at least allow determination of the degree of error involved in the usual procedure of evaluating only the direct use of resources at shadow prices.

While only a few shadow prices are of special importance in dealing with the industrial priority issues, the entire set of dual prices is of use through the determination of the marginal costs incurred in the primal by operating an activity not already in the solution. These marginal costs are, of course, the simplex criteria.[8] Section 4.1 noted that the primal solution allows distinction of two levels of priority: either a sector produces domestically and is a priority sector or it does not and is not a priority sector. Examination of simplex criteria, however, allows a greater degree of priority ranking for any single solution. If a sector produces domestically, the simplex criteria associated with importing its products will be negative; that is, the simplex criteria will indicate the marginal cost of importing rather than producing. When the costs of importing rather than producing are high, the sector in question is of high priority. Consequently, to rank producing industries by the absolute value of the simplex criteria of the alternative import activity will be equivalent to a priority ranking. Nonproducing sectors—importing sectors—can also be ranked according to the simplex criteria of the alternative producing activity.

The simplex criteria of the optimal solution are also significant in determining the sensitivity of the primal results to quantitative misspecification of parameters. The simplex criteria provide a measure of the degree of error which could be tolerated in parameters of a particular activity before that activity would be removed from the solution. If a sector is a producing one, the simplex criteria is the difference between the marginal cost of production and the marginal cost of importing; since the sector is a producing one, this simplex criteria is necessarily negative. From the dual it is assured that the marginal cost of production will equal the marginal product of the good; that is, the marginal cost of production is a dual variable. Therefore, it is possible to compute the percentage by which the marginal cost of importing exceeds the marginal cost of production. This percentage serves as a measure of the amount by which actual costs of production could exceed estimated costs of production without inducing a change in the source of supply. Although there is no basis for statistical significance tests, when the ratio of the simplex criteria of importing to the shadow price of the product is large, one can be confident that the industry in question should be one of those expanded domestically. This sensitivity test will be employed in Appendix B.

4.3 Basic Solution

Macroeconomic Aspects

The principal use of a complex planning model is to lay out alternative development programs. By obtaining solutions to the model based on alternative assumptions about important economic variables one can see the relationships among the assumptions, the goals, and the instruments of economic planning. The model serves as both an analytic function and a tool in the planning process —or in critique of the actual planning process. Comparison of the alternatives leads to an understanding of the economic relationships and serves as a basis for choosing the direction of a plan.

The basic solution—the solution to the model with the model, parameters, and predetermined variables precisely as specified in Chapter 3—serves as a reference point in carrying out the comparisons. The basic solution represents a "best guess" about the economic circumstances under which Pakistan's Fourth Plan must be formulated.

The national and regional accounts that the basic solution yields for the Pakistan economy are shown in Table 4.1. The base year accounts, implicit terminal year accounts, and situation envisioned in the Plan Document (Pakistan 1965a) for the year 1975 are also presented. (The terminal year variables are simply the base year values plus the increments obtained in the basic solution.) In Table 4.2 other descriptive macroeconomic variables are presented: per capita consumption, per capita income, population, the incremental aggregate savings rate, the incremental net and gross capital-output ratios, and the average annual rate of growth of GNP.

The growth rate of GNP of 7 percent called for in the plan is slightly higher than the 6.7 percent obtained in the basic solution. However, since the base year estimates of GNP used here are higher than those of the plan, the terminal year value of GNP from the model is 9 percent higher than the plan projection and the increment is about 5.6 percent greater. In the context of ten-year macroeconomic projections, these differences do not seem large; on this level the solution and the plan are in rough accord.[9]

Table 4.1. National and Regional Accounts

	Basic solution increments between 1964-65 and 1974-75			Base year 1964-65			Terminal year 1974-75			Plan projection 1975
	East Pakistan	West Pakistan	All Pakistan	East Pakistan	West Pakistan	All Pakistan	East Pakistan	West Pakistan	All Pakistan	All Pakistan
Consumption	18,865.9	17,455.9	36,321.8	19,447.4	23,530.6	42,978.0	38,313.3	40,986.5	79,299.8	74,635
Private	18,504.3	16,627.0	35,131.3	18,724.2	21,872.9	40,597.1	37,228.5	38,499.9	75,728.4	n.a.[a]
Government	361.6	828.9	1,190.5	723.2	1,657.7	2,380.9	1,084.8	2,486.6	3,571.4	n.a.
Gross investment[b]	5,523.4	4,910.7	10,434.1	4,163.8	7,064.4	11,228.2	9,687.2	11,975.1	21,662.3	19,180
Net investment[b]	4,567.0	3,315.9	7,882.9	3,326.3	5,245.6	8,571.9	7,893.3	8,561.5	16,454.8	n.a.
Replacement	956.4	1,594.8	2,551.2	837.5	1,818.8	2,656.3	1,793.9	3,413.6	5,207.5	n.a.
Foreign exports, FOB	1,345.0	1,209.0	2,554.0	1,268.1	1,139.6	2,407.7	2,613.1	2,348.6	4,961.7	7,300
Foreign imports, CIF	1,337.1	1,216.9	2,554.0	1,743.5	3,726.9	5,470.4	3,080.6	4,943.8	8,024.4	11,300
Competitive	501.6	880.1	1,381.7							
Noncompetitive	928.5	987.8	1,916.3							
Import substitution (−)[c]	93.0	651.0	744.0							
Net foreign trade surplus	7.9	−7.9	0.0	−475.4	−2,587.3	−3,062.7	−467.5	−2,595.2	−3,062.7	−4,000
Regional exports FOB[d]	1,710.0	1,819.5		536.1	856.4		2,246.1	2,675.9		
Regional imports CIF	1,819.5	1,710.0		856.4	536.1		2,675.9	2,246.1		
Competitive	1,635.6	1,486.1								
Noncompetitive	156.0	223.9								
Import substitution (−)[c]	−27.9									
Net regional trade surplus	−109.5	109.5	0.0	−320.3	320.3		−511.8	210.8		
Net capital inflow	101.6	−101.6	0.0	795.7	2,267.0	3,062.7	897.3	2,165.4	3,062.7	4,000
GNP	24,287.7	22,468.2	46,755.9	22,815.5	28,328.0	51,143.5	47,103.2	50,796.2	97,899.4	89,815

SOURCE: Base year data can be found in Appendix A and in *Plan Projections from the Third Five-Year Plan*, Pakistan (1965a).

[a] In this and subsequent tables n.a. means "not allowed."

[b] Includes change in working capital.

[c] Absolute import substitution is a negative increment to imports. Regional absolute import substitution is on net negative for East Pakistan because of the substitution of regional for foreign imports of wheat.

[d] Regional exports are divided among competitive, noncompetitive, and import substitution as are regional imports of the other region.

Table 4.2. Other Macrovariables

	Per capita private consumption (rupees)	Per capita income (rupees)	Population (millions)	Incremental gross aggregate domestic savings rate[a]	Incremental capital-income ratio (net gross)	Average annual rate of growth of GNP
Basic solution increment						
East Pakistan	144.9	197.3	21.5	22.3	2.17/2.66	7.5
West Pakistan	146.4	203.5	15.9	22.3	2.54/3.63	6.0
All Pakistan	144.4[b]	198.6	37.4	22.3	2.35/3.13	6.7
Base year 1964–65						
East Pakistan	309.5	377.1	60.5	14.8		
West Pakistan	423.1	547.9	51.7	16.9		
All Pakistan	361.8	455.8	112.2	16.0		
Terminal year 1974–75						
East Pakistan	454.0	574.2	82.0	18.7		
West Pakistan	569.5	751.4	67.6	19.3		
All Pakistan	506.2	654.4	149.6	18.9		
Plan assumption for 1975						
East Pakistan	n.a.	565.9[c]	81.1	n.a.	n.a.	7.7[d]
West Pakistan	n.a.	662.1[c]	66.3	n.a.	n.a.	6.2[d]
All Pakistan	n.a.	609.3[c]	147.4	23.5[d]	n.a. 2.90	7.0

SOURCE: Plan Assumptions for 1975 are from *The Third Year Plan*, Pakistan (1965a). Population estimates for the model computations are from a study by the Demographic Section of the Pakistan Institute for Development Economics, (1967). All other entries can be derived from these and Table 4.1.

[a]These are average rates for the base and the terminal years. Savings includes government savings.

[b]That the increment to national per capita consumption is less than either of the regional increments is due to the faster rate of population growth in East Pakistan.

[c]The Plan Document gives per capita income figures inconsistent with its aggregate GNP and population estimates. The estimate given here is based on the aggregate GNP data and population with the same regional breakdown as given by the Plan per capita figures.

[d]Arithmetic average of Third and Fourth Plan rates.

The underlying aggregate parameters of the plan and the basic solution are also similar in magnitude. The aggregate savings rates are 23.5 percent and 22.3 percent, respectively; the aggregate gross capital-output ratios are 2.9 and 3.13, respectively. That the savings rates and capital-output ratios are similar is not simply a corollary of the similar growth rates. In the basic solution the capital-output ratios are specified on a sectoral basis, and there is no reason for the optimal program to yield an aggregate ratio so close to the plan assumption. Of course, with a savings rate close to that of the plan, its growth rate would not be obtained were the capital-output ratio much different.

On a regional level the plan and the basic solution yield similar results. The disparity ratios from them are shown in Table 4.3. Although they both begin with different estimates of base year disparity, both prescribe large reductions of disparity over the plan period.

Table 4.3. Disparity Ratios from the Plan and the Basic Solution[a]

	1964–65	1974–75
Plan (in terms of per capita income)	1.34	1.17
Basic solution (in terms of per capita income)	1.45	1.31
Basic Solution (in terms of per capita private consumption)	1.37	1.25

[a]The disparity ratio is defined as the ratio of the West Pakistan value to the East Pakistan value.

Although the disparity reduction of the plan is a matter of policy, no politically based restriction on regional distribution is included in the basic solution. Disparity reduction there is an optimal economic program when national per capita consumption is the welfare criterion.

The result that it is economically optimal to move toward parity between two regions of the country requires some explanation.[10] Section 4.1 pointed out that the model operates at each step of consumption expansion to increase consumption in that region where it is "cheapest." East Pakistan being the poorer of the two regions has a larger share of agricultural goods in its marginal consumption bundle. These agricultural goods, especially rice, are relatively cheap to produce at low levels of growth. Therefore, in the beginning of the expansion process East Pakistan consumption is favored. When the costs of agricultural commodities begin to rise due to the constraints on the rate of growth of agricultural sectors, the model switches to favoring West Pakistan consumption. The resource availability of the basic solution is that which happens to (almost) equalize the increments to per capita consumption in the two regions. If resource availabilities were less (greater), the incremental reduction of disparity would be greater (less). That will become more evident when the basic solution is compared with alternative development programs.

What should be emphasized here is that it is the differential in the cost of providing consumption to the two regions that brings about the reduction in disparity. That should be contrasted with the more usual result of increased disparity being optimal due to the greater productivity of the advanced region (see, for example, Hirschman 1959). The point is that "productivity" of a region can be measured only in terms of what must be supplied in that region, that is, what is consumed.

East Pakistan's ex post production advantage is evident in that the disparity reduction in the basic solution does not carry with it a large transfer of resources from West to East Pakistan. The total inflow of capital to East Pakistan increases by 12.8 percent in the solution, and the inflow to West declines by 4.5 percent. In other words, the distribution of foreign funds between the two regions does not change greatly, and still East Pakistan is able to attain a more rapid rate of development.

East Pakistan grows more rapidly than West with less external resources because East has a lower requirement for capital. The incremental net capital-output ratio in East Pakistan is 2.16 and in the West, 2.54. The higher productivity of capital in East Pakistan exists primarily because of the very high capital costs of agricultural expansion in the West. While such costs in the East have been taken as much higher than average costs of agricultural production, costs in the West are still a good deal more (see Section 3.5). Whether East Pakistan really does have an over-all production advantage may be subject to some question; in particular, if skilled labor requirements and supplies were taken into account the situation might be significantly modified.

Though East Pakistan seems to have the advantage in terms of capital, the two regions are most equal in terms of their foreign exchange positions. East Pakistan has a slightly larger export increment (the East has traditionally supplied the majority of foreign exchange) but West Pakistan has far more absolute import substitution. That import substitution is primarily in wheat and is made possible by new wheat programs (see Section 3.10 and Chapter 6). In spite of the import substitution, however, West Pakistan's expansion of imports is almost as great as the East's in the basic solution; and the incremental propensity to import (as a percent of GNP) is about the same in both regions, about 5.5 percent. This propensity, it should be noted, is significantly below the base year average propensity to import of over 10 percent.

The macroeconomic results of the basic solution should not be endowed with undue significance. The coincidence of the results of the model and the plan does not serve to verify the plan since many of its basic assumptions are incorporated in the model. On the other hand, the model does tend to confirm that the plan is internally consistent in its macroeconomic aspects. The regional distribution results—the reduction of disparity—should only be viewed as a straightforward deduction from the assumptions upon which the model is built and not in themselves as offering "proof" of the optimality of disparity reduction.

Agriculture and Services

What the macroeconomic results provide is a best-guess picture of the over-all economy from which an analysis of industrial priority issues can proceed. In Tables 4.4 and 4.5 the sector-by-sector results of the basic solution are shown; that is, the solution values of all variables which enter the solution as explicit choice variables are shown. These sector-by-sector results are the key to the industrial priorities. Before dealing with the industrial sectors themselves, however, the agricultural and service sectors should be discussed.

The nonfoodgrain agriculture sectors all expand production to their full limits. This result is to be expected given the high growth rate of the economy. However, with the exception of jute, some choice does exist about the source of supply of these products. It is a reassuring feature of the result that tea, cotton, and other agriculture exhaust domestic production capability in preference to importing. Since land and labor costs are ignored in the model and since no substitution of land among sectors is allowed, it would be strange to find any of these sectors noncompetitive with imports.[11] In the absence of demand limits, it would also be an unacceptable result if the jute sector, so important in earning foreign exchange, were not to expand to its maximum.

With the foodgrain sectors, however, the limit to expansion lies on the demand side. In these sectors—East Pakistan rice and West Pakistan rice and wheat—85 percent, 64 percent, and 53 percent, respectively, of the potential expansion made possible by the new techniques is utilized.[12] While these sectors will be given special attention in Chapter 6, it is obvious at the outset that if the new rice and wheat programs are moderately successful, not only will Pakistan be self-sufficient by 1974–75, but it will also be exporting large quantities of foodgrains.[13]

The development of the service sectors is of little direct interest in this study. The results the model yields for them are explained by the over-all rate of growth of the economy and by the demand elasticities for those sectors that deliver directly (or are closely tied) to consumption. Some note should be taken, however, of the very rapid development of the electricity sector in East Pakistan and the housing sectors in both regions. The growth of those sectors is explained by their high income elasticities of demand and, in the case of East Pakistan elec-

Table 4.4. Basic Solution Increments to Production and Competitive Trade at Purchasers' Prices, East Pakistan
(in million rupees)

Sector	Production	Competitive foreign imports	Competitive regional imports	Foreign exports	Competitive regional exports	Absolute import substitution
1. Rice	6,262.0			225.0		77.1
2. Wheat			76.4[a]			67.0[a]
3. Jute	988.9			874.3		
4. Cotton	4.4		47.1			
5. Tea	200.0	48.5				
6. Other agric.	4,433.7		886.7			
7. Sugar		155.6	169.1			
8. Edible oils	945.9				208.7	
9. Tobacco		264.4				
10. Other food		87.3	335.9			
11. Cotton text.	834.3					
12. Jute text.	525.0			470.6		
13. Other text.	139.4	431.9		138.0	105.7	
14. Paper		197.6	98.8			
15. Leather	22.7		133.0			
16. Rubber	72.0					
17. Fertilizer	1,403.6				627.3	
18. Other chem.	1,616.9			18.2	888.3	
19. Cement	399.3					
20. Basic metals	100.0					100.0
21. Metal prod.	164.7		465.0			
22. Machinery	1,154.1					
23. Transport eq.	305.6					
24. Wood, etc.		240.4				
25. Const., houses	2,940.1					
26. Const., buildings	845.0					
27. Other Const.	350.4					
28. Misc. manuf.	533.6					
29. Coal, etc.	452.0					
30. Elec. and gas	442.6					
31. Transport	1,576.7					
32. Trade	2,829.9					
33. Housing	2,005.9					
34. Government	443.0					
35. Services	1,796.4					

[a]The substitution for foreign imports by West Pakistan production is shown as an increment to regional imports and as import substitution.

Table 4.5. **Basic Solution Increments to Production and Competitive Trade at Purchasers' Prices, West Pakistan**
(in million rupees)

Sector	Production	Competitive foreign imports	Competitive regional imports	Foreign exports	Competitive regional exports	Absolute import substitution
1. Rice	1,398.1			750.1		
2. Wheat	2,801.7			131.8	76.4	783.4
3. Jute						
4. Cotton	802.0			249.1	47.1	
5. Tea	213.0					
6. Other agric.	6,158.2			169.9	886.7	
7. Sugar	865.9				169.1	
8. Edible oils	802.0	6.8	208.7			
9. Tobacco		521.1				
10. Other food	541.2			26.1	335.9	
11. Cotton text.		807.2				
12. Jute text.			105.7			
13. Other text.	346.9	481.0		330.0		
14. Paper	381.0			19.4	98.8	
15. Leather	614.2			170.0	133.0	
16. Rubber	103.9					
17. Fertilizer			627.3			
18. Other chem.	93.1		888.3	91.0		
19. Cement	932.3					
20. Basic metals	337.7					100.0
21. Metal prod.	1,230.4				465.0	
22. Machinery	750.5					
23. Transport eq.	595.9					
24. Wood, etc.		115.4				
25. Const., houses	1,927.9					
26. Const., buildings	965.8					
27. Other const.	792.9					
28. Misc. manuf.	374.5					
29. Coal, etc.	687.1			20.7		
30. Elec. and gas	574.7					
31. Transport	1,974.1					
32. Trade	2,477.8					
33. Housing	1,666.2					
34. Government	934.1					
35. Services	2,259.6					
Special paper imports		143.5				

tricity, by the relative rise in the importance of industrial sectors (that is, electricity using sectors). The rapid growth of these very capital-intensive sectors no doubt has an important impact upon the availability of capital for the rest of the economy.[14]

Industrial Priorities

To begin developing a picture of the choice of industrial priorities, we distinguish four groups of industrial sectors for each region in the basic solution. These groups are defined in terms of the source of supply of their product. The sectors falling into each group are listed in Table 4.6.

1. supplied entirely from within the region (except for noncompetitive imports)
2. supplied entirely from foreign imports (except for production for noncompetitive regional export)
3. supplied entirely from regional imports (except for production for noncompetitive regional export)
4. mixed source of supply

Group 1 constitutes the set of priority industries for the region, that is, the manufacturing sectors that should be developed in the region. Industries in group 2 or group 3 are, from the point of view of one region, not priority sectors and should not be developed within the region. From the point of view of the nation, of course, group 3 industries are priority sectors, but only in one region. The sectors in group 4 are the special cases that were referred in Section 4.1.

The priority grouping of Table 4.6 provides only a group ranking of industries. There are two further distinctions that can be made. First, through variation of macroeconomic parameters—the savings rate, the export growth rate, the level of foreign funds inflow—a distinction can be made between those industries in group 1 that are priority sectors only under the special circumstances of the basic solution and those that are priority sectors under a wide variety of conditions. (These variations will be the subject of Chapter 5.) Second, the simplex criteria of the excluded import activities can be used to obtain a priority ranking of domestically producing sectors.

In Table 4.7 industries in group 1 are ranked according to the absolute value of the simplex criterion of the cheapest alternative source of supply. As explained in section 4.2, that is equivalent to a priority ranking. The group ranking of

Table 4.6.   Division of Manufacturing Sectors in the Basic Solution According to Competitive Source of Supply

East Pakistan	West Pakistan
1. Produced within the region	
8. Edible oils	7. Sugar
11. Cotton text.	10. Other food
12. Jute text.	14. Paper
16. Rubber	15. Leather
17. Fertilizer	16. Rubber
18. Other chem.	19. Cement
19. Cement	20. Basic metals
20. Basic metals	21. Metal prod.
22. Machinery	22. Machinery
23. Transport eq.	23. Transport eq.
28. Misc. manuf.	28. Misc. manuf.
29. Coal, etc.	29. Coal, etc.
2. Imported from abroad	
9. Tobacco	9. Tobacco
24. Wood, etc.	11. Cotton text.
	24. Wood, etc.
3. Imported from other region	
15. Leather	12. Jute text.
	17. Fertilizer
4. Mixed Source of supply	
7. Sugar	8. Edible oils
10. Other food	13. Other text.
13. Other text.	18. Other chem.
14. Paper	
21. Metal prod.	

Table 4.6 and the more detailed ranking of Table 4.7 have many interesting aspects. However, a full discussion of them is postponed until the effects of capital and foreign exchange supply upon priorities have been discussed. (A more complete picture of industrial priorities will emerge for analysis at the end of Chapter 5.)

Only a general comment on the pattern of the priorities will be offered at this point. The general picture reveals that the list of priorities is heavily dominated

Table 4.7. Priority Ranking of Domestically Producing Sectors in the Basic Solution

Region	Sector	Simplex criteria of cheapest alternative[a]	Rank
East Pakistan	8. Edible oils	0.08	8
	11. Cotton text.	.17	6
	12. Jute text.[b]		
	16. Rubber	.04	10
	17. Fertilizer	.30	2
	18. Other chem.	.26	3
	19. Cement	.18	5
	20. Basic metals	.51	1
	22. Machinery	.10	7
	23. Transport eq.	.20	4
	28. Misc. manuf.	.02	11
	29. Coal, etc.	.07	9
West Pakistan	7. Sugar	0.04	12
	10. Other food	.12	9
	14. Paper	.34	2
	15. Leather	.92	1
	16. Rubber	.12	9
	19. Cement	.18	4
	20. Basic metals	.16	6
	21. Metal prod.	.17	5
	22. Machinery	.12	9
	23. Transport eq.	.14	8
	28. Misc. manuf.	.16	6
	29. Coal, etc.	.24	3

[a]Simplex criteria are expressed in terms of units of aggregate consumption rather than in units of per capita consumption.
[b]Since no jute textiles import variable exists, jute textiles production cannot be ranked in this way. For comparison of jute and jute textiles production, see Chapter 5.

by capital goods, capital goods related sectors, and a few intermediate goods industries. Consumer goods industries, especially sectors closely tied to agriculture, are either low on the list of priorities or excluded entirely.

The industrial priorities picture is reflected in the export program the solution yields. However, the reflection is somewhat distorted. Industries whose products can be imported with a high tariff will be low in the ranking of Table 4.7 (like

West Pakistan other food) or not even in Group 1 of Table 4.6 (like other textiles), since the tariff gain makes the cost of importing relatively low. Nonetheless, such sectors may have greater foreign exchange earning per unit of production cost and will therefore be included in the export program before sectors
with higher production priorities. Aside from the dominance in the export
programs of agricultural products, the priority industries do appear as such, as
shown in Tables 4.4 and 4.5.

Dual Variables

Deciding whether to expand the production or import of a product can be
viewed as a cost minimization problem in which the dual variables are the input
and resource prices. An examination of the values of these variables can be a
guide to understanding the production and import decisions of the primal
solution.

For the basic solution, the complete set of dual variables or shadow prices is
presented in Table 4.8. The set of variables is arranged in groups according to
the primal constraints with which they are associated. The numeraire of the
shadow prices is aggregate consumption rather than per capita consumption,
the maximand of the problem. Therefore, as shown, a shadow price is the
amount of increase in aggregate consumption which would be obtained from a
unit increase in a resource.[15]

The first group of shadow prices in Table 4.8 (those associated with the interrelated capital and foreign exchange constraints) describes the position of the
economy with respect to these basic resources. The regional ratios of the shadow
price of capital to the shadow price of foreign exchange serve two descriptive
functions: (1) they indicate the relative importance of the two resources within
each region; (2) comparison of the ratios is a basis for comparing the economies
of the two regions with regard to their use of these resources.[16]

In the basic solution, these ratios—0.70 for East Pakistan and 0.54 for West
Pakistan—show that in both regions foreign funds have a larger impact through
the foreign exchange constraint than through the capital constraint, and that in
West Pakistan that impact is relatively greater than in the East. Alternatively, it
could be said that foreign exchange is scarcer (more valuable) in the West than
in the East. The dominance of the exchange constraint over the capital constraint
is a function of the entire cost structure and resource supply conditions of the
economy. The difference between the regions is explained by the greater foreign
exchange component in East Pakistan's consumption bundle. As Table 4.4

Table 4.8. Basic Solution Shadow Prices

	East Pakistan	West Pakistan
Basic capital and foreign exchange constraints		
Foreign funds	4.72[a]	4.72[a]
Capital	1.94	1.66
Foreign exchange	2.78	3.06
Regional foreign exchange earning limit	1.74	1.34
Agricultural production and import constraints		
Jute production	0.76	
Cotton production	.60	1.05
Tea production	1.49	
Other agric. production	2.08	0.63
Cotton imports		
Other agric. imports	0.82	
Active sectoral foreign exchange earning limits		
1. Rice	0.82	1.01
2. Wheat		1.38
10. Other food		0.55
12. Jute	.07	
13. Other text.		.03
14. Paper		.43
15. Leather		.93
18. Other chem.	.50	.31
29. Coal, etc.		.13
Special constraints		
Basic metals import substitution	0.07	0.16
Special limit on edible oils		.52
Special paper supply		.95
Regional paper import limit	.22	
Commodity balance constraints		
1. Rice	.10	.43
2. Wheat	.08	.22
3. Jute	.82	

	East Pakistan	West Pakistan
Commodity balance constraints (*continued*)		
4. Cotton	1.27	1.37
5. Tea	1.82	1.79
6. Other agric.	1.90	1.17
7. Sugar	0.43	0.55
8. Edible oils	.86	1.17
9. Tobacco	− .58[b]	− .31[b]
10. Other food	.29	0.42
11. Cotton text.	.89	1.33
12. Jute text.	.73	1.11
13. Other text.	− .20[b]	0.05
14. Paper	.60	.61
15. Leather	.25	.37
16. Rubber	.58	.79
17. Fertilizer	1.14	1.57
18. Other chem.	0.28	0.59
19. Cement	.66	.93
20. Basic Metals	.94	1.54
21. Metal prod.	.72	0.89
22. Machinery	.92	1.18
23. Transport eq.	.94	1.26
24. Wood, etc.	.42	0.70
25. Const., houses	.32	.38
26. Const., buildings	.57	.76
27. Other const.	0.55	1.06
28. Misc. manuf.	.49	0.70
29. Coal, etc.	.52	.70
30. Elec. and gas	3.45	2.25
31. Transport	0.53	1.25
32. Trade	.08	0.15
33. Housing	3.16	2.78
34. Government	0.22	0.29
35. Services	.10	.16

[a]Represents the total for East and West.

[b]Because of the large tariff on these commodities, it would be profitable to import excess quantities to earn the tariff. Excess imports are prevented by specifying the balance constraint as an equality. Negative shadow prices result.

shows, East Pakistan's imports—foreign and regional taken together—consist far more of consumption goods than do West Pakistan's. That more foreign exchange is required to create an additional unit of consumption in the East than in the West means the productivity—the shadow price—of foreign exchange will be lower in the East. Relatively then, the consumption bundle in West Pakistan requires more capital per unit of consumption.

It is interesting to examine the priority results of the basic solution in relation to this resource cost structure exhibited in the dual. First, the optimality of the domestic expansion of several high capital cost sectors is clear when the high relative price of foreign exchange is revealed. With a unit of foreign exchange being 43 percent more dear than a unit of capital in the East and 85 percent more dear in the West, it is understandable that few sectors rely totally or even mainly upon imports for supply. Second, the greater scarcity of foreign exchange in the West explains the decision to expand certain sectors in the West even though they are expanded in the East at lower (in terms of 1964–65 prices) capital costs, for example, rubber products, cement and concrete, and transport equipment.[17]

The priority decisions can be further understood by considering the shadow prices of agricultural growth constraints and the commodity shadow prices for agricultural products. The effect of the growth constraints on nonfoodgrain agricultural sectors is to force up the cost of agricultural commodities. Consequently, industrial sectors closely tied to agriculture are low-priority sectors. This effect is most significant in the East Pakistan other agriculture sector, as can be seen by the high shadow price on its growth limit. The high cost of agricultural raw materials is part of the explanation of the general pattern of priorities which emerges in the basic solution: in general, capital and intermediate goods-producing sectors appear more favorable than consumer goods sectors. In alternative solutions, the relative importance of the agricultural growth limits can be seen by comparing their shadow prices with the shadow price of funds.

The resource prices obtained in the basic solution will differ from those resulting from the operation of the private market. In the case of foreign exchange, for example, the black market, the limited free market (that is, the bonus voucher market), and the trade margin earned on imported goods indicate that the private economy values foreign exchange at a price 75 percent to 100 percent above its official price. The private valuation of foreign exchange through these private markets is often used as an estimate of the shadow price of foreign exchange to make social cost calculations. The private economy, however, treats labor as a scarce factor and operates with a positive wage rate. If the model used here is accurate in treating labor as a socially free resource, then the shadow price obtained for foreign exchange will necessarily be higher than that indicated by the free market. In fact, the shadow price of foreign exchange in the basic solution is about 200 percent greater than its official value and about 50 percent greater than the price in the private economy. As long as the assumption of socially free labor is correct, the higher shadow price for foreign exchange would be appropriate in social cost calculations.

As with an analysis of industrial priorities, it is best to forego a detailed discussion of the export limit shadow prices and the commodity shadow prices until alternative solutions have been presented. These prices are, of course, closely tied to the priority issues. The shadow prices of the sector specific export limits indicate where expansion of export limits has the greatest payoff; that is, they establish the export priorities.

While discussion of particular aspects of the commodity shadow prices will be postponed, there are certain general observations about these prices which should be discussed now. First, for all tradable goods the shadow price is higher in West Pakistan than in East Pakistan.[18] That result is a direct corollary of the higher shadow price of foreign exchange in the West than in the East. East-to-West trade will continue only to the point where the benefits of trading the goods are equal to the cost of transferring the foreign exchange from West to East. While, in the other direction, trade will continue until the loss incurred in trading the goods is just compensated for by the benefit of transferring the foreign exchange from East to West.

A second interesting aspect of the commodity shadow prices is their wide divergence from the 1964–65 price, unity in all cases, and that the divergence is in both directions. This is a result of several factors. The 1964–65 prices do not accurately reflect opportunity costs, that is, there is disequilibrium in the base year.[19] The cost structure of the model is not the same as the cost structure of the base year. The agricultural sectors are particularly interesting in this respect. On the one hand, the decline in costs of foodgrains production shows up in the very low shadow prices for rice and wheat. On the other hand, the shadow prices of other agricultural consumables are high because of the high incremental costs of production and the rise in costs of supply forced by the agricultural growth limits. Though their effects may be easily traced, these agricultural production cost changes are not the only structural changes that have been incorporated in the model. The entire set of production cost data is incremental rather than average, and the entire set of shadow prices is affected. There is another reason for the divergence of the shadow prices which can be attributed to a deficiency of the model. The fixed structure of the consumption bundle does not allow price-induced substitution among consumables. Were price substitution taken into account, there is no doubt that the variation of the commodity prices would be greatly reduced. Any general or specific conclusions based on those commodity shadow prices must be qualified by that shortcoming of the model.

The wide variation of the commodity shadow prices has some significance for approaches to sectoral and project planning. It seems likely that if planners make calculations using shadow prices only for direct use of basic resources, they may be subject to serious errors when commodity inputs are a large portion of costs. This issue, however, will be taken up in a subsequent chapter.[20]

Finally, the commodity shadow prices have a use in a comprehensive sensitivity analysis of the results obtained in the basic solution. Appendix B describes and presents the results of the analysis.

4.4 A Development Plan and Development Plans

Section 4.3 provides a development plan for the Pakistan economy. That is, it provides a set of targets on a sectoral and regional basis which are mutually consistent and which place the economy on the highest feasible consumption path. If targets are the basis of a sound development program, they have been laid down.

But targets per se are not the basis of a sound development program. A good development program is one that specifies directions of expansion—perhaps in terms of targets—on the basis of the interrelationships between the general economic situation and the planners' instruments and goals. And, of course, the plan must be reformulated as the economic circumstances change. Therefore, to organize a sound development program, it is necessary to consider alternative development possibilities.

5 | Resource Availabilities and Industrial Priorities

It is now possible to examine the relationship between resource availabilities and industrial priorities. In the first part of this chapter alternative solutions to the model are examined. Each alternative is based on a different set of assumptions regarding the ability of the economy to generate savings, the ability of the economy to earn foreign exchange, and the availability of foreign funds. The analysis is designed to point out the changes in industrial priorities that occur when resource availabilities are altered.

From the alternative solutions, it becomes possible to derive a priorities program for the Pakistan economy. In the latter part of this chapter, the priorities program is discussed in detail. The positions on the priority list of several industries are examined in relation to the past experiences of the industries and in relation to where they stand on the priority lists of the Pakistan Planning Commission and of other analysts of Pakistan development.

5.1 Savings Rate Effect

A change of the savings rate assumption can be expected to have two general implications for the optimal development program. First, a change in the ability of the economy to generate capital will affect the over-all level of performance. A higher savings rate will allow a higher rate of growth, and a lower savings rate will force a lower rate of growth. Second, the availability of capital will change relative to foreign exchange. Consequently, a change in the savings rate will tend to effect a shift in the operation of the economy—toward capital-using activities if the savings rate rises and away from capital-using activities if the savings rate falls.

Solutions to the model have been obtained for four different savings rate assumptions. In one of these, the basic solution, the assumed savings rates are 14 percent of value added in agricultural sectors and 24 percent of value added in other sectors. The other three solutions are based on assumptions of 12 percent, 15 percent, and 17 percent, respectively, for the agricultural sectors; and 22 percent, 25 percent, and 27 percent, respectively, for value added in other sectors. The solutions will hereafter be referred to as 12/22, 14/24 (The basic solution), 15/25, and 17/27.[1]

In Table 5.1 the macroeconomic results obtained in the alternative savings rate solutions are shown. In terms of national income growth, the change in the savings assumption from 12/22 to 17/27 brings about a rise from 6.3 percent per annum to 7.1 percent per annum. Since the aggregate marginal rate of savings changes from 20.3 percent to 24.8 percent in those two solutions, the effect of a 22 percent change in the marginal rate of savings is to bring about a 17 percent change in the ten-year increment to GNP. The effect of the savings rate rise on income is somewhat dampened by the rise in the capital-output ratio that accompanies the growth. Because foreign exchange availability does not change, expansion requires investment in higher and higher capital cost sectors.

The rise in national income that accompanies the rise in the savings rate takes place almost entirely in West Pakistan. As the savings rate rises, there also is a strong shift in the allocation of consumption towards West Pakistan. To the extent that income does grow in the East as the savings rate rises, the surplus is transferred to finance consumption in the West. Changes of the savings rate have their major impact on West Pakistan because, once the limits to direct expansion of agricultural supply are binding in the East, consumption is more cheaply supplied in the West. Furthermore, once the agricultural supply limits begin to have effect, increments to consumption in the East can only be supplied by importing agriculture-based commodities. Therefore, as savings becomes more plentiful and foreign exchange relatively more scarce, the distribution of consumption shifts toward the West. The rise in income in the West necessarily accompanies the rise of consumption (see Chapter 4).

Nonetheless, in all solutions East Pakistan is growing more rapidly than West, and when compared to 1964–65 there is a reduction in the disparity between the two. Were the savings rate raised still higher, a point would be reached

Table 5.1. Macroeconomic Results of Alternative Savings Rate Solutions

	12/22	14/24[a]	15/25	17/27
Aggregate marginal savings rate				
East Pakistan	21.3%	22.3%	23.3%	24.5%
West Pakistan	19.0	22.3	23.5	24.9
All Pakistan	20.3	22.3	23.4	24.8
Increment to per capita consumption				
East Pakistan	Rs147.8	Rs144.9	Rs143.0	Rs138.9
West Pakistan	112.3	146.4	158.1	173.0
All Pakistan	130.7	144.4	148.8	153.2
Disparity ratio				
Incremental	.76	1.02	1.11	1.25
Terminal year	1.17	1.26	1.29	1.33
Incremental capital inflows (millions)				
East Pakistan	+Rs256.5	+Rs106.6	−Rs100.7	−Rs284.9
West Pakistan	− 256.5	− 106.6	+ 100.7	+ 284.9
Rate of growth of GNP (per annum)				
East Pakistan	7.5%	7.6%	7.6%	7.7%
West Pakistan	5.2	6.1	6.4	6.8
All Pakistan	6.3	6.8	6.9	7.1
Incremental net capital-output ratio				
East Pakistan	2.10	2.16	2.17	2.21
West Pakistan	2.47	2.54	2.62	2.69
All Pakistan	2.29	2.34	2.39	2.46

[a]Basic solution.

where agricultural supply would become as important a constraint in the West as in the East. If such a point could be reached, then further expansion would not (necessarily) be biased in favor of the West.

The general effects of changes in the savings assumptions are reflected in the dual variables of the alternative solutions. Table 5.2 shows dual variable ratios that indicate the relative scarcity of capital and foreign exchange in each region

Table 5.2. **Some Shadow Price Relationships of the Alternative Savings Rate Solutions**

Solution	Capital ÷ foreign exchange		Funds ÷ average of agricultural growth Limits
	East Pakistan	West Pakistan	
12/22	0.90	0.79	7.54
14/24	.70	.54	4.28
15/25	.36	.30	2.26
17/27	.16	.15	1.73

and the relative importance of the supply of funds and the agricultural growth limits. The first ratio is of the shadow price of capital to the shadow price of foreign exchange for each region and the second is of the shadow price of funds to the average shadow price of the agricultural growth constraints.

The decline in the relative importance of the capital constraint as the savings rate rises is marked in both regions. The marginal value of a unit of capital is almost as great as that of foreign exchange in solution 12/22, but in solution 17/27 the marginal value of capital is only one-sixth that of foreign exchange. In all these solutions, however, the relative positions of the East and the West with respect to these resources remain the same: foreign exchange has the greater productivity in the West and capital has the greater productivity in the East. As stated in Chapter 4, this is most easily explained by the larger (direct and indirect) role of imports in East Pakistan's incremental consumption bundle. As the savings rate rises, however, West Pakistan's growth rate approaches that of the East, and it is forced to rely more heavily upon imports for consumption goods. Thus the two regions become more similar in terms of their requirements for foreign exchange and capital.

The increase in importance of the agricultural growth constraints as the savings rate rises is shown by the decline of the ratio of the shadow price of funds to the average shadow price of these constraints (Table 5.2, last column). At the high rates of growth induced by the high savings rate, the slow growth of the nonfoodgrain agricultural sectors becomes a greater and greater burden. The economy is forced to use more and more foreign exchange in order to meet supply requirements for these goods.[2]

The changes in industrial priorities which accompany the changes in the savings rate assumption can be explained both in terms of changes in resource supply and in terms of relative prices of resources. The general tendency as the savings rate is raised is a shift toward domestic production where choices exist. It may be said that this results either from the increased supply of capital or from the decline in the price of capital. In the opposite direction from this general tendency, there are some cases where agriculture-based industries shift from domestic toward foreign sources of supply. This results either from the relative decline in agriculture supply possibilities or from the rise in the price of agricultural goods relative to the price of foreign exchange.

In Table 5.3, tradable commodities for each region have been classed into four groups according to their source of supply in the alternative savings rate solutions.

The group 4 industries, those that switch among alternate sources of supply, are of most interest here. The priority sectors, group 1, and the import sectors, group 2 and group 3, will be given attention in Section 5.5.

For both regions, first in the columns of the switching sectors are certain agricultural sectors: East Pakistan cotton, tea, and other agriculture and West Pakistan cotton. In all solutions these sectors are producing up to the limits allowed by the agricultural growth constraints. In East Pakistan, cotton, tea, and other agriculture are also imported in all the solutions; however, as the savings rate and rate of growth rise, East Pakistan shifts from regional imports to foreign imports of cotton and other agriculture. Concomitant with East Pakistan's switch to foreign supply of cotton, West Pakistan begins to import cotton to supplement its domestic supply. These switches all occur between solution 15/25 and solution 17/27.

Although the agricultural growth limits are absolute, it is not "necessary" for these agricultural commodities to be imported. The alternative exists to import commodities that use these products as raw materials (edible oils, cotton textiles). The model must determine in the case of each agriculture using industry whether to import its product or its raw materials. At low rates of growth, low prices of agricultural products relative to the price of foreign exchange tend to favor domestic production of agriculture-using sectors. The low rate of growth, however, is the result of a low savings rate and is, therefore, accompanied by a high shadow price of capital relative to the price of foreign exchange. This relationship between capital and foreign exchange price tends to favor the importing of agriculture-using sectors. At high rates of growth, the situation is equally ambiguous—a high ratio of agricultural prices to foreign exchange price but a low ratio of capital price to foreign exchange price (see Table 5.2). Under these circumstances, the model prescribes different choices for different agriculture-

Table 5.3. Grouping of Sectors According to Source of Supply in Alternative Savings Rate Solutions

East Pakistan	West Pakistan

1. Only producing within region in all Solutions

East Pakistan	West Pakistan
1. Rice	1. Rice
3. Jute[a]	2. Wheat
8. Edible oils	5. Tea[b]
11. Cotton text.	6. Other agric.
12. Jute text.[a]	14. Paper
16. Rubber	15. Leather
17. Fertilizer	20. Basic metals
18. Other chem.	22. Machinery
19. Cement	23. Transport eq.
20. Basic metals	29. Coal, etc.
22. Machinery	
23. Transport Eq.	
28. Misc. Manuf.	
29. Coal, etc.	

2. Only importing from abroad in all solutions

East Pakistan	West Pakistan
9. Tobacco	9. Tobacco
24. Wood, etc.	

3. Only importing from other region in all Solutions

East Pakistan	West Pakistan
2. Wheat	12. Jute text.[a]
15. Leather	17. Fertilizer
	18. Other chem.

4. Switching between alternative sources of supply[c]

East Pakistan	West Pakistan
4. Cotton	4. Cotton
5. Tea	7. Sugar
6. Other agric.	8. Edible oils
7. Sugar	10. Other food
10. Other food	11. Cotton text.
13. Other text.	13. Other text.
14. Paper	16. Rubber
21. Metal prod.	19. Cement
	21. Metal prod.
	24. Wood, etc.
	28. Misc. manuf.
	Special paper imports

[a]Jute and jute textiles have no possible alternative source of supply.
[b]Tea is hardly to be counted as a priority sector in the West since it is based entirely on tea imported noncompetitively from the East.
[c]Noncompetitive imports and production for noncompetitive regional export are ignored.

based industries. In each case, of course, the decision is a function of the cost structures of the individual sectors.

The sugar industry is a case in which domestic production on the basis of agricultural inputs takes place at low growth rates; but, at high growth rates, there is a switch to importing. Sugar is never a producing sector in East Pakistan, but it is an active sector in West Pakistan in solutions 12/22 and 14/24. However, at higher savings rates, sugar supply is imported.

West Pakistan cotton textiles production, on the other hand, is a case in which no production takes place at low rates of saving. When the savings rate rises to 17/27, the relative price of capital drops sufficiently to allow domestic production even though a part of domestic production must be based on imported raw cotton.[3] West Pakistan wood, cork, and furniture (24), also closely tied to agriculture, follows the same pattern as the cotton textiles sector, coming into production only at the highest savings rate solutions.

The changing source of imports of edible oils to West Pakistan illustrates the countervailing effects of the agricultural price changes and the capital price changes. While production of edible oils in West Pakistan takes place in all solutions, additional imports of edible oils to that region are always required. That is necessary because the edible oils sector is dependent upon cotton by-products for inputs and the limits placed on the output of the cotton sectors affect the output of edible oils (see Section 3.11). At the low levels of growth of solution 12/22, these imports are provided entirely from East Pakistan: the low price of agricultural goods offsets the high price of capital and justifies the necessary production in the East. However, in the 14/24 and 15/25 solutions, the rise in the price of agricultural goods begins to have effect, and a portion of the supply originates abroad. Finally, in the 17/27 solution, the price of capital has fallen sufficiently to offset the rising price of agricultural inputs, and imports are again supplied entirely from the East. Though small quantities of foreign imports are involved, the switching and reswitching of source of supply are an interesting example of the effects of the relative resource supply changes.

The remaining sectors heavily dependent upon agriculture for raw materials are the tobacco products sectors in both regions and the wood, cork, and furniture sector in the East. None of these is ever a producing sector; in no solution does the capital cost drop sufficiently to offset the cost of agricultural inputs.[4]

There are several manufacturing sectors for which the switch from foreign to domestic source of supply can be explained simply as a response to the decline in the availability of foreign exchange relative to capital (or as a result of the rise in the price of foreign exchange relative to the price of capital). In

West Pakistan, the sectors in which domestic production replaces foreign supply as the savings rate rises are: other food, other textiles, cement, metal products, and miscellaneous manufacturing. Except in the cases of cement and miscellaneous manufacturing, the switch from foreign imports to production in the West is accompanied by a switch from foreign to regional imports for the East. There is only one sector in the East where supply shifts from foreign import to domestic production as the savings rate rises; this is the paper sector. Simultaneously, West Pakistan switches its source of supply of noncompetitive special paper imports from abroad to the East.[5]

There are two final but interesting cases of switching industries. When the savings rate rises to 17/27, West Pakistan reduces production of rubber products and transport equipment and begins to import them from the East. Up to that point, both had been producing sectors in each region. The explanation of this switch lies in the increasing similarity between the two regions in the relative productivity of foreign exchange and capital which comes about as the savings rate rises (see Table 5.2). As that rate rises and the rate of growth of West Pakistan approaches that of East Pakistan, the relative productivities of capital and foreign exchange in the two regions approach one another. When the productivity of foreign exchange in the West drops toward the level in the East, the cost differential that will justify trade between the two also drops. In the 17/27 solution, a point is reached where the higher cost of producing those two products in the West is no longer offset by the high productivity of foreign exchange in the West. Therefore, interregional trade begins (see Section 4.3).

Shifts among producing and importing sectors caused by alteration of savings rate assumptions are accompanied by shifts in the export programs. In all four solutions the same total and sectoral export limits have been employed. But priority shifts and the rising level of consumption do carry certain shifts in export priorities (see Section 3.9). The rising level of consumption has the effect of reducing the availability of agricultural goods for export; or, alternatively, the rising level of consumption carries with it a rise in the price of agricultural goods relative to foreign exchange. Either development yields the same result: fewer agricultural commodities are exported. Agricultural exports are replaced by manufactured exports that become profitable as the price of capital declines relative to the price of foreign exchange.[6]

Switching from agricultural exports at high growth rates leads to a significant decline in the gain from a rise in the over-all export limit in West Pakistan. Without agricultural exports, the West exports relatively high cost goods. Such an effect, though evident, is not nearly so strong in the East, since jute exports remain large. The shadow prices of the over-all regional export limits in the four solutions are shown in Table 5.4. It should be pointed out that were a marginal expansion in the over-all limit accompanied by proportional expansions in the sectoral limits, the benefits of the expansion would be much larger. Such situations will be considered when the export limits are systematically examined.

Table 5.4. Shadow Prices of the Over-all Export Limits in the Alternative Savings Rate Solutions

Solution	East Pakistan	West Pakistan
12/22	1.83	2.21
14/24	1.74	1.34
15/25	1.10	0.29
17/27	1.01	.08

First, however, some general observations are in order. It may be concluded from the previous discussion that alternative savings rate assumptions imply quite different development programs. The direct effect upon the rate of growth is of no particular interest in itself.[7] What is important is the shift in the regional allocation of consumption and income which the growth carries with it *and* the shift in the priority program resulting from the interaction of capital, foreign exchange, and agricultural limits. It is becoming evident that the establishment of an industrial priorities program is necessarily tied to the resource programs.

5.2 Export Effect

Foreign exchange earning possibilities are another important aspect of the resource program on which the industrial development program must be based. But a change in the assumptions regarding the export growth rate is not parallel to a change in the assumptions regarding the savings rate. The latter change raises the availability of capital and the growth rate of the economy but does not affect the absolute level of foreign exchange available. Therefore, there is a relative decline in the availability of foreign exchange as the savings rate is raised. A rise of the export growth rate effects a higher growth rate of income which, in turn, effects a greater absolute availability of capital. Since income growth will be concentrated in the nonagricultural sectors where the savings rate is higher, the raising of the export growth rate will raise the aggregate savings rate (see Table 5.5).

Solutions to the model have been obtained for three different export growth rate assumptions. In the basic solution it is assumed that total foreign exchange earnings in each region can grow at 7.5 percent per annum over the ten-year plan period. The two additional solutions have been based upon assumptions of 6.5 percent and 8.5 percent. The sector specific export limits have been proportionally adjusted.[8] The three solutions are designated hereafter as 6.5, 7.5, and 8.5.

The macroeconomic description of these solutions in Table 5.5 show that the change from a 6.5 percent to an 8.5 percent growth rate of exports results in a

Table 5.5. Macroeconomic Results of Alternative Export Rate Solutions

	6.5	7.5[a]	8.5
Aggregate marginal savings rate			
East Pakistan	22.3%	22.3%	22.8%
West Pakistan	20.7	22.3	23.1
All Pakistan	21.6	22.3	22.9
Increment to per capita consumption			
East Pakistan	Rs145.3	Rs144.9	Rs145.3
West Pakistan	130.8	146.4	155.9
All Pakistan	137.7	144.4	149.0
Disparity ratio			
Incremental	.90	1.02	1.07
Terminal year	1.22	1.26	1.27
Incremental capital inflows (millions)			
East Pakistan	+Rs160.0	+Rs106.6	+Rs70.8
West Pakistan	− 160.0	− 106.6	− 70.8
Rate of growth of GNP (per annum)			
East Pakistan	7.6%	7.6%	7.6%
West Pakistan	5.7	6.1	6.3
All Pakistan	6.6	6.8	6.9
Incremental net capital-output ratio			
East Pakistan	2.17	2.16	2.18
West Pakistan	2.52	2.54	2.55
All Pakistan	2.33	2.34	2.37

[a]Basic solution.

change in the rate of growth of income from 6.3 percent to 7.1 percent. The export limit growth effect is somewhat dampened—as was the savings rate effect—by the high incremental capital cost of expansion. That cost is reflected in the change in the incremental capital-output ratios (Table 5.5).

As in the case of the savings rate effect, almost all of the growth takes place in West Pakistan. However, the shift in the allocation of consumption is not so dramatic. Unlike in the case of a rising savings rate, the level of per capita consumption does not fall in East Pakistan when it rises in the West—though East's per capita consumption does not grow either.

Why the shift in the allocation of consumption is less marked than with the savings rate effect is explained by the dual variable ratios in Table 5.6. The ratios of the shadow price of capital to the shadow price of foreign exchange in both regions and the ratio of the shadow price of funds to the average shadow price of the agricultural growth limits indicate there is not much variation among solutions in the relative shadow prices of capital and foreign exchange in the two regions. This lack of variation is a direct result of the phenomenon, pointed out above, that as the export growth rate is increased, the availability of capital also rises.

However, the data in Table 5.6 show the growth that does take place brings about a significant decline in the importance of the funds constraint relative to the agricultural growth limits. The change in the distribution of consumption between the regions can therefore be explained primarily in terms of the changing relative cost of agricultural goods. But, since there is no large change in the relative prices of capital and foreign exchange, the shift toward the West—where consumption is less foreign exchange intensive—is not as great as it was when the savings rate was raised.

Since there is little change in the relative prices of foreign exchange and capital, few industrial priority shifts occur when the export growth rate is varied.

Table 5.6. Some Shadow Price Relationships in the Alternative Export Growth Rate Solutions

	Capital ÷ foreign exchange		Funds ÷ average of agricultural growth Limits
Solution	East Pakistan	West Pakistan	
6.5	0.62	0.59	5.80
7.5	.70	.54	4.28
8.5	.71	.53	3.38

Some of those shifts that do occur bear an interesting relationship to the shifts that were observed when the savings rate was varied.

In West Pakistan the switches occurring for three sectors as the export growth rate is raised are the reverse of switches occurring when the savings rate was raised. Rubber and transport equipment are imported to the West from the East when the export growth rate is low; they are produced within the region when that rate, and the rate of growth of income, rise. The explanation of this shift lies in the difference of the regional ratios of the shadow price of capital to the shadow price of foreign exchange, which increases when the availability of foreign exchange rises. When the regional ratios are similar in the two regions, the productivity of foreign exchange is similar and interregional trade in these commodities is justified. When the productivity of foreign exchange in the West rises relative to the level in the East, the import by the West is no longer justified (see Section 5.1). The switch that occurs for the wood, cork, and furniture sector in the West is also in the opposite direction from the switch that occurs when the savings rate is varied. When that rate was raised, the rising price of agricultural goods was outweighed by the falling price of capital, and this sector became a producing sector. However, when the export growth rate is raised, the agricultural prices dominate, and wood, cork, and furniture becomes an importing sector.

The switches occurring in East Pakistan's priority set can be interpreted as consequences of the rising relative price of capital in that region and of the fall in the price of foreign exchange in the region relative to the price of foreign exchange in the West. Those two factors combine to effect a shift toward the regional import, rather than production, of metal products and miscellaneous manufacturing.

The other shifts in industrial priorities which take place when the export limits are raised are the unambiguous result of the rise in the price of agricultural products. Sugar is no longer produced in the West and is imported from abroad. And West Pakistan's supplemental requirement of edible oils shifts from regional to foreign import.

Although the industrial priority shifts resulting from export limit variation are not great, each alternative export growth solution yields a very different export program. At low rates of over-all export growth, the export program is dominated by agricultural exports. The effective limits on agricultural exports are the domestic production limits less domestic demand. At low levels of over-all export growth, not only are the agricultural limits relatively high, but the economy is growing slowly and domestic demand is low. When the rate of growth of exports is raised, both regions are forced to turn to manufacturing sectors for exports. Because East Pakistan's opportunities for exporting manufactured goods are neither numerous nor large, it is forced to turn to high-cost sectors, resulting in a very low shadow price on the over-all export limit, as can be seen in Table 5.7. The problem is not nearly so great in the West, as can also be seen from Table 5.7.

Table 5.7.   Shadow Prices of the Over-all Export Limits in the Alternative Export Growth Rate Solutions

Solution	East Pakistan	West Pakistan
6.5	2.05	2.03
7.5	1.74	1.34
8.5	0.13	1.16

The implication of the decline in the productivity of the over-all export ability is that the important problem is to find markets for the profitable exports rather than to emphasize efforts to raise exports per se. If the economy reaches a point at which it must move away from its dependence upon agricultural exports, then developing opportunities for the export of low-cost manufactured goods becomes a real issue. Were a greater rise in the savings rate to accompany the rise of the export growth limit, however, the production costs in manufacturing might drop sufficiently to raise the profitability of some of those industrial sectors.

Since relative costs of foreign exchange and capital are not so greatly changed when the export limits are altered—that is, relative availabilities of the two resources are not greatly changed—the shifts in industrial priorities are not as dramatic as when the savings rate assumptions were altered. Nonetheless, the results of alternative export growth rate solutions reexhibit the dependence of the industrial priorities upon the relative availabilities of capital and foreign exchange.

5.3 Foreign Funds Effect

The availabilities of capital and foreign exchange are dependent on the foreign funds flowing into the economy as well as on the country's own ability to generate savings and earn foreign exchange. Foreign funds—which are defined here as including all net public and private funds flowing into the economy—are a supplement to both domestic savings and earned foreign exchange. Since it is assumed that export limits and the domestic savings rate (as a percentage of value added) are independent of the level of foreign funds available, an incremental unit of foreign funds directly raises foreign exchange availability by a unit and, through providing more goods without raising consumption, raises capital availability by a unit (see Sections 2.1 and 3.9).

Beside that effect of foreign funds on foreign exchange and capital supplies, there is an additional indirect effect that must be taken into account. When the availabilities of these resources rise, income also rises. That rise effects a larger supply of domestically generated savings. And, as with the growth resulting from raising export limits, the rise in income will be concentrated in nonagricultural sectors and will cause the domestic savings rate to go up.

The basic solution, assumes the plan period increment to the annual inflow of foreign funds to be zero. Several alternative solutions have been obtained with this increment ranging from −Rs1000.0 million to Rs1000.0 million (in the base year, the level of foreign funds inflow was Rs3062.7 million).[9] Macroeconomic data from the two extreme solutions and the basic solution, 0, are presented in Table 5.8.

Again, the resource variation effect upon consumption and income in East Pakistan is small. In all solutions it is optimal to expand in the East up to the limit imposed by the agricultural supply limits and then expand in the West. The rise in the growth rate of national income—from 5.8 percent to 7.3 percent—which takes place when foreign funds are raised is accompanied by a rise in the savings rate and in the incremental capital-output ratio. Thus, the general resource expansion effect is qualitatively the same as with the savings rate and export growth rate expansion.

The variation of foreign funds increment from −Rs1000.0 million to Rs1000.0 million amounts to a change in per capita foreign funds of Rs13.4. The increment to national per capita consumption resulting from this change is Rs64.9. Thus, the average productivity for foreign funds over this range is Rs4.8.

It is interesting to examine the way in which the productivity of foreign funds varies with the level of foreign funds and how this productivity is divided between foreign exchange productivity and capital productivity. In Table 5.9 the shadow prices of foreign funds and of foreign exchange and capital in each of the regions are shown for several levels of the increment to foreign funds. The marginal productivity curves these prices define are shown in Figure 5.1.

The most striking feature of the productivity of foreign funds curve in Figure

Table 5.8. Macroeconomic Results of Alternative Levels of Aid Solutions

	−Rs1000	Rs0[a]	Rs1000
Aggregate marginal savings rate			
East Pakistan	22.7%	22.3%	22.6%
West Pakistan	18.6	22.3	23.2
All Pakistan	21.2	22.3	22.9
Increment to per capita consumption			
East Pakistan	Rs145.0	Rs144.9	Rs148.2
West Pakistan	57.3	146.4	197.3
All Pakistan	104.4	144.4	169.3
Disparity ratio			
Incremental	.40	1.02	1.33
Terminal year	1.06	1.26	1.36
Incremental capital inflows (millions)			
East Pakistan	Rs61.5	Rs106.6	Rs164.9
West Pakistan	−1,061.5	− 106.6	835.1
Rate of growth of GNP (per annum)			
East Pakistan	7.6%	7.6%	7.6%
West Pakistan	4.1	6.1	7.0
All Pakistan	5.8	6.8	7.3
Incremental net capital-output ratio			
East Pakistan	2.17	2.16	2.18
West Pakistan	2.47	2.54	2.65
All Pakistan	2.28	2.34	2.42

[a]Basic solution.

5.1 is the large productivity decline that occurs when the increment to foreign funds is raised above −Rs300 million. It is at this point that growth in West Pakistan rises to a height where the growth limit on the other agriculture sector becomes binding. When more foreign funds are made available and the growth rate in West Pakistan rises further, agricultural exports must be reduced, and imports of agriculture-based goods must be increased. Consequently, the economy is forced to import substitute and to export in relatively high-cost

Table 5.9. **Shadow Prices for Foreign Funds, Foreign Exchange, and Capital in Alternative Foreign Funds Inflow Solutions**[a]

Level of increment to foreign funds inflow (million rupees)	Funds	Foreign exchange		Capital	
		East Pakistan	West Pakistan	East Pakistan	West Pakistan
−1000	7.14	4.16	4.12	2.98	3.02
− 790	6.27	3.72	3.71	2.55	2.56
− 586	6.19	3.63	3.68	2.57	2.52
− 298	6.02	3.51	3.60	2.51	2.42
− 73	5.22	3.19	3.30	2.03	1.92
	4.72	2.78	3.06	1.94	1.66
133	4.30	2.75	3.00	1.55	1.30
394	3.61	2.68	2.78	0.93	0.83
614	3.52	2.60	2.77	.92	.75
910	3.38	2.59	2.75	.78	.63
1000	3.35	2.59	2.76	.75	.59

[a]Note that the shadow prices of foreign exchange and savings (capital) within a region necessarily add up to the price of funds. When this is not the case, it is due only to rounding.

industrial sectors. Ergo the relatively sharp decline in the productivity of additional funds.

While the precise level at which that process begins is determined by the arbitrary specification of the agricultural growth limits, the phenomenon is a real one. The actual process, of course, would be more gradual. As the growth rate rises, costs in agricultural sectors will rise, and shifts to high-cost industrial sectors will take place. Concomitantly, the productivity of capital and of foreign funds will fall.

The shift from low- to high-cost exports is reflected in the decline in the shadow prices of the regional export limits for the alternative foreign funds solutions. These shadow prices are shown in Table 5.10. While the shift is somewhat less marked in the East than in the West due to the dominance of jute and jute textiles exports in the East, the changes are significant in both regions.[10]

With the decline in the productivity of funds, there is a decline in the productivity of capital relative to the productivity of foreign exchange. At low levels of foreign funds inflow, the incremental impact of foreign funds is slightly greater due to its role in augmenting foreign exchange than to its role in augmenting savings. At high levels of foreign funds inflow, however, the effect upon foreign exchange availability is far more important (see Table 5.9 and Figure 5.1). The decline in the productivity of capital relative to foreign exchange is the result of the secondary effect of foreign funds expansion. As income rises,

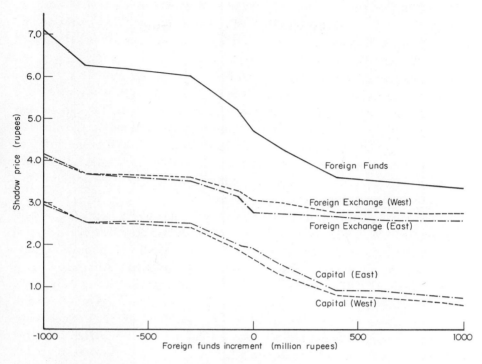

Figure 5.1   Shadow Price of Foreign Funds and of Its Foreign Exchange and Capital Components

Table 5.10.   Shadow Price of Regional Export Limits in Alternative Foreign Funds Solutions

Level of increment to foreign funds inflow (million rupees)	East Pakistan	West Pakistan
−1000	2.82	3.20
− 790	2.50	2.74
− 586	2.41	2.70
− 298	2.33	2.62
− 73	1.95	1.82
	1.74	1.34
133	1.50	1.01
394	1.06	0.28
614	1.02	.24
910	0.93	.18
1000	.91	.16

domestic savings rise, but domestic earning of foreign exchange does not rise. The absolute decline in the productivity of capital is concomitant with the decline in the productivity of foreign funds: as the economy expands, investment in more costly activities must be undertaken.

With due consideration given to the rising cost of agricultural goods, the industrial priority shifts taking place when the availability of funds is raised can be explained from the changes in the relative prices of capital and foreign exchange. Little will be added to the findings of the sections on the effect of savings and the effect of exports (5.1 and 5.2) by any detailed examination of the priority shifts occurring when the availability of funds is varied. What will be useful is a comparison of individual solutions in order to consider alternative programs which yield the same aggregate outcome.

Before leaving this section, however, there are some policy issues that should be presented. While the point of view of this study has been that of the central planner, the findings may be of some use to those outside Pakistan whose decisions affect its development, that is, those giving foreign aid. Although foreign funds include private foreign funds as well as aid, all that has been said about the effect of marginal units of funds applies equally to marginal units of foreign aid.

From the point of view of an aid-giver dealing with the problem of allocating aid among recipient countries, a qualitative lesson may be derived from the productivity of funds curve in Figure 5.1. If the primary constraints to growth for the developing country are the ability to generate capital and to earn foreign exchange, the productivity of aid can be very high. However, when other limits to growth become important, for example, the agricultural growth limits, the productivity of aid drops significantly. These "other limits" could be several things beside the agricultural growth constraints considered here; skill limitations would likely be of importance. It makes intuitive sense that aid has its greatest impact when the capital and foreign exchange constraints are dominant because foreign aid directly augments these two resources.[11] The problem for those giving aid is to determine when, for a particular recipient country, the "other limits" become effective.

A second lesson may be derived from a comparison of the effects of foreign funds and the effects of exports. Reduction of trade barriers is often the suggested alternative to the giving of aid. At low levels of growth, aid plays an important role by contributing to capital as well as to foreign exchange. Lowering trade barriers cannot substitute for the capital-augmenting role of aid. Although the capital constraint becomes relatively less important than the foreign exchange constraint at higher rates of growth, a general expansion of export opportunities will not have much affect, since the export expansion must come from high-cost sectors (see Tables 5.4, 5.7, and 5.10). What can have a powerful impact, however, is a selective policy that allows expansion of exports from low-cost sectors. In Table 5.11 the shadow prices on the sector specific export limits for the highest growth rate solutions of this and the previous two sections are shown. Clearly, a reduction of trade barriers will have a strong effect when it allows expansion of exports from the foodgrain agricultural sectors; from other chemicals; from other food, leather, and paper in the West; and from jute textiles in the East.

Table 5.11. Shadow Prices on Sector Specific Export Limits for Three High Growth Rate Solutions[a]

	Savings rate 17/27		Export growth 8.5		Foreign funds increment of Rs1,000 million	
	East	West	East	West	East	West
1. Rice	1.62	2.34	2.32	1.11	1.49	2.09
2. Wheat	[b]	2.57	[b]	1.47	[b]	2.33
7. Sugar						
8. Edible oils		0.20	0.68			
10. Other food	0.16	1.73	1.15	0.65	0.10	1.50
11. Cotton text.			0.92			
12. Jute text.	.81	[b]	1.04	[b]	.69	[b]
13. Other text.		0.81	1.50	.13		0.64
14. Paper	.07	1.76	0.04	.55		1.49
15. Leather		1.79	.29	1.00		1.61
16. Rubber	.39	1.03	1.09		.33	0.83
18. Other chem.	.92	1.43	1.97	0.43	.89	1.27
21. Metal prod.	.27	1.27	1.15	.04	.35	1.08
22. Machinery		0.78	0.77		.02	0.61
23. Transport eq.	[c]	.73	.57			.53
24. Wood, etc.		.21				.11
28. Misc. manuf.	.52	1.42	1.20		.45	1.12
29. Coal, etc.	.43	1.28	1.36	.26	.43	1.12
Regional limit	1.01	0.08	0.13	1.16	.91	0.16

[a]See Tables 5.1, 5.5, 5.8.
[b]No exports possible.
[c]Positive shadow price but less than .01.

5.4 Alternative Programs with the Same Aggregate Outcome

Sections 5.1–5.3 attempted to establish the dependence of the optimal industrial priorities program upon the relative availabilities of capital and foreign exchange. The relationship between industrial priorities and those resources has, however, been somewhat obscured by the influence of the rate of growth of income and by the influence of the agricultural growth limits. In this brief section, alternative solutions are compared in which the aggregate growth of income and consumption are similar but in which the relative availabilities of capital and foreign exchange are different.

The first comparison is between the solution in which the savings rate assumption is 15/25 and the solution in which the export growth rate assumption is 8.5 percent (all else being as in the basic solution). The income growth rate in both these solutions is 6.9 percent per annum over the plan period, and the increments to national per capita income are Rs148.8 and Rs149.0, respectively. Thus, on a national level, these two programs lead to the same aggregate outcome.

In Table 5.12 the shadow price of foreign funds, the regional ratios of the shadow price of capital to the shadow price of foreign exchange, and the ratio of the shadow price of funds to the average shadow price of the agricultural growth limits are shown for the two solutions. The ratio of the shadow price of capital to the shadow price of foreign exchange is, of course, much larger in the solution with export growth at 8.5 percent. That is, capital is more scarce when this level of income and consumption is achieved by the high export growth rate than when achieved by the high savings rate. The lower productivity of funds in the high savings solution can be viewed as the result of the higher savings

Table 5.12. Shadow Price Relationships in Savings Solution 15/25 and Export Solution 8.5

Solution	Funds	Capital ÷ foreign exchange		Funds ÷ average of agricultural growth Limits
		East Pakistan	West Pakistan	
15/25	3.65	0.36	0.30	2.26
8.5	4.56	.71	.53	3.38

rate; the greater availability of domestic savings reduces the capital impact of foreign funds.

The difference between the two solutions in terms of industrial priorities follows directly from the difference in capital and foreign exchange scarcity.[12] In solution 8.5, West Pakistan's supplies of supplemental edible oils and of special paper are imported from abroad. In solution 15/25 the source of supply for both those products shifts toward East Pakistan production. In solution 15/25, West provides East with other food products; in solution 8.5 the source of East's supply of other food products shifts toward foreign import. A final priority difference is brought about because, in comparing solution 8.5 to solution 15/25, capital is relatively more scarce in East than in West. Consequently, in the 8.5 solution, East imports miscellaneous manufacturing products from the West though it produced them in solution 15/25.

A similar comparison can be made between solution 17/27 and the solution in which the level of the increment to foreign funds inflow was raised to Rs394 million. The rates of income growth for these solutions are 7.1 percent and 7.0 percent, respectively; and the increments to national per capita consumption are Rs153.2 and Rs155.4, respectively.[13]

The difference in availability of capital and foreign exchange in these two solutions is reflected in the different ratios of the shadow price of capital to the shadow price of foreign exchange. In solution 17/27 those ratios are .16 in the East and .15 in the West. In solution Rs394 million these ratios are .35 in the East and .30 in the West. Consequently, some industries that tend to be importing sectors in the Rs394 million solution switch toward production in 17/27, and imports of agricultural products are larger. Those switching sectors are paper in the East and cotton textiles; other textiles; and wood, cork, and furniture in the West. Also, West's supply of supplemental oils and special paper switch from foreign import to import from the East. The difference in the interregional differential in foreign exchange productivity brings about a change in regional trade patterns: in solution 17/27, West imports some rubber products and transport equipment from the East, while it relies totally on its own production in solution Rs394 million.

The comparisons just examined should finally establish the point, which has been developed throughout this chapter, that industrial priorities programs and capital and foreign exchange programs must be developed simultaneously. The proper choice of priorities is dependent upon the costs of both those resources. If decisions are made without consideration of the relative costs of capital and foreign exchange, those decisions will often be erroneous.

5.5 Derivation of a Priorities Program for Pakistan

In a priorities program, or priorities ranking, industries are ranked according to the desirability of their development. A high priority sector is one for which the benefits of production, as opposed to importing, are high.

The preceding sections of this chapter have established that a priorities program is sensitive to resource conditions, and, therefore, that a set of priorities should not be presented without a statement of the resource assumptions on which it is based. Sections 5.1–5.4 have shown both the general and specific ways in which any priorities ranking for Pakistan is sensitive to resource availabilities and thereby serve to qualify that priority ranking.

In this section priorities rankings are presented for the manufacturing sectors in the economy of each region and for the manufacturing sectors in the Pakistan economy taken as a whole. The national ranking is presented to abstract from peculiarities resulting from regional comparative advantage and to gain an over-all qualitative picture.

The resource conditions on which these rankings are based are the assumptions of the basic solution. However, the ranking of that solution is qualified on the basis of the results of the alternative solutions to the model. The derivation of the ranking is begun by establishing six groupings of industries:[14]

 I. Industries producing within the region (nation) in all solutions and never importing.

 II. Industries that are producing within the region (nation) and not importing in the basic solution but are importing in one or more of the alternative solutions.

 III. Industries that are both producing and importing in the basic solution and are producing and not importing in one or more of the alternative solutions.

 IV. Industries that are both producing and importing in the basic solution but are never only producing sectors in any of the alternative solutions (these sectors are those producing only to export and obtain the remainder of their supply from imports).

 V. Industries that are importing and not producing in the region (nation) in the basic solution but are producing in one or more of the alternative solutions.

 VI. Industries that are not producing in either the basic solution or in any of the alternative solutions.

Within each of these groups, sectors are ranked using the simplex criteria and dual variables of the basic solution; though on the basis of that solution's costs, no industry in one group is ranked above (below) any industry in a higher (lower) group. Sectors producing and not importing in the basic solution—groups I and II—are ranked by the absolute value of the simplex criteria of the cheapest alternative source of supply. When an industry is in group I or II in terms of the nation, the simplex criteria of foreign importing to the region where the product is produced more cheaply is the basis of ranking. In neither of the regional rankings is there more than one group III industry, so intragroup ranking is unnecessary. In the national rankings, there are two group III industries. Since they are both West Pakistan producing sectors, the relative rankings of West are used. Industries producing only to export—group IV—are ranked within their group according to the benefits that would be gained from exporting an extra unit; those benefits can be computed from the shadow prices on the sector specific foreign exchange earning constraints and the foreign exchange price of exports. Industries not producing in the basic solution—groups V and VI—are ranked inversely by the absolute value of the simplex criteria of the unused production activities.[15]

The groupings and rankings are shown for each region and for the country as a whole in Table 5.13. In the national ranking it has been necessary to distinguish edible oils, cotton textiles, and paper industries separately for the two regions. For each of these sectors interregional trade from the more cheaply producing region is in some way limited (see Sections 3.7 and 3.11).

The priority rankings in Table 5.13 present an interesting picture of the Pakistan economy. In general they give high positions to capital goods and capital-goods related sectors while the position of intermediate goods and consumption goods industries is rather mixed.

The policy implications of the priorities program must be appropriately qualified before proceeding further. First, the sector classification used in this study includes what would be large aggregates from the point of view of those who formulate specific policy. That one of the sectors in this study is given high (low) priority does not exclude the possibility that there are low (high) priority industries within that sector. Second, the data used in this study, although incremental in principle, are based on past performance. A case might be made, for example, that an industry shows low priority in this study because its past performance has been bad and that a proper set of policies could greatly improve the industry's performance. The low-priority position of such a sector should not lead to its exclusion from future development programs so long as the

Table 5.13. Regional and National Priority Rankings of Manufacturing Industries in Pakistan

Sector	East Pakistan Group	East Pakistan Rank	West Pakistan Group	West Pakistan Rank	All Pakistan Group	All Pakistan Rank
7. Sugar	VI	20	II	13	III	18
8. Edible oils						
East	II	11			II	16
West			I	2	I	4
9. Tobacco	VI	18	VI	19	VI	23
10. Other food	V	15	II	11	III	17
11. Cotton text.						
East	I	6			I	11
West			V	16	V	20
12. Jute textiles	I	9			I	12
13. Other textiles	IV	14	IV	15	IV	19
14. Paper						
East	V	17			V	22
West			I	3	I	9
15. Leather	V	16	I	1	I	2
16. Rubber	I	10	II	12	I	10
17. Fertilizer	I	2	VI	18	I	1
18. Other chem.	I	3	IV	14	I	3
19. Cement	I	5	II	6	II	13
20. Basic metals	I	1	I	5	I	5
21. Metal prod.	III	13	II	7	II	15
22. Machinery	I	7	II	10	I	6
23. Transport eq.	I	4	II	9	I	7
24. Wood, etc.	VI	19	V	17	V	21
28. Misc. manuf.	II	12	II	8	II	14
29. Coal, etc.	I	8	I	4	I	8

relevant policies are introduced. With these qualifications established, the following analysis of this priorities program can be appropriately viewed.[16]

5.6 The Program and Past Growth

The priorities program prescribed here for the manufacturing sectors calls for some changes in the industrial pattern Pakistan has developed. Pakistan's industrial structure has, of course, not been static, and some of the changes called for by the priorities ranking are not inconsistent with recent trends.

Particularly notable are the changes indicated for the textile sectors. Cotton textiles, a West Pakistan-based industry, is the largest manufacturing sector in the country, and jute textiles is the second largest. Cotton textiles played an important role as an import-substituting industry during the industrial growth of the 1950s and has become a large exporting sector. Jute textiles has increasingly become an important exporter, the most important among Pakistan's manufacturing industries. The other textiles sector has also grown significantly and has increasingly become a source of foreign exchange earnings (see Soligo 1965; Khan 1963; Pakistan 1967a, 1966c).

Nonetheless, as a group the textile industries showed a significant decline in their growth rates during the early 1960s, and the priority rankings prescribe further de-emphasis in the future. Other textiles and cotton textiles in the West rank fifteenth and sixteenth, respectively; other textiles in the East ranks fourteenth. Jute textiles and cotton textiles are in the upper half of East Pakistan's ranking, but jute textiles is ninth and cotton textiles drops to eleventh in the national ranking.

That the priorities ranking calls for de-emphasis of the textile industries does not necessarily mean that any errors have been made in past policy. The first part of this chapter demonstrated that the proper priorities choice depends on the resource availabilities; and the resource position of the economy in the past was not that which has been assumed for the future. In examining the alternative solutions to the model, it was found that the development of that entire set of textile industries tends to be more desirable when foreign exchange is scarce relative to capital. It is possible that Pakistan's past is better characterized by such a situation than by the assumptions of the basic solution of the model. However, there is some indication that the textile industries were not growing simply in response to actual opportunity costs. A study of Pakistan tariffs finds the textile industries to be the most heavily protected group of industries (Soligo and Stern 1965; Lewis and Guisinger 1966).

Another group of industries that grew rapidly in the pre-1965 period, but are rated as low priority for future development, are, with the exception of West Pakistan edible oils, consumer goods producing sectors, which are heavily dependent upon the other agriculture sector for inputs. None of these sectors is in the upper half of the rankings; and East Pakistan sugar and wood, cork, and furniture and the tobacco sectors of both regions are in group VI. Again, the divergence between past events and prescriptions for the future can be explained as a reflection of different resource circumstances in the two periods or as a result of discriminatory tariff policies. The alternative solutions to the model show

129

that the desirability of developing these industries is inversely correlated with the price of agricultural goods. The relatively low price of agricultural goods in the mid 1950s would have been a favorable impetus to the growth of these industries. The high price of agricultural goods obtained in the basic solution, consistent with the trend of the late 1950s and early 1960s (Lewis and Hussain 1967), reverses the circumstances; and these sectors become low priority. On the other hand, this group of sectors is very heavily protected, and this protection rather than the objective resource circumstances could explain their growth (Soligo and Stern 1965).

Among those sectors with high priority rankings are the important capital goods sectors and capital goods related sectors—machinery, transport equipment, basic metals, and cement.[17] The past experience of these sectors is somewhat unclear and has been the subject of controversy (see Lewis and Soligo 1965; Power 1963; and Khan 1963). The dispute is whether or not these sectors are discriminated against by Pakistan's import policies and whether or not these sectors have grown sufficiently relative to the other manufacturing sectors. Implicit in the controversy is the assumption that a relative increase in the importance of the capital goods industries would be a desirable development. The priorities ranking certainly calls for a direction of development in favor of the capital goods industries: these four sectors are in the upper half of both regional rankings, and only the cement sector drops to the lower half in the national ranking.

Regarding other high ranking sectors, it is difficult to offer generalizations. These sectors include fertilizer, leather, and other chemicals at the top of the list and coal and petroleum products, West Pakistan paper, and rubber at a slightly lower level. The fertilizer sector, although growing rapidly, remains small. Its priority position calls for continuation of the growth and a consequent rise in its importance. Leather exports have been one of the most rapidly growing sources of foreign exchange earning. That sector's high priority position and the assumption of growing opportunities for foreign exchange earnings should further raise the significance of the industry. The priority positions of other chemicals and coal and petroleum products indicate the desirability of a continued emphasis on sectors that have grown quite rapidly in the previous decade (although the other chemicals sector seems to have lagged slightly in the early 1960s). Rubber, a rapidly growing sector, and West Pakistan paper, a more slowly growing sector, are both very small industries. Their priority positions call for an increase in their importance.

In summary, the priorities program calls for a de-emphasis of the large textile industries and several agriculture-based industries in favor of a number of relatively small sectors. The favored sectors include the capital goods industries and a number of intermediate goods industries. The change in the structure of the manufacturing sector which is called for does not necessarily imply a criticism of past policy. The past patterns of industrialization may well have been justified under existing resource conditions. Nonetheless, among the lower priority industries are several which have received heavy protection. A change in the pattern of development designed to conform to the changing resource circumstances would require some policy changes.

5.7 The Program and the Plan

The principle of balanced growth seems to have been an overriding constraint under which the Pakistan Planning Commission formulated its industrial development program for the third Five-Year Plan. The plan calls for growth in production corresponding to growth in demand in many sectors, with no apparent attempt to consider the relative costs of alternative sources of supply (Pakistan 1965a; 448, 459–488).

The over-all strategy of the plan does call for a high rate of import substitution in capital good sectors rather than in intermediate and consumer goods sectors. It does not seem unreasonable to infer, however, that for the Planning Commission, the high rate of import substitution in capital goods sectors follows directly from its estimate of a relatively high rate of growth of demand for capital goods (Pakistan 1965a: 32, 35, 80, 85).

It is possible to justify a balanced growth approach to industrial development. The availability of industry specific skills may cause costs to go up sharply as the growth rate in any one industry becomes high. Therefore, it would be desirable to develop all industries at similar rates of growth rather than relying upon imports to supply some products and rapid growth to supply others. Also, the expectation of an eventual deterioration of the foreign exchange position of the country and limits on the rate at which the economy could adjust itself to the change would justify a balanced program. The move to self-sufficiency in fifteen years could carry with it just such a deterioration of the foreign exchange position of the economy.[18] A balanced industrial development program could also be justified on political grounds: it may be desirable to maintain a diversified import program to avoid dependence upon foreign supply. Indeed, the benefits of avoiding such a dependence can be economic as well as political.

Nonetheless, if unbalanced development is feasible, it would seem that in choosing a balanced growth program, it would be helpful to know the costs involved in that choice. It is interesting to examine the marginal costs involved in the plan's decisions to expand some of the sectors that, in the program derived here, have particularly low priority rankings. The simplex criteria of excluded production activities in the basic solution provide those marginal costs.

In Table 5.14, the basic solution simplex criteria (see Section 4.4) are shown for the production activities of several importing sectors.[19] The simplex criteria is the cost in terms of aggregate consumption of producing rather than importing one unit of the good. If production is expanded and resources become more scarce, these marginal costs would rise. The marginal costs of production vary from sector to sector according to rank. Expanding production of cotton textiles or wood, cork, and furniture in the West would not be very costly at the margin. The expansion of sugar; paper; or wood, cork, and furniture in the East or of tobacco products in either region would involve a substantial sacrifice. In all of these industries, the targets of the Third Plan are rapid expansion of domestic production.

The model of development being employed in this study and the one that seems to be implicit in the Pakistan plan embody different views of the planning process. But the model used here employs those plan assumptions that imply

Table 5.14. Basic Solution Marginal Costs of Expanding Production for Several Low Ranking Sectors

Sector	Rank	Marginal cost[a]
East Pakistan		
7. Sugar	20	1.088
9. Tobacco	18	0.543
10. Other food	15	0.118
14. Paper	17	0.619
24. Wood, etc.	19	0.624
West Pakistan		
9. Tobacco	19	0.548
11. Cotton text.	16	0.064
17. Fertilizer	18	0.200
24. Wood, etc.	17	0.066

[a]In terms of aggregate private consumption.

conditions of relative foreign exchange scarcity, and competitive import activity and the elimination of incremental production in the solution are confined to a relatively few sectors. Except for those sectors, the model is not so different from the plan prescription of balanced growth. Still, within those sectors the cost of the plan's decisions may be substantial. It would not seem unwarranted to suggest that plan formulation could be improved by considering the possibility of relying more heavily upon imports for some products that have previously been produced domestically. Regardless of which decision is ultimately made, considering the alternatives should lead to a better understanding of costs and benefits.

5.8 The Program and Other Priority Rankings

The Pakistan Planning Commission has begun to develop the concept of a priorities ranking. In a recent study carried out at the Planning Commission by Tims (1967), a priorities ranking was developed to evaluate the proposed revisions in the Third Plan's industrial investment schedule. The rankings were used as an aid in determining where further investment could be expected to have the greatest pay-off. The basis of the ranking in the Tims study is the benefit per unit of foreign exchange required in expansion.

Another priorities ranking for Pakistan was carried out at the Pakistan Institute of Development Economics by Khan and MacEwan (1967b). The Khan-MacEwan ranking was developed primarily as an analytic rather than as a prescriptive tool. The concern was to establish in which sectors capital costs of previous development had been high, and the criteria for ranking are the capital costs per unit of income generation in each sector.

The Tims study implicitly assumes that the availability of foreign exchange is the dominant constraint to development, and the Khan-MacEwan study implicitly assumes that the availability of capital is the relevant limit. The present study assumes that both capital and foreign exchange constraints should be taken into account in formulating industrial priorities and does not prejudge which limit is more important. The Tims study and the Khan-MacEwan study represent two special and extreme cases of the more general approach used here, and an examination of some of the differences among results obtained in the three studies are useful.

The problem with comparing the results of the three studies involves the many differences among them beside the differences regarding scarcity of capital and foreign exchange. First, data in the three studies are different.[20] Not only are the basic sets of data different, but the Tims and the Khan-MacEwan data are averages of past (though recent) years.[21] Second, in both those studies, existing prices of commodities are used as though they reflect social opportunity costs, though in the Tims study some adjustments are made of basic resource costs. Third, in both studies, regional rankings are obtained separately; the desirability of regional specialization is not considered.

Finally, Tims uses a more disaggregated sector classification scheme than that employed here; for comparison it has been necessary to aggregate his results.[22] Those differences do limit the usefulness of the comparisons.

Table 5.15 shows the three priority programs for East and West Pakistan. Although for some sectors the three programs give similar rankings, the differ-

Table 5.15. Three Priority Rankings for East and West Pakistan Manufacturing Industries

Sector	East Pakistan			West Pakistan		
	This study	Tims[a]	Khan-MacEwan	This study	Tims[a]	Khan-MacEwan
7. Sugar	20	5	16	13	10	5
8. Edible oils	11	11	5	2	4	9
9. Tobacco	18	3	1	19	6	2
10. Other food	15	17	6	11	9	6
11. Cotton text.	6	6	15	16	2	17
12. Jute text.	9	1	12			
13. Other text.	14	8	17	15	11	14
14. Paper	17	10	19	3	5	8
15. Leather	16	2	4	1	1	1
16. Rubber	10	18	9	12	15	13
17. Fertilizer	2	7	18	18	3	19
18. Other chem.	3	4	2	14	8	7
19. Cement	5	15	13	6	12	16
20. Basic metals	1	16	3	5	18	15
21. Metal prod.	13	12	7	7	16	4
22. Machinery	7	9	10	10	14	10
23. Transport eq.	4	19	8	9	19	18
24. Wood, etc.	19	13	11	17	7	3
28. Misc. manuf.	12	14	14	8	17	12
29. Coal, etc.	8			4	13	11

[a]The Tims study has been adjusted to the sector classification used in this study.

ences are far more striking. Some specific examples will illustrate the probable reasons for the differences.

1. Tims' high ranking of sugar in East Pakistan can be explained by his failure to take into account the high capital costs, the high costs of agriculture inputs, and the low cost of importing sugar.

2. Both Tims and Khan and MacEwan rank tobacco high in East and West Pakistan. They are correct in finding costs of expansion low in those sectors relative to expansion costs in other sectors, but they fail to take into account the high costs of expansion relative to the costs of imports.

3. The high ranking that Tims obtains for jute textiles is probably best explained as a direct result of his neglect of capital costs. Nonetheless, it is surprising that he obtains such a high ranking, since a large quantity of capital equipment for jute textile production is imported. The imports of capital equipment should weigh heavily against the sector according to Tims' criteria.

4. Tims and Khan and MacEwan rank leather high in both regions. This study, however, gives a low ranking to East Pakistan leather, since, compared to West Pakistan leather, it is not so desirable. Neither Tims nor Khan and MacEwan take the possibility of such regional specialization into account in formulating their rankings.

5. Tims ranks fertilizer high in both regions. Again, this study suggests the desirability of regional specialization. Khan and MacEwan rank fertilizer low in both regions, since its direct capital requirement has been so large. They fail, however, to note that relative to other products the cost of importing fertilizer is high.

6. The low rankings which Tims and Khan and MacEwan obtain for the cement and basic metals sectors are at odds with the findings of this study. Again the difference is probably explained by the fact that both studies measure expansion in terms of domestic prices, and for those sectors the high cost of importing is obscured. (Khan and MacEwan dismiss their low ranking for basic metals in the East as having little significance.)

7. Tims' high ranking of the West Pakistan cotton textiles sector is probably explained by failure to take capital costs into account. However, both for cotton and jute textiles, Tims is probably working with different data than have been employed in this study or by Khan and MacEwan.

8. Finally, both Tims and Khan and MacEwan rank the wood, cork, and furniture sectors high relative to the rankings they are given in this study. The difference can again be traced to their failure to compare costs of importing as well as costs of production expansion.

The chief fault of both the Tims and the Khan and MacEwan studies is not that they have failed to take into account both the capital and foreign exchange limitations, although their concentration on single constraints surely leads to errors. The main problem is that both studies developed rankings by comparing the relative costs of expanding domestic production in different sectors while measuring expansion in domestic prices. Since the differential between domestic price and import price varies quite significantly among sectors, that procedure leads to serious "misranking" of sectors. For example, the cost of producing a unit of a product measured in domestic prices may be high relative to costs in other sectors, but the cost of importing a domestic price unit may be even more dear relative to the cost of importing other products. Both Tims and Khan and MacEwan would give a low ranking to such a sector. The present study, however, by simultaneous consideration of production cost differences and import cost differences will give a high rank to such an industry.

5.9 Validity of the Program

The validity of the priority rankings derived in this study is supported by both comparison with alternative priority rankings and the findings of studies of protection and efficiency in Pakistan. In the many instances that the results obtained here were contradicted by the alternative rankings of Tims and of Khan and MacEwan, the differences could be explained by the limitations of the other studies. The analyses of tariffs and efficiency in Pakistan by Soligo and Stern (1965) and Lewis and Guisinger (1966) indicate that several sectors, especially textiles and food sectors, which this study ranks low, are highly protected and are not competitive at world prices. Thus, the past rapid growth of some of these sectors cannot be taken as contradicting the validity of their low priority rankings.

There are, nonetheless, some reservations which should be stated regarding the rankings of certain sectors. Particularly questionable are the low rankings that some sectors are given in one region because they compare poorly with their counterpart in the other. For example, development of both West Pakistan other chemicals and East Pakistan leather would be preferable to foreign imports of these products. The model by its aggregation necessarily obscures opportunities that probably exist for regional specialization in certain subsectors of these industries.[23] The model's prescription for regional specialization in fertilizer production is also questionable. Cost estimations for that sector are poor, and the cost difference between the two regions can probably be considered insignificant.[24] Finally, the qualifications regarding the high level of aggregation and the possibilities for changing performance of sectors should be recalled (see Section 5.5 and Appendix C).

Regardless of those reservations, for these sectors that rank either very high or very low in the priority program, confidence can probably be placed in the accuracy of their general positions. In addition, the more general empirical results of the priority analysis should be equally accepted. The low position of the food industries, the low position of the textiles sectors, and the high position of the capital goods producing sectors would seem to be most significant.

6 | Agricultural Change and Industrial Planning

6.1 Interdependence between Agriculture and Industry

There are several kinds of events directly affecting the availabilities of capital and foreign exchange. Changes in tax structure, increases in foreign aid, and changes in trade policies would be examples. The experiments of Chapter 5 were designed to determine the impact of such events on industrial priorities.

There are other types of events, whose impact on capital and foreign exchange, and consequently on industrial priorities, is more indirect; expansion of housing and electricity generation projects, changes in defense expenditures, and changes of agricultural production techniques are examples. This chapter will examine the impact of one such program—the introduction of new techniques in the production of foodgrains—on industrial development decisions.

The foodgrains production program in Pakistan is centered around the introduction of new seed varieties in the production of rice and wheat. Those new varieties have higher yields than the traditional varieties, regardless of the intensity of cultivation. However, the yield differential between modern and traditional seed varieties increases with greater application of modern inputs—fertilizer, pesticides, and capital for water control. The high pay-off to the use of modern inputs which accompany the new seed varieties will, it is hoped, induce general changes in the methods of cultivation.[1]

The most immediate impact of the foodgrains production program on resource availability is its affect in saving foreign exchange. Achievement of the primary goal of the program, self-sufficiency in foodgrains, will release foreign exchange for use elsewhere in the economy. Beyond self-sufficiency is the possibility of expanding foreign exchange earnings with foodgrain exports. The foreign exchange providing function of technical change in agriculture is similar to the labor providing role that is usually emphasized (see W. A. Lewis 1954; Fei and Ranis 1964; Mellor 1966). The technical change directly increases the resources available to the industrial sector. In the case of labor the increase in availability comes through releasing labor from the agricultural production process. In the case of foreign exchange, the availability is increased through releasing foreign exchange from the agricultural supply process and, perhaps, through generating foreign exchange by exporting.

The technical change in agriculture, however, has ramifications other than those transmitted by the direct provision of foreign exchange (or labor) to the industrial sector. The additional effects come from two sources. First, the change creates demands for inputs from the industrial sector. Second, the change raises the level of income and thereby has the dual effect of changing consumption demand and raising the availability of capital through raising domestic savings. The provision of foreign exchange, the creation of demand for industrial inputs and consumption goods, and the generation of additional capital will have a manifold impact upon the industrial sector. Aside from the general rise in output that will result from the technical change in agriculture, it is not possible to make an a priori judgment about how the industrial sector will be affected by the change.

In other words, the effect of agricultural change upon the direction of industrial development, that is, upon industrial priorities, is a complex issue. The provision of foreign exchange through agricultural import substitution and export expansion will tend to increase foreign exchange using activity in the industrial sector. On the other hand, the generation of capital resulting from the general rise of income will tend to increase capital using activity in the industrial sector. And the foreign exchange and capital using effects of the changes in intermediate and consumption demand cannot be directly determined. Derivation of the effects of technical change in agriculture upon the direction of industrial development, it seems, requires the use of a general equilibrium approach.

The general equilibrium programming model used in this study has been designed to facilitate consideration of alternative degrees of success of the foodgrains production program. Separate production functions are specified for land under traditional cultivation and under modern cultivation. The assumption regarding the degree of adoption of the new program is prespecified in terms of the share of land to which each production function applies. Solutions to the model determine only the degree of intensity of operation with the new techniques. By obtaining alternative solutions to the model, each based on a different assumption regarding the degree of adoption of the new program, it is possible to examine the effects of the agricultural change on the economy in general and on the direction of industrial development in particular (see Section 3.10). It should be emphasized, however, that intra-agricultural choices are excluded from consideration in the model.

Within the framework of the model, the technical change in agriculture can be classed as: (1) foreign exchange savings and capital using, that is, the change brings about a rise in the ratio of the marginal product (shadow price) of capital to the marginal product (shadow price) of foreign exchange; (2) foreign exchange using and capital saving, that is, the change brings about a decline in the ratio the marginal product (shadow price) of capital to the marginal product (shadow price) of foreign exchange; or (3) neutral with respect to foreign exchange and capital, that is, the change does not alter the ratio of the marginal products of capital and foreign exchange.[2] To class technical change in the production of foodgrains in these terms is, of course, to set it in the context of Chapter 5. The changes in agriculture can then be seen as operating through the capital and foreign exchange constraints—capital using, foreign exchange using, or neutral —to effect the proper choice of industrial priorities.

6.2 Alternative Degrees of Success for the Foodgrains Program

The model has been designed to allow consideration of technical change in three sectors—rice in East Pakistan and rice and wheat in West Pakistan. Alternative solutions to the model have been obtained, each with a different assumption about the degree of adoption of the new techniques in these three sectors.[3] For purposes of discussion it is useful to define the degree of success assumed in the basic solution as 100 percent. In terms of acreage, "100 percent" means 6 million of East Pakistan's 23 million rice acres, 2 million of West Pakistan's 3.5 million rice acres, and 6 million of West Pakistan's 13 million wheat acres are under modern cultivation, and the remainder are under traditional cultivation. Other solutions are defined in relation to the basic solution norm, for example, 75 percent success means 4.5 million acres, 1.5 million acres, and 4.5 million acres, respectively, of the three crops are under modern cultivation. It should be noted that in all variations the number of acres under modern cultivation in each crop remains in fixed proportion to the area of each of the other crops under modern cultivation; that is, no differential success is considered. In addition to the basic solution with an assumption of 100 percent success, solutions have been obtained based upon assumptions of 50, 62.5, 75, 90, and 150 percent success.

The impact of the technical change on the economy in general can be seen in the relationship—shown in Figure 6.1—between the degree of adoption of the new techniques and the level of the increment to national per capita consumption, the maximand of the model. The slope of the curve in Figure 6.1 is, in a rough sense, the marginal return to the introduction of the new techniques, and the leveling-off of the curve shortly before 100 percent reflects a diminishing return to the adoption of the new techniques. The diminishing return effect is easily explained by examining the alternative solutions. At the lowest level of success, 50 percent, the economy is forced to import rice to East Pakistan and, though self-sufficient in the West, does not produce sufficient surplus to take full advantage of its export opportunities for West Pakistan rice.[4] In the next solu-

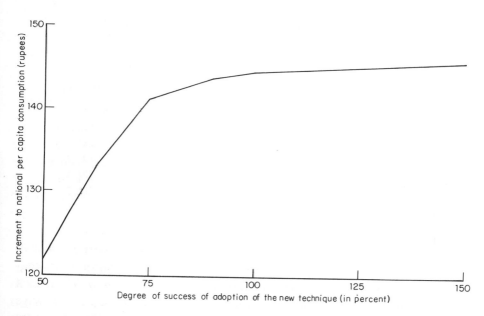

Figure 6.1 Impact of Technical Change in the Production of Foodgrains on the Increment to National Per Capita Consumption

extent that foreign exchange earning through foodgrains exports requires less of the marketing resources than does foreign exchange earning through alternative exports, the experiments of this chapter understate the foreign exchange saving effect of the technical change in the production of foodgrains. Nonetheless, some limit to foreign exchange earning through foodgrain exports, or at least a declining rate of return, surely exists. Though the change might take place at a higher degree of adoption of the new techniques, the switch in the nature of the technical change from foreign exchange saving to capital saving is probably a real phenomenon.

A second deficiency of the model in dealing with the impact of technical change in foodgrains production is that no account is taken of transfers of land from foodgrain production to production of other agricultural products. In all solutions it is assumed that the total acreage devoted to each crop remains unchanged, though the distribution of the acreage between traditional and modern techniques of cultivation changes. Clearly, when the productivity of land in foodgrains sectors rises and the value of additional foodgrains supply falls, it would be desirable to transfer land to other types of agricultural activities. In failing to take account of the land-releasing effect of technical change in foodgrains production, the model understates the impact of the change.

The changes the model does show in the capital and foreign exchange intensity of the economy as techniques in agriculture change are not large. Consequently, few changes are induced in the optimal direction of development in the industrial sector. At very low levels of adoption of the new techniques, when the price of foreign exchange in the West is high relative to that in the East, East Pakistan obtains its supply of rubber, miscellaneous manufacturing, and coal and petroleum products from the West. When the level of technical change is raised and the price of foreign exchange rises relatively in the East, those regional imports are replaced by production within East Pakistan. East Pakistan switches the source of supply of its sugar from regional toward foreign imports and its supply of other food from regional toward foreign import and then back toward regional import as the degree of adoption of the new techniques is raised. In West Pakistan the assumed increase of progress in the foodgrains sector effects a shift from domestic production to foreign import of wood, cork, and furniture and the beginning of a switch from foreign import to domestic production of cotton textiles.

The sum of all these changes, however, is not large. Within the limitations of the model, the technical change in agriculture can be taken as having a nearly neutral effect on industrial priority decisions.

6.3 Impact of Technical Change in the Production of Foodgrains

The degree of success of the foodgrains production program postulated in the basic solution is not unreasonable, yet the model indicates that payoffs to further progress in the foodgrains sectors would be low. With the low-income elasticities of demand for foodgrains, the attainment of self-sufficiency does not seem to be far off. Once that is attained, further improvements in foodgrains production techniques could affect aggregate consumption (income) through expanding exports and through releasing land for the cultivation of other crops. The design of the model employed in this study may lead to an understatement of the export expansion effect and takes no account of the land-releasing effect. While the solutions to the model are probably accurate in indicating that the greatest returns to technical change in foodgrains production come in attaining self-sufficiency, a comprehensive analysis of the impact of the change should consider the other effects.

The model is probably more accurate in evaluating the impact of agricultural change on industrial priorities than in measuring the impact of the change upon aggregate variables. The understatement of the export expansion and land-releasing effects of technical change in foodgrains production should not lead to a large distortion of the relative scarcities of capital and foreign exchange. Export expansion would lead to a greater availability of foreign exchange, and land releasing would probably have a parallel effect by allowing import substitution for other agricultural commodities. Nevertheless, the changes would generate a rise in income, and the resulting rise in savings would tend to counteract the direct foreign exchange saving nature of the change. The over-all implication of the export expansion and land-releasing effects for capital and foreign exchange productivity would likely tend to be neutral.[5]

The failure of technical change in foodgrains production to seriously affect industrial priorities should not be taken as counterevidence to the hypothesis that industrial priorities are dependent on relative scarcities of capital and foreign exchange. What is shown is that the relative scarcities of capital and foreign exchange are not very sensitive to the sort of agricultural change examined here.

Although relative scarcities of capital and foreign exchange and, consequently, optimal interindustry allocation decisions are not very different in the alternative cases considered in this chapter, regional allocation decisions are sensitive to alternative assumptions regarding the success of the foodgrains program. Because of the importance of rice in East Pakistan's consumption bundle, a failure to attain foodgrain self-sufficiency would make expansion of consumption in that region very costly. Under such circumstances, therefore, consumption in West Pakistan is favored, and resources are allocated to the West. The assumption of success of the foodgrains program would call for a much larger allocation to East Pakistan, for then consumption in that region could be provided more cheaply. Thus, the success of the foodgrains program is certainly not neutral in terms of its impact upon allocation of resources between the two regions.

Regarding the operation of the model itself, it may be concluded that the results of the basic solution are relatively insensitive to a misspecification of the degree of success of adoption of the new techniques in foodgrains production.[6] As can be seen from Figure 6.1 and Tables 6.1 and 6.2, aggregate variables are not sensitive to changes in the foodgrains assumptions of the basic solution. As would be expected, an examination of priorities in the various solutions reveals that the optimal industrial development program is also not very sensitive to changes in the assumptions regarding the spread of the new techniques. Given the degree of uncertainty about the progress of the foodgrains production program, it is reassuring to be able to conclude that the results obtained in the previous chapter are not dependent upon the particular assumptions postulated for foodgrains production.

7 | Interregional and Intersectoral Allocation

7.1 The Regional Problem in Pakistan

Pakistan has an especially severe regional problem. In form it is not unlike the regional problems of other large countries: an unequal allocation of income and political power between the regions and no significant improvement over time. The problem in Pakistan is an extreme one because the peculiar geographic nature of Pakistan makes the issue so visible.

Consequently, much of the economic planning in Pakistan is carried out on an explicitly regional basis. The reduction of regional income disparity is put forth as a high priority planning goal, and the target is the complete elimination of disparity by 1985.[1] The attainment of that goal will require the reversal of a trend. Although data are poor, it is generally agreed that disparity has increased significantly since the early 1950s. Whereas the West Pakistan real per capita income then exceeded that in the East by less than 20 percent, in 1964–65 the difference was at least 30 percent.[2]

The economic differences between the two regions can be seen in several indices of economic development in addition to income level. Comparison of the structure of the two regions' economies, of the composition of their industrial output, of the degree of urbanization, of the extent of financial institutions, of the extent of transport facilities, would all reveal the differences between the two regions in the level of economic development.[3]

The difference in the levels of development is consistent with the pattern of distribution of resources between the regions. Although East Pakistan has in every year since 1952–53 earned the greater share of the nations foreign exchange, the majority of those earnings have been used to finance imports for West Pakistan. Unequal allocation of foreign exchange between the two regions cannot be attributed simply to market forces; that allocation is in large part determined by granting of import licenses. The transfer of foreign exchange from East to West has been partly offset by a net deficit in East Pakistan's trade with the West. However, because foreign exchange is undervalued and domestic prices, that is, the prices of goods traded between the regions, greatly exceed world prices, East's regional trade deficit does not offset the transfer of foreign exchange as much as it would appear. Even at the official exchange rates, West Pakistan's total trade deficit has consistently run two to three times that of the East. (The net inflow of foreign funds to the nation allows both regions to run a deficit.)

A second important aspect of resource allocation between the regions is the disbursement of government development funds. The regional allocations of those funds for the three plan periods are shown in Table 7.1. (While not directly relevant to the regional problem, the very rapid growth of the government development expenditures should be noted.) Although East Pakistan's share of such expenditures did rise between the First and Second Plan periods, and during the Third Plan East Pakistan is scheduled to receive the majority of government funds, the figures in Table 7.1 do not reveal a disparity reduction program of the sort implied by the plans' statements of goals. Furthermore, given the actual disbursements for the first fiscal year of the Third Plan, the projected allocations can hardly be taken seriously.

Table 7.1. Regional Allocation of Public Development Expenditures in the Three Plan Periods
(million rupees)

	Actual allocation			Planned allocation
	First plan 1955–1960	Second plan 1960–1965	1965–66	Third plan 1965–1970
East Pakistan	3320	6210	1421	16000
West Pakistan	5940	7790	1782	14000

SOURCE: For the first plan, Rahman (1966); for the second plan, Pakistan (1966f); for the third plan, Pakistan (1965a); for 1965–66, Pakistan (1967b).

It does not seem unreasonable to infer that the unequal growth of the two regions of Pakistan has been affected directly by the unequal distribution of resources, and that the distribution of resources between the regions has, in turn, been effected by government policy.[4]

If an attempt is made to design government policy toward the elimination of regional disparity, part of the effort could well be spent in developing complementarities between the regions. East and West Pakistan are not natural trading partners in that each does not traditionally produce goods that the other traditionally imports.[5] In formulating an industrial development program for the nation, attention should, of course, be given to determining and exploiting the comparative advantages of the two regions. Comparative advantage, however, is not independent of the relative emphasis that is placed on the development of each of the regions.

7.2 Alternative Regional Allocation Programs

The model being employed in this study determines the comparative advantage of each region while finding an optimal national development program. In the experiments undertaken in the preceding chapters, solutions have been based on the political assumption that increments to national per capita consumption have equal value regardless of the region in which they originate. In this section, several alternative solutions to the model are compared, each based on a different assumption about the relative emphasis placed on development in the two regions.

The maximand of the programming model may be written as:

$$W = \delta^e q^e p^e + \delta^w q^w p^w$$

where p^e and p^w are per capita increments to consumption in East and West Pakistan, respectively; q^e and q^w are population shares of each region; and δ^e and δ^w are weights representing the political valuation of increments to national per capita consumption originating in each. In the basic solution and in all of the others so far discussed, the δ's have both been taken as unity (what is important is that they have been taken as equal to one another). By varying the relative values of the δ's, alternative political situations can be simulated. Using a linear objective function and holding the relative weights constant at all levels of consumption to simulate the alternative political situations is of somewhat questionable validity. However, as a simple pragmatic device to generate the alternative possibilities, that is, a regional incremental consumption frontier, the method is certainly appropriate.

In addition to the basic solution, five others have been obtained, each with different relative valuation of increments to national per capita consumption originating in the East and in the West. With δ^w as unity, the values of δ^e in the six solutions are 2.00, 1.22, 1.00 (the basic solution), 0.79, 0.68, and 0.60. The segment of the incremental regional consumption frontier which these solutions imply is shown in Figure 7.1, and values of increments to per capita consumption obtained are shown in Table 7.2.

Table 7.2.   Increment to Per Capita Consumption under Alternative Relative Valuations of Consumption in the Two Regions

East (δ^e)	West (δ^w)	East Pakistan	West Pakistan	All Pakistan
2.00	1.00	Rs162.3	Rs120.3	Rs142.3
1.22	1.00	150.4	138.3	143.9
1.00	1.00	144.9	146.6	144.4
0.79	1.00	143.8	147.2	144.3
.68	1.00	105.9	181.5	139.0
.60	1.00	70.4	208.3	131.6

The segment of the regional consumption frontier in Figure 7.1 is obtained by linear interpolation between the six points obtained by the solutions. The slope of the frontier is the quantity of per capita consumption which must be given up in the West in order to expand consumption in the East by one unit, that is, the slope of the frontier is the marginal rate of transformation of per capita consumption in the West for per capita consumption in the East. It is an interesting property of the consumption frontier that the marginal rate of transformation is close to unity over a wide range. Consequently, in terms of national per capita consumption, no great loss would result from placing strong emphasis on the development of one of the regions.

Movement along the frontier involves a transfer of resources from one region to the other, which can take place in two ways. First, there can be a direct transfer of resources by a change in the net flow of capital between the regions. The capital serves to finance investment in and imports to the receiving region. Second, a transfer of foreign exchange between the regions can be effected by

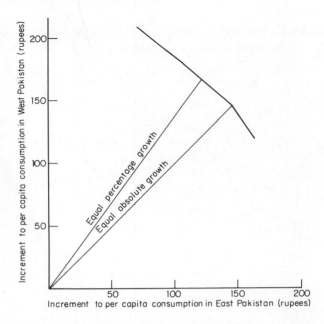

Figure 7.1 Incremental Regional Consumption Frontier

adjusting trade patterns. That is, the region that is favored runs a regional trade surplus in order to finance a foreign trade deficit. The other region, accordingly, must run a foreign trade surplus and a regional trade deficit. The foreign trade surplus region is forced to produce commodities that it would otherwise import and to regionally import commodities it would otherwise produce. That is, one region saves foreign exchange that is then used by the other region.

Both processes of resource transfer are exhibited in the movement between the solution points on the consumption frontier in Figure 7.1. In Table 7.3, the regional, foreign, and total trade deficits of each region are shown. In moving from the basic solution toward a greater emphasis on development in East Pakistan, resources are first shifted to the East by a direct transfer of capital and by a decline in the East's net regional trade deficit. The next shift toward the East—from weights 1.22 and 1.00 to weights 2.00 and 1.00—is accomplished completely by adjustment of the trade patterns. In fact, in the solution which favors the East more the capital inflow to the East is less. At the extreme solution, the expansion of East is very intensive in foreign imports. In order to finance the increase of foreign imports in the East, capital is transferred to the West and used for import substitution there. The foreign exchange thus saved in the

Table 7.3. **Trade Deficits and Surpluses under Alternative Valuations
of Consumption in the Two Regions**
(in million rupees)

East (δ^e)	West (δ^w)	Total incremental capital inflow to East = total incremental capital outflow from West	Incremental foreign and regional trade deficits for East = incremental foreign and regional trade surplus for West	
			Foreign	Regional
2.00	1.00	Rs38.5	Rs868.4	−Rs829.9
1.22	1.00	142.7	153.5	− 10.8
1.00	1.00	101.6	− 7.9	109.5
0.79	1.00	91.1	− 18.4	109.5
.68	1.00	− 458.2	− 322.0	− 136.2
.60	1.00	− 890.0	− 693.6	− 196.4

West is then transferred to the East by running a large regional trade surplus in the East.

Moving in the other direction from the basic solution—towards programs favoring the West—resources are transferred to the West by direct capital transfer. In fact, as the West is favored more, both the West's net regional trade deficit and its net foreign trade deficit rise. Emphasis on the development of either region brings about a rise in that region's foreign trade deficit and a rise in the other region's foreign trade surplus. However, the alternative solutions to the model illustrate that the deficit for the favored region can be financed by capital transfers from the other region or by import substitution in and foreign exchange transfers from the other region.

The nonparallel nature of resource transfers can be explained by the difference in the requirements of the two regions as output expands. It has been pointed out in preceding chapters that from the point of the basic solution, expansion of the East tends to require more foreign exchange than does expansion of the West. When emphasis on development in the East is increased, the economy is forced upon a more import intensive path. Most important is the requirement of agricultural based imports, that is, edible oils.[6] Since foreign exchange earnings and capital inflow are fixed, the increase in the requirement for agriculture based imports must be accompanied by import substitution in some other sectors. Industries importing in the basic solution in which import substitution is most efficient are West Pakistan industries, that is, cotton textiles and wood, cork, and furniture.[7] Therefore, substitution for foreign imports takes place in the West. Simultaneously, production in certain East Pakistan industries—rubber, transport equipment, metal products—is expanded to replace either production in the West and regional imports to the East from the West or both. By this process, the foreign exchange saved by the West is transferred to the East.

When West Pakistan expands, the need for additional imports is offset by the contraction of the East Pakistan economy and the consequent release of foreign exchange. The expansion in West does not carry with it the need for elimination of some foreign imports so that expansion is effected by a direct transfer of resources from the East.

The movement from the basic solution toward greater emphasis on West Pakistan development does, however, result in some changes in interregional trade patterns and in the change of the location of expansion for some industries. Expansion of the West cannot be accomplished by a balanced expansion because of the limits on the production of agricultural goods. West Pakistan is forced to import other agriculture products and edible oils from the East. To offset the increased requirement for those imports, West Pakistan substitutes its own production for the regional import of rubber and fertilizer. Furthermore, West Pakistan production of cement, machinery, miscellaneous manufacturing, and coal and petroleum products is expanded to replace production of those products in the East by regional trade (although in the case of machinery the elimination of production in the East is only partial).

The switches taking place when the relative weights on consumption in the two regions are changed illustrate the changes in comparative advantage which result from variation of the regional emphasis of a national development program. Although some of the solutions considered may not be politically reasonable, the tendency of comparative advantage to shift will not be eliminated when only the less extreme solutions are considered. The switching seems to be a clear illustration of the interdependence between regional and sectoral allocation programs.

7.3 Economic Determinants of Regional Development

Although the degree of emphasis placed on development in each of the regions is primarily a political decision, that decision is influenced and constrained by economic circumstances. A regional allocation program may be viewed as the result of an interaction between political and economic forces. In the case of political decision makers having no preference for one region relative to the other—the case assumed in the previous chapters—it may be said that economic circumstances will determine regional allocation.

In Section 7.2, a set of economic circumstances which defined an interregional consumption frontier were taken as given, and the implications of alternative political decisions were examined. This section examines the relation between the shape of the consumption frontier and specific economic factors.

The basic solution calls for a development program that brings about a significant reduction in disparity, the resulting increment to per capita consumption being about the same in each of the regions. Chapter 4 showed that the disparity reduction program was a result of economic circumstances rather than any political allocation decisions. That is, in the basic solution, increments to national per capita consumption are weighted equally regardless of the region of origin. Growth in the East is then favored so long as a unit of consumption there can be provided more "cheaply" than a unit of consumption in the West. The primary reason consumption in the East is "cheap" is that the consumption bundle is, relative to that of West, very foodgrain intensive and the technological change assumed for the foodgrains sectors makes foodgrain production very cheap.[8] Consumption in the East becomes more "expensive" when nonfoodgrain agricultural production limits are reached and it becomes necessary to import agriculture based goods. In terms of the consumption frontier of Figure 7.1., the marginal rate of transformation of consumption in the West for consumption in the East rises above unity at the point where the East begins to import substitute for edible oils.

Reduction of the savings rate in the East relative to that in the West would raise the relative cost of producing East Pakistan consumption. However, it seems that the differential between the savings rate in the two regions would have to be large before a shift toward the West is effected. A solution to the model was obtained with a 12/22 savings rate for East and a 15/25 savings rate for the West.[9] The resulting change from the basic solution was a decline in total resource availability and a resulting decline in consumption in the West. In some East Pakistan sectors the fall in the savings rate was sufficient to eliminate production, and in some West Pakistan sectors the rise in that rate led to some import substitution. However, resources are shifted to the East by a rise in the net capital flow from West to East.

Differential assumptions about the export possibilities of the two regions will not effect a change in regional allocation of consumption. It is possible, of course, that a decline in the assumed level of export expansion for the East would reduce or eliminate certain exports. However, because foreign funds can be transferred between the regions, the decline in export possibilities would have no more effect on over-all costs in the East than would a decline in export earnings in the West or a general decline in export opportunities. A solution to the model was obtained in which the export growth rate for the East was reduced to 6.5 percent per annum while the export growth rate in the West was maintained at 7.5 percent. As compared to the basic solution, consumption in the West was reduced and consumption in the East was unaffected, that is, the result is the same as that obtained when exports for both regions are lowered (see Section 5.2).

Although the distribution of consumption away from the East is not effected by a decline in the savings rate (of the magnitude considered) or export growth rate in the East, such a change in distribution is effected by a resource change that raises the availability of capital relative to the availability of foreign exchange. The alternative savings rate solution obtained in Section 5.1 shows that the regional distribution of consumption shifts toward the West as the scarcity of capital declines. Consumption in the East is relatively less capital intensive, and a relative increase in capital availability will shift the regional consumption frontier so that the politically neutral assumptions of the basic solution lead to more development in the West. Although a complete consumption frontier has not been obtained under a set of economic assumptions implying greater relative capital availability, it is easy to show how the new consumption frontier would differ from that obtained with the economic assumptions of the basic solution.

In Figure 7.2 the relationship between the two consumption frontiers is illustrated. The curve AA' represents the consumption frontier under conditions of relative capital scarcity. BB' represents the consumption frontier under conditions of relative foreign exchange scarcity. As capital becomes less scarce, the consumption space shifts upward and to the left; and, with WE representing the line with slope of minus unity, the solution point shifts from P to P'.

A shift in the consumption frontier that will lead to a shift in the allocation of consumption toward the West would also result from an assumption of relatively poor performance in East Pakistan agriculture. Chapter 6 showed that less success (as compared to the basic solution) of the new foodgrains production techniques would force the East to import rice and thereby raise the cost of consumption in the East. Under those circumstances a large shift of consumption toward the West resulted (see Section 6.2). Also, if the performance of the nonfoodgrains agricultural sectors is less than that assumed in the basic solution,

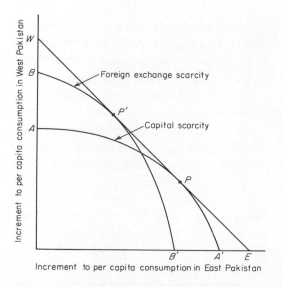

Figure 7.2 Different Consumption Frontier Positions under Alternative Relative Capital and Foreign Exchange Availabilities

the point on the frontier at which the marginal rate of transformation rises above unity is moved upward and to the left. A solution was obtained in which the growth of the East Pakistan other agriculture sector was limited to 4.5 percent per annum over the plan (rather than the 5 percent of the basic solution). The result was to change the per capita consumption increment in the East to Rs118.9 and the per capita consumption increment in the West to Rs160.3. In the basic solution per capita consumption increments in the two regions were Rs114.9 and 146.6, respectively.

On the basis of those observations it can be seen why the macroeconomic results obtained in this study differ in their regional aspect from the results obtained in other studies of Pakistan development that include a regional dimension.

Khan (1967a), using a seven sector regional programming model to investigate problems of development during Pakistan's Third Plan (1965–1970), obtained results implying that a reduction of income disparity between the regions is not optimal when the political objective is to maximize national income (that is, increments to per capita income in the two regions are weighted by population shares). Although Khan's model does not include a savings constraint, it does include agricultural growth limits and operates like the model used in this study.

The difference between the two studies arises because Khan does not specify rice production as a sector separate from other agricultural sectors and does not consider the cost reductions in rice production resulting from the introduction of the new techniques.[10] When the agricultural growth limits are binding in both regions and agricultural goods must be imported, the Khan model chooses to expand further in the region in which industrial development costs are less. According to his data, that region is West Pakistan. In this study, however, because rice can still be produced within East Pakistan, even when the nonfood-grain agricultural growth limits are binding, some further expansion of the region is warranted.

A study by Stern (1968) also shows that an optimal national growth policy will lead to an increase of regional disparity. Stern's optimizing model, however, distinguishes only two sectors and it thereby obscures the differences in the relative costs of consumption bundles in the two regions.[11] Furthermore, Stern assumes a generally more optimistic set of resource use and resource generation parameters for the West than for the East. With East's advantage on the consumption side eliminated by aggregation and with the assumption of a more favorable set of production possibilities in the West, the regional allocation results that Stern obtains follow automatically.

Comparison with the Khan and Stern studies brings out one of the important aspects of disaggregation. When working with more sectors it is possible to take account of more differences between the regions. Such a procedure can reveal important implications for regional allocation decisions.

7.4 Conclusions on Regional Allocation

The regional allocation of consumption (or income) is a function of the interplay between economic circumstances and political motives. The purpose of this chapter has been to determine the implication of alternative sets of political decisions regarding the relative emphasis to be placed upon development in each of the regions and to investigate the economic factors most important in determining the range of possibilities within which decision makers must act. Several conclusions can now be drawn.

1. The comparative advantage of each region is a function of the relative emphasis placed upon development in the two regions. That is, the set of industries which should be active within each region cannot be determined independently of the interregional consumption allocation program. One interesting

aspect of the changing comparative advantage associated with changing regional consumption allocation programs is the possibility of import substitution taking place in one region to finance increased requirements for imports in the other region.

2. The relative costs of expanding production in the two regions are not significantly affected by differences between the two regions in savings or foreign exchange earning abilities. Regardless of where resources are generated, they will be used to expand consumption in the region where the consumption bundle is cheapest. Furthermore, within a reasonable range, the changes in relative costs of consumption resulting from a difference in regional savings rates is not sufficient to offset the importance of low cost agricultural goods in East Pakistan's consumption bundle.

3. Although differential savings and export performance in the two regions have little effect upon the relative costs of supplying consumption, major changes in the relative national supplies of capital and foreign exchange will affect changes in the relative costs of the consumption bundles. In particular, if the availability of capital rises relative to foreign exchange, the cost of consumption in the West will drop relative to the cost of consumption in the East.

4. Changes in the performance in agricultural sectors significantly affect the relative costs of consumption expansion in the two regions. If the performances of the rice sector or of the other agriculture sector or of both sectors in the East do not meet the expectations implicit in the basic solution, the reduction in disparity will not be as great as in the basic solution.

5. The differences between the regions in terms of costs of consumption can be seriously obscured by aggregation of the agriculture sectors. Were the rice sector in East Pakistan not specified as an individual sector, the lower costs of East Pakistan consumption would probably be overlooked.

These conclusions seem to be a realistic description of some of the problems related to interregional development in Pakistan. The particular regional allocation program that the basic solution yields may be subject to question. It should be clear, however, which assumptions are most important in determining the basic solution results and how changes of these assumptions change the regional and sectoral allocation programs.

8 | Development Alternatives and Development Policy[1]

8.1 Development Planning and Comparative Advantage

Many poor countries are constrained in their development by shortages of investment funds and foreign exchange earning opportunities and by limited agricultural growth possibilities. The principal and most general purpose of this study has been to demonstrate how industrial comparative advantage, and therefore the optimal industrial development program, is determined by the relative importance of those growth-limiting factors.

In formulating long-term development plans, it is not possible to project precisely what resource limitations will be or to carefully examine the resource requirements of each industry. The procedure employed here of determining which industries are most sensitive to the variation of the resource program can, therefore, be a useful aid in planning. By obtaining several alternative solutions to a programming model, each based upon a different assumption about relative resource availabilities, it is possible to distinguish three broad groups of industries: (1) those for which domestic production is preferable to importing under all realistic resource programs; (2) those for which importing is preferable to domestic production under all realistic resource programs; (3) those for which production is sometimes preferable and importing is at other times preferable.[2] By using a model to specify those groups, a general picture of the country's comparative advantage can be obtained. Furthermore, the classification distinguishes those marginal industries that need special examination—the industries in the third group.

In addition to these "operational" implications obtained by examining the interrelationship between resource availabilities and comparative advantage, there are several interesting aspects of this relationship that should be pointed out.

First, any alteration of the resource program has a secondary effect on domestic savings (that is, capital supply) and therefore on comparative advantage. Because the level of savings is a function of the level of income, any change in resource supply that changes income will have the secondary effect of changing savings; that change in savings will then again affect the level of income, and so on.

The secondary savings effect is directly analogous to the multiplier effect of aggregate demand theory. In aggregate demand theory it is the level of demand that constitutes the principal economic problem, and the multiplier process is initiated by an exogenous change in demand. For an economy like Pakistan's, it is more reasonable to assume that the growth constraints are resource supply. The model that results from such an assumption necessarily embodies a supply-initiated multiplier process.

In the model used here, the multiplier, or secondary savings effect, plays an important role in determining the comparative advantage implications of any change in resource supply. For example, although the direct impact of a rise in foreign exchange earning possibilities would be to shift the industrial priorities program toward foreign exchange using activity, the secondary savings effect dampens—and sometimes reverses—the direction of that shift. On the other hand, a relatively small change in the savings rate results in a relatively large change in the industrial priorities program because the direct effect on the capital supply is augmented by the secondary savings effect (see Section 5.1, 5.2, 5.3).

A related aspect of the interconnection between resource programs and comparative advantage is the way the inflow of foreign funds affects the economy. When the inflow of foreign funds is raised, both capital supply and foreign exchange supply are augmented. The capital supply is then again increased through the multiplier process. The growth that follows from an increase in the flow of funds is, therefore, not balanced in its use of capital and foreign exchange. Investment takes place in more capital intensive sectors that had previously been importing sectors. Consequently, the productivity of capital falls, and further additions to the inflow of funds will have less value, that is, the marginal productivity of foreign funds declines (see Section 5.3).

The concomitant decline in the productivity of capital and foreign funds is especially marked due to the agricultural growth limits. The rise of the inflow of foreign funds can raise the level of income and consumption, but that leads to a rise in the domestic absorption of agricultural goods. Foreign exchange previously earned by agricultural exports must then be earned by exporting capital intensive industrial products: thus the sharp decline in the productivity of capital and foreign funds (see Section 5.3).

Bruno (1966) and Tendulkar (1968), by employing multisectoral programming models, also obtain the result that the productivity of additional foreign funds is high when the domestic savings constraint is active. However, neither Bruno nor Tendulkar notes the full extent of the interaction between the capital supply and the foreign funds supply. That is, they do not point out that as the availability of foreign funds is raised, the supply of capital is more than proportionally affected by the multiplier process, the productivity of capital falls, and the importance (productivity) of further additions to the supply of foreign funds declines.

Another factor in the expansion of foreign funds supply is that the productivity of funds is low when constraints other than the capital and foreign exchange are important. In this study, the "other constraints" are agricultural growth limits. In the Tendulkar study, the important role of agricultural growth limits is also noted, although their relationship to the productivity of foreign funds is not made explicit. In the Bruno study, labor constraints play a similar role; when labor limitations become important, the productivity of foreign funds declines.

While the general phenomena observed here regarding changes in comparative advantage might hold in many countries, the specific priority rankings and groupings obtained for Pakistan will not necessarily be applicable elsewhere. There are, however, some properties of the Pakistan program that shed light on general issues of development planning.

First, the Pakistan groupings cut across the traditional categories of consumer goods, intermediate goods, and investment goods. Pakistan's comparative advantage cannot be said to lie with any one such category of products. Although Pakistan could constitute the exception to a general rule, it seems more likely that its case is an illustration of the invalidity of such a generalization. Within each of those categories—consumption goods, intermediate goods, and investment goods—there is probably as much difference in capital costs and foreign exchange requirements as there is between categories.[3]

The present study, however, does not deal with economies of scale, an issue often raised in support of the argument that poor countries should not develop capital goods industries. The small size of the market in many poor countries may not be large enough to support plants of an efficient size. But for a country as large as Pakistan, the scale arguments would seem to have limited importance.

Using a very similar model for analysis of development problems in Mexico, Manne (1966) found that size factors in capital goods industries seem to have very little effect on the optimality of developing capital goods industries. For most of the capital goods sectors with which he dealt, the Mexican market was sufficiently large to support plants of an efficient size.[4] Westphal (1968) employed a more sophisticated programming model to determine whether or not South Korea should develop certain large petrochemical and steel complexes in which economies of scale are important. He found that under the expected resource conditions of the South Korean economy, the size factor would not prohibit the construction of those complexes. However, the construction was marginal, and under alternative assumptions regarding resource availability, they would not have been optimal.[5]

Two other aspects of the Pakistan comparative advantage results that could have importance for development decisions in other countries are the low-priority positions of agriculture-based manufacturing industries and of some industries that have grown quite rapidly in the past. Wherever agriculture growth limits are important, the cost of agricultural inputs to manufacturing sectors will be high. Agriculture-based industries will then not be favorable candidates for expansion. Such a situation is more likely to occur at higher growth rates of the economy, when the differential is great between the possible agricultural growth rate and the actual growth rate of the economy.

Part of the reason that low priority should be given to certain industries in Pakistan that have grown rapidly in the past is that they are dependent upon agriculture for raw materials. There is, however, a second possible reason for their low position. These sectors have attained their rapid growth rates under very high levels of protection. It is not unlikely that maintaining such levels of protection and other policies favoring these industries has led to the development of inefficiencies and monopoly profits or both. The infant industry argument by which protection is often rationalized can be a justification only for short-run protection. If the policies are not changed, such industries may become heavy weights for the economy to carry.

8.2 Implications for Planning in Pakistan

In addition to the general lessons for development planning that have been derived from this study, a great deal of information has been obtained which can be of use for planning in Pakistan. The results do not lead to precise and specific policy, but the information presented here can aid in the formulation of guidelines.

In establishing a development and trade policy for Pakistan, there seems to be good reason to follow a path of industrialization in the sense of reducing the economy's dependence on imported manufactured goods. Furthermore, the comparative advantage of Pakistan seems to lie with a number of industries that have not hitherto played a large role in the growth of the economy. Among those are some capital goods and capital goods related industries, certain important intermediate goods industries, and a few consumer goods industries. The consumer goods industries in general, however, should not maintain the favored position they have been given in the past. Under the protection policies that have been followed, several industries developed that are not efficient when compared to the alternative of importing their products.

One reason a program of industrialization is called for is the limited growth opportunities in the agricultural sector. Rapid growth of the economy will require the use of foreign exchange for the import of agricultural goods and agricultural-based goods, necessitating a greater reliance on domestic production for industrial goods. Furthermore, the limited agricultural growth opportunities and the rising domestic absorption of agricultural products will require that the economy rely more and more on the industrial sector for the earning of foreign exchange. Thus foreign exchange must be both saved and earned by the industrial sector.

The second explanation of the optimality of an industrialization program for Pakistan is that the outlook for capital supply appears more favorable than the outlook for foreign exchange supply. This set of expectations is embodied in two basic assumptions of the model: (1) that the economy will be able to attain a marginal savings rate well above the average savings rate; and (2) that the rate of growth of exports will not rise above that which has been maintained over the past several years.

The favorable outlook for capital supply relative to the outlook for foreign exchange supply should not, however, be construed as deriving from the assumption that the level of Pakistan's foreign aid will fail to rise in the coming decade. Were the level of aid to rise, an even greater degree of industrialization would be called for because the supply of capital would be affected more than the supply of foreign exchange.

Although the broad program of industrialization and the reasoning behind it might be generally accepted, the specific industrialization and trade program

163

that the model yields is subject to some skepticism. In any case, the translation of the priority results of the programming model to policy prescriptions is subject to two qualifications.[6]

First, the sectors in this programming model, and in most similar programming models,[7] are aggregates of the industries that would constitute the actual decision units. The result that a particular sector is not a priority sector does not mean that all of the individual industries in that sector are not priority industries. An examination on a more disaggregated level may find certain industries in the sector that should be developed. In those industries constituting the marginal priority group, such distinctions could be especially important.

Second, although the cost data in the model are incremental, their estimation has been based on past performance. Therefore, the result that an industry has low priority does not necessarily mean that the industry should not be developed. It may be possible for the efficiency of that industry to be improved. The appropriate policy prescription, therefore, is that if efficiency cannot be improved, the industry should not be developed.

Thus, as a tool in the planning process, a programming model of the sort used in this study must be complemented by more precise industry studies and project analyses. In more precise planning exercises, the principles of choice in the model should continue to prevail. First, the rankings of industries should depend not simply on a comparison of the costs of production in different industries, but on a comparison of costs of production with costs of importing. Second, in computing benefits and costs, resources should be valued at their opportunity costs (shadow prices), which may differ significantly from their nominal price.

An important specific use of the results of the model is precisely in carrying out benefit-cost analyses. Such exercises first require an estimate of the shadow prices of resources. The model provides these shadow prices. However, in order to take account for the indirect as well as the direct cost of resources in any project, it is necessary to have shadow prices for the various goods—inputs and outputs. These the model also provides. It is possible to determine the importance of evaluating the indirect as well as the direct use of resources with shadow prices. Such an exercise has been carried out by comparing for a few sectors the results obtained by the model with results that would have been obtained by using the resource shadow prices of the model to evaluate direct capital and foreign exchange costs and using base year prices to evaluate commodity costs and benefits.[8] The results of the exercise are shown in Table 8.1.

Although in a few cases the partial and general equilibrium analyses yield almost the same results, in most of the cases the difference between the outcomes

Table 8.1. Results of Production and Import Net Benefit Comparisons
(excess of net benefit of a rupee of production over net benefit of a rupee of import)

Sector	All inputs at shadow prices	Only direct capital and foreign exchange inputs at shadow prices
East Pakistan		
8. Edible oils	0.08	0.57
17. Fertilizer	1.34	1.42
20. Basic metals	0.51	0.34
24. Wood, etc.	− .56	− .35
West Pakistan		
7. Sugar	.04	.58
11. Cotton text.	− .06	.07
19. Cement	.39	.08
22. Machinery	.45	.59

cannot be dismissed as insignificant. The greatest differences in the results of the two approaches come in sectors where agricultural raw materials are important inputs, for example, in the edible oils and sugar sectors. For agricultural inputs, the model indicates that past prices are especially poor indicators of future opportunity costs. On the other hand, the two approaches yield most similar results in that sector where current inputs are least important—the fertilizer sector. In general, when direct resource costs are large (and current input costs are small), the difference between the general and partial approaches will not be great.

It is evident from this little exercise that the commodity shadow price that the model yields may be of some value in carrying out benefit-cost analyses (refer, however, to Section 4.3). Furthermore, the exercise is evidence of the importance of developing and using a complete programming model rather than relying on many independent benefit-cost exercises to determine industrial priorities.

The use of a complete programming model has made it possible to investigate numerous problems of development planning. This study has emphasized the interrelationships between resource availabilities and industrial priorities and the determination of a set of industrial priorities for the Pakistan economy. The findings of the study should be of use in understanding planning problems in many poor countries and should be an aid in dealing with particular planning problems in Pakistan.

Appendices
Notes
References
Index

Appendix A: Data for 1964–65

Tables A.3 and A.4 at the end of Appendix A provide a complete set of 1964–65 supply and demand data for East and West Pakistan on a thirty-five sector basis. These tables were built with the Khan-MacEwan (1967a) 1962–63 input-output tables as their base. However, numerous other data and many assumptions were required to create the 1964–65 set of data. The general procedure was to obtain production and intermediate demand by up-dating the Khan-MacEwan 1962–63 data. Trade data were obtained from official sources. The residual supply was divided among consumption, inventory changes, and investment on the basis of various data and assumptions. The purpose of this appendix is to explain in some detail how Tables A.3 and A.4 were constructed.

Production

For each sector a 1964–65 quantum production index with 1962–63 equal 100 was estimated. The indices for East and West Pakistan are presented in Table A.1. These indices were constructed as follows.

Agriculture Actual output figures for rice, wheat, jute cotton, and East Pakistan tea were obtained from the *Monthly Bulletin* (CSO *Bulletin*) of the Central Statistical Office (Pakistan 1967a), or from the *Pakistan Statistical Yearbook, 1964* (Pakistan 1966b) or from both. The index for West Pakistan tea (which only is a processing industry based on imports from the East) was arbitrarily taken to be 100.00. The indices for all other agriculture were determined from the 1962–63 regional accounts in Khan and Bergan (1966) and the national accounts for 1964–65 were divided between the regions on the basis of Khan-Bergan trends and on the basis of separate CSO *Bulletin* data for certain major crops. Also, it was necessary to exclude from the accounts data the output of rice, wheat, cotton, jute, and tea.

Manufacturing Indices for large-scale manufacturing sectors are based on either CSO *Bulletin* reports of data collected by the Central Board of Revenue or the *New Index of Industrial Production* (Pakistan 1966c). In some cases sector classifications did not coincide, and rough averages were taken. No direct information was available on growth of the small-scale parts of manufacturing sectors between 1962–63 and 1964–65. The assumption was made that the elasticity of small-scale output with respect to large plus small scale output was 0.5 between 1962–63 and 1964–65.* The output of the cottage part of sectors was assumed not to grow between 1962–63 and 1964–65. While this, of course, yields a downward bias in the 1964–65 data, it should not affect any of the conclusions of this study since cottage activity is excluded from analysis.

---

* This was not done for East Pakistan paper, rubber, and other chemicals, where the small-scale part of the sector was very small and its growth ignored. Also, though East Pakistan cement output fell over the period, brick output was raised by 5 percent.

168

Table A.1.   Quantum Index of Production for 1964–1965 with 1962–63 Equal to 100.0[a]

Sector	East Pakistan	West Pakistan
1. Rice growing and processing	118.4	123.3
2. Wheat growing and processing	65.9	105.5
3. Jute growing and baling	84.5	
4. Cotton growing and ginning	100.0	103.3
5. Tea growing and processing	112.0	100.0
6. All other agriculture	106.6	104.1
7. Sugar refining	102.6(A)	101.2[b]
8. Edible oils	124.3(B)	125.0(A)
9. Tobacco products	111.2(B)	123.8(B)
10. Other food and drink	133.2(B)	112.2(B)
11. Cotton textiles	109.0(A)	112.6(B)
12. Jute textiles	97.0(A)	
13. Other textiles	300.00(A,B)	220.9(A,B)
14. Paper and printing		
Paper	123.4(B)	121.5(B)
Printing	116.1(B)	110.6(B)
15. Leather and leather products	120.5(B)	130.0[c]
16. Rubber and rubber products	159.4(B)	217.5(B)
17. Fertilizer	100.4(A)	107.7(A)
18. Other chemicals	149.6(B)	123.5(B)
19. Cement, concrete, and bricks	59.6(A)	118.0(A)
20. Basic metals	236.1(B)	165.0(B)
21. Metal products	89.3(B)	151.3(B)
22. Machinery	336.5(B)	180.8(B)
23. Transport equipment	97.8(B)	220.3(B)
24. Wood, cork, and furniture	231.2(B)	177.1(B)
25. Construction of residential houses	148.2	120.1
26. Construction of nonresidential buildings	148.2	120.1
27. All other construction	148.2	120.1
28. Miscellaneous manufacture	113.6(B)	134.9(B)
29. Coal and petroleum products		209.2(B)
30. Electricity and gas	126.7	142.5
31. Transport	109.7	108.0
32. Trade	113.8	113.8
33. Ownership of dwellings	104.8	105.7
34. Government[d]	116.8	115.7
35. Services n.e.s.[e]	106.7	108.2

[a]Indices for large-scale manufacturing sectors are based on either (A) CSO *Bulletin* reports of data collected by the Central Board of Revenue or (B) the *New Index of Industrial Production* (Pakistan 1966c). Each index is appropriately labeled (A) or (B).
[b]Crop data from CSO *Bulletin*.
[c]Estimated on the basis of export data.
[d]Public administration and defense.
[e]Not elsewhere specified.

Construction An index of construction activity was obtained for each of the regions from the *Evaluation Report on the Second Five-Year Plan* (Pakistan 1966f). The index was applied to all three construction sectors.

Electricity and Gas Indices for electricity and gas were constructed from CSO *Bulletin* physical output data.

Transport services, services n.e.s., and housing For each of these sectors the trends of the Khan-Bergan data were used to divide the 1964–65 national accounts figures between the regions. With the Khan-Bergan data for 1962–63 it was then possible to construct indices.

Government services An index was obtained from an analysis of the government budget data in the *Economic Survey of Pakistan 1966–67* (Pakistan 1967c).

Trade Total trade output was computed as equal to trade margins on all outputs of other sectors plus trade margins on imports.

Prices

For each sector it was also necessary to have a price index of 1964–65 with 1962–63 as 100. For all physical commodities, indices were obtained from the CSO *Bulletin* (though classification was not identical in many cases.) For other sectors, the price indices implicit in the national accounts in the CSO *Bulletin* were used. The indices are presented in Table A.2.

Trade Data

Foreign trade data—imports CIF and exports FOB—and regional trade data—CIF region at delivery—were obtained from the CSO *Bulletin*. For regional trade data, the total trade and transport margin ratio from the Khan-MacEwan tables were used. This margin was divided between transport and trade for each type of goods by assuming the transport cost rate was the same as for goods of that type produced within the region. For import from abroad, the tariff rates and total markups were obtained from Lewis and Guisinger (1966). By making the same assumption about port to user transport margins as about regional trade, the total margin could be split between tariffs, trade, and transport. The FOB foreign export data required no adjustment.

Intermediate Demand

Intermediate demand was determined by first price adjusting the 1962–63 Khan-MacEwan large-scale, small-scale, and cottage coefficient matrices to 1964–65 prices. Then the 1964–65 output estimates were multiplied by the appropriate coefficients to determine intermediate deliveries. By computing intermediate deliveries separately for

Table A.2. Price Indices for 1964–65 with 1962–63 equals 100.00

	East Pakistan	West Pakistan
1. Rice	92.42	106.92
2. Wheat	99.98	120.80
3. Jute	136.91	
4. Cotton	98.29	118.03
5. Tea	79.86	88.75
6. Other agric.	107.00	109.25
7. Sugar	108.77	115.01
8. Edible oils	148.62	161.56
9. Tobacco	115.15	111.29
10. Other foods	107.00	109.25
11. Cotton text.	96.00	105.00
12. Jute text.	113.27	114.32
13. Other text.	115.31	115.31
14. Paper	105.00	104.76
15. Leather	84.67	100.00
16. Rubber	107.63	107.93
17. Fertilizer	128.64	93.77
18. Other chem.	110.48	97.37
19. Cement	103.03	103.10
20. Basic metals	99.92	102.64
21. Metal prod.	99.92	102.64
22. Machinery	105.81	104.43
23. Transport eq.	99.92	104.43
24. Wood, etc.	104.08	101.47
25. Const., houses	102.36	102.36
26. Const., buildings	102.36	102.36
27. Other const.	102.36	102.36
28. Misc. manuf.	104.08	101.47
29. Coal, etc.	114.07	113.90
30. Elec. and gas	110.17	110.17
31. Transport	110.12	110.12
32. Trade	106.18	106.18
33. Housing	107.53	107.53
34. Government	106.38	106.38
35. Services	106.99	106.99

large-scale, small-scale and cottage parts of each sector, aggregation problems were avoided.*

Final Demand

In addition to exports (foreign and regional), final demand is divided into consumption, inventory changes, and investment in fixed capital. (The division of fixed investment between net investment and replacement is discussed below.) After total supply had been estimated for each sector and exports subtracted from this total, the problem remained of dividing the residual into the three categories of domestic demand. For items which are neither consumption nor investment goods—for example, fertilizer, cement, raw cotton—the entire residual was allocated to inventory changes. The residual for all service sectors was also easily allocated, that is, to consumption. And all of the construction residuals were allocated to investment. There remain, however, several goods for which inventory changes can be expected and which are delivered to consumption or to investment or to both. For these sectors, the general procedure was to begin with an estimate of inventory changes obtained as follows: Let θ_i be the ratio of inventories of final product to total supply in the ith sector (see Section 3.7); let q_i be the 1964–65 quantum index of production, 1962–63 equal 1.00 (from table A.1); and let X_i be 1964–65 total supply. Then the change of X_i during 1964–65 may be approximated by $X_i (1 - q_i)/2$. And the inventory change is given by

$$W_i = \frac{\theta_i X_i (1 - q_i)}{2}$$

This procedure worked reasonably well in most cases; that is, it yielded seemingly reasonable results but required adjustment in some special sectors. For example, in East Pakistan rice and wheat sectors, though the 1964–65 index was greater than 1.00 with 1962–63 as the base, crops declined between 1963–64 and 1964–65; therefore, inventory changes in these sectors were taken as zero. Or, for another example, while output rose rapidly in the West Pakistan coal and petroleum products sector, imports in 1964–65 were relatively quite low; to obtain a reasonable estimate of consumption it was necessary to show a negative stock change. There are a few other special cases. Once the inventory change estimate was established for noninvestment good sectors, the remaining residual was allocated to consumption. In the four manufacturing sectors producing investment goods as well as some consumption and intermediate goods, the division between investment and consumption was based on investment

* A problem arose in computing intermediate demand for fertilizer, since fertilizer input coefficients are relatively unstable. In 1962–63, the year for which the coefficients were originally estimated, fertilizer availability in West Pakistan and, therefore, fertilizer input coefficients were very high. Since 1964–65 fertilizer availability in the West was much lower, the use of the 1962–63 coefficients resulted in the fertilizer demand being far greater than supply. The difference was much too great to be explained by a change in stocks. Only by reducing fertilizer requirements to 75 percent of the original could reasonable 1964–65 figures be obtained for West Pakistan.

data from the CSO.* In the most important of these sectors, machinery, the CSO data gave a reasonable result. Some adjustment was necessary in the other three cases so that the consumption estimate would not be unreasonable.

Replacement

From the Planning Commission's *Evaluation Report of the Second Five-Year Plan* (Pakistan, 1966 f) an estimate of investment on a regional basis can be obtained for the years 1959–60 through 1964–65. While these investment estimates have certain deficiencies, they provide a good estimate of an index of investment for those years and thereby form the basis for an estimate of replacement. To extend the index back from 1959–60, it was assumed that the rate of growth of investment had been 5 percent per year. It was also assumed that the composition of investment remained constant so that the index applied to all components of investment. The deterioration of capital assumptions of Khan and MacEwan (1967b)† were applied to the index for each type of capital good using the following average length of life estimates: building (not including housing), 40 years; other construction, 20 years; machinery, 12 years; transport equipment, 5 years; and other assets, 12 years.‡ It was thus possible to obtain an estimate for each year of the percentage of investment which was replacement. These percentage rates were then applied to the investment estimates obtained above. Obviously the resulting replacement estimates are very crude. For the housing construction sector, repair and maintenance charges are shown as a current input to the housing sector. No additional allowance was made for replacement.

* The CSO data are based on the results of a recently completed, but as yet unpublished, survey of investment activity.

† The deterioration assumptions can be summarized as follows: (1) For some time after its installation, an asset's productive value declines very slowly. A 25 percent loss of value spread evenly over the first half of the asset's life has been assumed. (2) A point is reached when the value of an asset begins to deteriorate rather rapidly. A greater amount of time is lost in breakdowns or in maintenance or in both; new parts are required; even when repaired, the old asset is not as efficient as a new one. Finally, the asset is retired even though it maintains some productive value. A 65 percent loss of value spread evenly over the second half of the asset's live and 10 percent value remaining at the time of retirement have been assumed.

‡ U.S. Treasury Department data (1964) on average life of various kind of assets were used, and it was assumed that all assets in a particular category lasted exactly the average.

Table A.3.　East Pakistan 1964–65 Supply and Demand

Sector	Production	Foreign imports CIF	Duty on imports	Trade margin on imports	Transport margin on imports	Imports at purchasers' prices	Regional imports CIF
1. Rice	8,229.0	36.2		16.7	1.4	54.3	13.8
2. Wheat	15.2	49.1		17.9		67.0	5.7
3. Jute	1,201.4						
4. Cotton	7.0	3.3	0.3	0.2	0.1	3.9	81.3
5. Tea	231.8						
6. Other agric.	7,049.9	90.4	10.8	22.8	2.5	126.5	181.9
7. Sugar	562.2						0.4
8. Edible oils	447.5	126.2	59.3	69.3	5.2	260.0	16.1
9. Tobacco	194.1	0.2	0.6	0.1		0.9	41.9
10. Other food	256.7	1.0	1.1	.5	0.1	2.7	2.8
11. Cotton text.	1,142.7	17.1	9.2	1.7	.4	28.4	254.5
12. Jute text.	641.3						
13. Other text.	538.5	12.4	22.3	5.8	.4	40.9	7.4
14. Paper	212.6	14.6	11.2	1.9	.6	28.3	46.9
15. Leather	96.3	0.6	0.3	0.1		1.0	4.0
16. Rubber	17.1	6.6	2.7	6.8	.6	16.7	6.8
17. Fertilizer	57.5	8.6		0.2	1.0	9.8	
18. Other chem.	308.3	143.7	58.9	53.7	5.2	261.5	52.4
19. Cement	183.8	64.3	34.7	6.4	13.5	118.9	0.1
20. Basic metals	200.1	375.2	63.8	178.6	42.9	660.5	3.2
21. Metal prod.	203.0	40.8	26.9	8.6	3.2	79.5	13.9
22. Machinery	132.5	411.5	51.4	275.9	38.9	777.7	38.3
23. Transport eq.	58.0	139.7	17.5	101.6	5.3	264.1	12.9
24. Wood, etc.	176.2	1.4	1.3	0.4	0.1	3.2	
25. Const., houses	981.6						
26. Const., buildings	543.2						
27. Other const.	1,034.0						
28. Misc. manuf.	191.1	36.1	22.0	30.7	1.8	90.6	68.7
29. Coal, etc.		122.9	70.0	41.1	20.4	254.4	3.4
30. Elec. and gas	164.9						
31. Transport	1,211.3	36.3				36.3	
32. Trade	2,408.3						
33. Housing	1,099.6						
34. Government	797.9						
35. Services	1,050.7	5.3				5.3	
Total	31,645.3	1,743.5	464.3	841.0	143.6	3,192.4	856.4

Trade margin	Transport margin	Regional imports at purchasers' prices	Total supply	Intermediate deliveries	Inputs to processing of imported wheat	Trade and transport margins on imports	Consumption
8.4	0.6	22.8	8,306.1	1,095.5			7,210.6
0.5		6.2	88.4	27.6			60.8
			1,201.4	237.2			26.5
30.1	3.2	114.6	125.5	131.0			
			231.8	4.0			32.6
74.0	7.9	263.8	7,440.2	2,538.5			4,723.8
		0.4	562.6	36.3			516.7
2.6	0.6	19.3	726.8	53.6			668.6
5.8	1.2	48.9	243.9				242.8
1.1	0.1	4.0	263.4	3.1			248.9
18.0	5.5	278.0	1,449.1	555.7			871.1
			641.3	38.7			2.0
0.6	0.1	8.1	587.5	194.3			321.8
4.0	2.7	53.6	294.5	80.1			117.8
0.6	0.1	4.7	102.0	9.4			55.4
.8	.4	8.0	41.8	14.8			26.4
			67.3	69.6			
5.8	1.2	59.4	629.2	252.6	0.3		325.2
		0.1	302.8	322.7			
0.3	0.2	3.7	864.3	357.4			
1.7	.5	16.1	298.6	147.4			142.1
2.1	1.7	42.1	952.3	107.3	.9		185.0
0.7	0.6	14.2	336.3	16.3			19.6
			179.4	16.9			133.9
			981.6	323.2			
			543.2				
			1,034.0				
6.6	2.3	77.6	359.3	76.9			246.1
0.4	0.3	4.1	258.5	155.9			100.2
			164.9	107.6			57.3
			1,247.6	758.9	2.5	172.8	313.4
			2,408.3	1,413.6	8.0	986.7	
			1,099.6				1,099.6
			797.9	74.7			723.2
			1,056.0	80.0			976.0
164.1	29.2	1,049.7	35,887.4	9,300.8	18.4	1,159.5	19,447.4

Table A.3. (*continued*)

Sector	Stock changes	Gross invest-ment	Net invest-ment	Replace-ment	Foreign exports FOB	Regional exports CIF of other region	Total demand
1. Rice							8,306.1
2. Wheat							88.4
3. Jute	104.4				833.3		1,201.4
4. Cotton	−10.3				4.8		125.5
5. Tea					10.0	185.2	231.8
6. Other agric.	39.1				90.7	48.1	7,440.2
7. Sugar	2.0					7.6	562.6
8. Edible oils	4.4				0.2		726.8
9. Tobacco	0.2					0.9	243.9
10. Other food	11.4						263.4
11. Cotton text.	10.4				5.4	6.5	1,449.1
12. Jute text.	214.5				282.2	103.9	641.3
13. Other text.	40.0				18.9	12.5	587.5
14. Paper	5.2				5.5	85.9	294.5
15. Leather	2.3				12.4	22.5	102.0
16. Rubber	0.6						41.8
17. Fertilizer	−4.4				2.1		67.3
18. Other chem.	18.6				0.7	31.8	629.2
19. Cement	−19.9						302.8
20. Basic metals	506.9						864.3
21. Metal prod.		9.0	5.4	3.6	.1		298.6
22. Machinery	26.9	631.8	379.1	252.7	.4		952.3
23. Transport eq.		300.0	129.0	171.0	.4		336.3
24. Wood, etc.	21.7	6.9	4.1	2.8			179.4
25. Const., houses		658.4	658.4				981.6
26. Const., buildings		543.2	456.3	86.9			543.2
27. Other const.		1,034.0	713.5	320.5			1,034.0
28. Misc. manuf.	4.1				1.0	31.2	359.3
29. Coal, etc.	2.4						258.5
30. Elec. and gas							164.9
31. Transport							1,247.6
32. Trade							2,408.3
33. Housing							1,099.6
34. Government							797.9
35. Services							1,056.0
Total	980.5	3,183.3	2,345.8	837.5	1,268.1	536.1	35,887.4

Table A.4. West Pakistan 1964–65 Supply and Demand

Sector	Production	Foreign imports CIF	Duty on imports	Trade margin on imports	Transport margin on imports	Imports at purchasers' prices	Regional imports CIF
1. Rice	1,101.9						
2. Wheat	2,580.5	594.2		189.2		783.4	
3. Jute							
4. Cotton	1,275.3	9.4	.9	0.7	0.3	11.3	
5. Tea	95.6						185.2
6. Other agric.	9,792.0	198.3	23.8	50.0	5.5	277.6	48.1
7. Sugar	2,088.4	46.1	28.6	118.2	3.9	196.8	7.6
8. Edible oils	1,097.7	131.6	61.9	72.2	5.4	271.1	
9. Tobacco	761.1	0.7	1.9	0.3	0.1	3.0	0.9
10. Other food	183.1	6.2	6.7	3.0	.3	16.2	
11. Cotton text.	2,553.2	7.0	3.8	0.7	.2	11.7	6.5
12. Jute text.							103.9
13. Other text.	781.5	89.1	160.4	41.6	2.9	294.0	12.5
14. Paper	186.8	39.1	30.1	5.1	1.5	75.8	85.9
15. Leather	344.7	5.8	3.2	0.6	0.2	9.8	22.5
16. Rubber	57.7	63.2	25.9	64.9	5.9	159.9	
17. Fertilizer	91.2	1.8		0.1	0.2	2.1	
18. Other chem.	473.3	330.7	135.6	123.6	12.0	601.9	31.8
19. Cement	653.8	22.8	12.3	2.3	4.8	42.2	
20. Basic metals	501.3	627.9	106.7	298.8	71.8	1,105.2	
21. Metal prod.	508.6	59.6	39.3	12.6	4.6	116.1	
22. Machinery	649.1	852.7	106.6	571.7	80.6	1,611.6	
23. Transport eq.	821.5	397.4	49.7	289.0	15.0	751.1	
24. Wood, etc.	115.1	4.1	3.9	1.2	0.4	9.6	
25. Const., houses	972.4						
26. Const., buildings	726.9						
27. Other const.	2,055.1						
28. Misc. manuf.	183.4	103.7	63.3	88.1	5.2	260.3	31.2
29. Coal, etc.	640.3	79.4	45.3	26.6	13.1	164.4	
30. Elec. and gas	561.2						
31. Transport	2,148.5	51.6				51.6	
32. Trade	4,370.2						
33. Housing	1,090.2						
34. Government	1,823.5						
35. Services	2,272.3	4.5				4.5	
Total	43,557.4	3,726.9	909.9	1,960.5	233.9	6,831.2	536.1

Table A.4. (*continued*)

Sector	Trade margin	Trans- port margin	Regional imports at purchasers' prices	Total supply	Inter- mediate deliveries	Inputs to processing of imported wheat
1. Rice				1,101.9	104.7	
2. Wheat				3,363.9	637.6	
3. Jute						
4. Cotton				1,286.6	956.1	
5. Tea	83.9	1.3	270.4	366.0	75.9	
6. Other agric.	33.5	1.3	82.9	10,152.5	3,615.8	
7. Sugar	0.5	0.1	8.2	2,293.4	13.4	
8. Edible oils				1,368.8	164.7	
9. Tobacco	.2		1.1	765.2		
10. Other food				199.3	17.1	
11. Cotton text.	3.5	.1	10.1	2,575.0	859.8	
12. Jute text.	5.0	1.1	110.0	110.0	89.4	5.4
13. Other text.	8.0	0.3	20.8	1,096.3	318.5	
14. Paper	24.8	1.2	111.9	374.5	159.9	
15. Leather	19.2	1.1	42.8	397.3	84.4	
16. Rubber				217.6	106.0	
17. Fertilizer				93.3	105.6	
18. Other chem.	10.6	0.7	43.1	1,118.3	492.6	
19. Cement				696.0	794.7	
20. Basic metals				1,606.5	1,054.0	
21. Metal prod.				624.7	505.0	
22. Machinery				2,260.7	352.8	
23. Transport eq.				1,572.6	544.1	
24. Wood, etc.				124.7	1.9	
25. Const., houses				972.4	158.6	
26. Const., buildings				726.9		
27. Other const.				2,055.1		
28. Misc. manuf.	4.4	.8	36.4	480.1	53.5	
29. Coal, etc.				804.7	719.7	2.4
30. Elec. and gas				561.2	440.9	8.0
31. Transport				2,200.1	973.6	45.8
32. Trade				4,370.2	2,333.0	72.3
33. Housing				1,090.2		
34. Government				1,823.5	165.8	
35. Services				2,276.8	295.5	
Total	193.6	8.0	737.7	51,126.3	16,194.6	133.9

Trade and transport margins on imports	Consumption	Stock change	Gross invest- ment	Net invest- ment	Replace- ment	Foreign exports FOB	Regional exports CIF of other region	Total demand
	830.7	30.0				122.7	13.8	1,101.9
	2,601.0	117.6				2.0	5.7	3,363.9
		−67.0				316.2	81.3	1,286.6
	287.4	2.7						366.0
	6,142.1	31.2				181.5	181.9	10,152.5
	2,270.5	4.2				4.9	0.4	2,293.4
	1,179.3	8.6				0.1	16.1	1,368.8
	722.0	1.3					41.9	765.2
	175.2	0.6				3.6	2.8	199.3
	1,148.9	37.1				274.7	254.5	2,575.0
	2.0	8.5				4.7		110.0
	552.0	185.3				33.1	7.4	1,096.3
	161.1	6.4				0.2	46.9	374.5
	235.0	17.6				56.3	4.0	397.3
	62.7	40.0				2.1	6.8	217.6
		−12.7				0.4		93.3
	535.8	20.1				17.4	52.4	1,118.3
		−103.4				4.6	0.1	696.0
		544.6				4.7	3.2	1,606.5
	99.1	−20.0	20.0	11.8	8.2	6.7	13.9	624.7
	146.8	100.0	1,609.0	949.3	659.7	13.8	38.3	2,260.7
	111.5	300.0	600.0	216.0	384.0	4.1	12.9	1,572.6
	98.4	9.0	15.0	8.8	6.2	0.4		124.7
			813.8	813.8				972.4
			726.9	603.3	123.6			726.9
			2,055.1	1,418.0	637.1			2,055.1
	288.7	15.3				53.9	68.7	480.1
	100.1	−52.4				31.5	3.4	804.7
	112.3							561.2
241.9	938.8							2,200.1
1,964.9								4,370.2
	1,090.2							1,090.2
	1,657.7							1,823.5
	1,981.3							2,276.8
2,206.8	23,530.6	1,224.6	5,839.8	4,021.0	1,818.8	1,139.6	856.4	51,126.3

Appendix B: Two Sensitivity Tests

Interpretation of the results of any empirical analysis is aided by knowledge of the sensitivity of those results—both general and particular—to possible errors in the estimation of parameters and exogenous variables. Two sensitivity tests are reported in this appendix. The first is designed to determine the sensitivity of the product-or-import decision in each manufacturing sector to possible errors in the estimation of cost parameters for that sector. The second is designed to measure the sensitivity of the set of optimal activities that constitute the basic solution to possible errors in the estimation of certain important exogenous variables.

The first sensitivity test uses the simplex criteria and shadow prices to determine the percentage by which the marginal cost of production differs from the marginal cost of importing in the Basic Solution. If for a particular manufacturing sector supply is obtained by production, it follows from the properties of the dual problem—see section 4.2.—that the shadow price of the product (π) will be equal to the marginal cost of production (mc_1). The simplex criterion of the excluded export activity (s) is the cost that would be incurred were that activity introduced at unit level. But when the import activity is introduced, the production activity will be reduced. The simplex criterion will then equal the marginal cost of importing (mc_2) less the cost (q) that will be saved by reducing production. Because production will be decreased by more than a unit when importing is increased by a unit, the cost q will be greater than the marginal cost of production. Therefore, the ratio:

$$P = 100 \, s/\pi = 100 \, (mc_2 - q)/\pi < (mc_2 - mc_1)/\pi$$

provides a lower limit to the percentage by which the estimate of the relative costs of production and importing, measured at the shadow prices of the basic solution, could be in error without affecting the optimality of the production decision.

The test may be carried out whether it is the production activity, the foreign import activity, or the regional import activity that is included in the basic solution as the source of supply. Each excluded activity is compared with the included activity by computing the P ratio of the absolute value of the simplex criteria of the excluded activity to the shadow price of the product. When there is more than one source of supply for a product, each source of supply will have the same marginal cost and any excluded source of supply can be compared with any of the included activities.

For the manufacturing sectors of East and West Pakistan, respectively, the P ratios have been computed for excluded activities and are shown in Tables B.1 and B.2. P ratios for sources of supply included in the basic solution are denoted by 0 in the tables.

The interpretation of the P ratios is simple: a high P ratio implies that the source of supply decision is relatively insensitive to errors of cost estimation; a low P ratio implies that the source of supply decision is relatively sensitive to errors of cost estimation. However, there seems to be no way in which the P ratios can be used to establish any sort of rigorous statistical confidence intervals.

Table B.1. Marginal Supply Cost Comparisons, East Pakistan

Sector	Production	P ratios of foreign import	Regional import
7. Sugar	253.5		
8. Edible oils		9.3	15.1
9. Tobacco	a	a	a
10. Other food	41.4		
11. Cotton text.		19.1	41.6
13. Other text.			a
14. Paper	103.3		
15. Leather		304.0	
16. Rubber		44.8	6.9
17. Fertilizer		117.5	26.3
18. Other chem.		296.4	92.9
19. Cement		51.5	27.3
20. Basic metals		54.3	62.8
21. Metal prod.		11.1	
22. Machinery		52.3	10.9
23. Transport eq.		47.9	21.3
24. Wood, etc.	147.6		28.6
28. Misc. manuf.		36.7	4.1
29. Coal, etc.		65.4	13.5

[a] P ratios cannot be computed when shadow prices are negative (see Table 4.8).

A ranking of the *P* ratios would correspond roughly to the priority rankings obtained in Chapter 5. Where the produce-or-import choice is insensitive to errors in cost estimates, it will also be insensitive to changes in the costs of resources. A few specific points regarding the *P* ratios deserve comment.

1. For the fertilizer sector, the source of supply for both regions in the basic solution is East Pakistan production. The *P* ratio for foreign importing of fertilizer is quite high in both regions, indicating that foreign importing would be preferable to domestic production only if the cost estimates for the fertilizer sector used in this study have large errors. The *P* ratios of production in the West and of regional importing in the East, however, are not large. Given the poor quality of the data used in estimating fertilizer production costs, the desirability of production in the West cannot be ruled out.

2. There are several sectors for which production takes place in both regions in the basic solution. For these sectors the *P* ratio of foreign imports is usually a good deal higher than the *P* ratio for regional imports. Again, some confidence can be placed in the result that domestic production is desirable, although the regional location of production is subject to question.

181

Table B.4. **Estimates Used and Limits of the Toleration Range for Certain Exogenous Variables of the Basic Solution, West Pakistan** (million rupees)

	Estimate	Upper limit	Lower limit
Base year investment from			
21. Metal prod.	20.0	457.6	− 7.9
22. Machinery	1,609.0	1,943.7	1,587.7
23. Transport eq.	600.0	853.6	581.6
24. Wood, etc.	15.0	130.6	− 75.2
25. Const., housing	813.8	2,519.1	530.1
26. Const., buildings	726.9	1,137.4	686.5
27. Other const.	2,055.1	2,243.3	2,034.0
Plan period increment to replacement from			
21. Metal prod.	7.2	35.1	− 430.4
22. Machinery	578.5	599.8	243.8
23. Transport eq.	336.8	355.2	83.2
24. Wood, etc.	5.3	95.5	− 110.3
25. Const., housing			
26. Const., buildings	108.3	148.7	− 302.2
27. Other const.	558.7	579.8	370.5
Plan period increment to government expenditures	828.9	921.3	− 50.7

Appendix C: Some Limitations of the Model

Were an analysis of the sort presented in this study to be undertaken by a planning authority and used in plan formulation, certain limitations of the model could be eliminated. The purpose of this appendix is to point out briefly those limitations that might be corrected with a greater investment of research resources than has been available for this study.

1. The results the model yields are based upon a weak set of data. Cost estimates for some sectors are obtained from observations of a small set of firms, and in some cases it has been necessary to fill in for missing data by rather arbitrary methods. The data that are (probably) least reliable are fixed capital costs, working capital costs, and import costs. Nonetheless, most of the data have the attribute of having been estimated in a consistent fashion; at least the data set has few, if any, internal contradictions. In Appendix B some sensitivity analysis was undertaken that allows identification of those industries where misspecification of costs will affect the production or import decision (See MacEwan 1968 for a complete description of how the data were prepared).

2. Several of the decision variables of the model are aggregates of many actual decision variables. The results obtained for residual sectors—other food, other textiles, other chemicals, and miscellaneous manufacturing—are of very little use in formulating policy. It would be a significant improvement to the model to further disaggregate these and some of the other sectors. However, a model of this sort cannot be expected to yield precise industrial policies. Project analyses cannot be replaced by general equilibrium analysis, and increasing disaggregation should not be allowed to become a fetish.

3. It would be a useful addition to the model to allow consideration of alternative techniques of production in some of the sectors having relatively homogenous products. Such a modification would bring the model closer to an accurate simulation of the actual substitution possibilities in the economy. To introduce alternative production activities would require the use of data from other countries or data from project proposals. In either case it would be necessary to depart from the procedure that has been adhered to consistently in the study of using actual observations on the Pakistan economy.

4. There is a great need for more analysis of the labor requirement problems of the Pakistan economy, and it would be useful to include such analysis as part of this study. A relatively simple but interesting exercise would be to estimate labor requirements of each sector—either from Pakistan data or international data—and compute the employment implications of alternative development programs. A more difficult, but also more useful, extension of the model would be to include skilled labor requirements as explicit constraints. But until more data becomes available, both on demand and supply of different skills in the Pakistan economy, such an exercise would be strictly illustrative. It would be advisable, however, in attempting to make any planning use of the results of this study, at least to make a casual appraisal of the skilled labor requirements and training contribution of different industries, because there is no doubt that skilled labor shortages constitute a bottleneck for development in Pakistan.

5. The treatment of nonfoodgrain agricultural production and the agricultural

production limits in the model could be improved. A weakness of the model is its sensitivity to the level of the agricultural production limits. One possible improvement would be to specify rising costs rather than an absolute limit to agricultural production. The empirical basis of a theoretically more accurate specification of agriculture would, however, be quite weak.

6. One way to reduce the sensitivity of the model to the agricultural production limits would be to employ a more sophisticated treatment of consumption. Rather than specifying exact consumption proportions, it might be better to allow consumption proportions to vary within some narrow range and to add a constraint forcing the parts of the consumption bundle to sum to the total. That method would avoid the empirical and computational problems of explicitly introducing price elasticities, but would allow the consumption bundle to vary somewhat as relative prices change.

7. Another modification of the model that would reduce its sensitivity to peculiarities of particular parts of the economy would be to make the welfare function nonlinear. There is no doubt that the linear welfare function used does not accurately reflect political preferences. It would be more realistic to reduce the relative value of increments to consumption in a region as consumption in that region rises relative to consumption in the other region. Introducing a nonlinear welfare function would involve computational difficulties, but not insurmountable ones.

8. Another part of the model where nonlinearities might usefully be introduced would be in the specification of foreign exchange earning possibilities. For some of the important exports—especially jute and jute textiles—it would be interesting to experiment with a falling export demand function. It should be pointed out, however, that by systematic variation of the fixed export limits, it has been possible to discern most of the effects that would be brought about by an alternative specification of export demand.

9. Another shortcoming of resource supply specification in the model is the failure to take into account the interindustry differences in savings propensities. There is no doubt that a complete study of savings would reveal different rates of savings in different sectors and different taxation possibilities in different sectors. Such findings might lead to important changes in the industrial priorities program that has been obtained. Complete lack of data has prevented a more meaningful treatment of savings in this study.

10. In the treatment of capital requirements, the model is weak in areas where extremely large, multipurpose investment projects have been or are being undertaken. The procedure used in estimating sectoral capital coefficients probably resulted in an understatement of total capital requirements because projects such as Tarbela Dam in West Pakistan and the Sea Walls in East Pakistan were not accurately accounted for. The best procedure would be to specify those very large projects as exogenous to the model.

Notes

1. Setting Industrial Priorities

1. Pakistan is unique in its regional division into two districts sharing the population on a 55:45 basis and separated by 1000 miles of foreign territory. (For trade purposes the relevant distance is the 3000 miles that separate the major ports of the two regions.)

2. There is also the problem of skilled labor requirements (see Chapter 2).

3. The rise was steady over the period. Pakistan received in per capita terms about five times as much aid as India in the same period.

4. A Prebisch-type argument appears appropriate.

5. Data for 1967–68 have become available since this was written. For West Pakistan wheat, the breakthrough now seems real rather than anticipated. West Pakistan wheat production for 1967–68 was 43 percent above the previous peak of 1964–65.

6. It must be pointed out that if the foodgrains programs are successful in getting the farmers to adopt modern agricultural techniques for rice and wheat, there should be some spill-over effect to the cultivation of other crops.

7. This rural-urban differential is not especially large when compared with other countries. The rural-urban differential which emerges from a comparison of the Khan (1967b) and Bose (1968) studies is a good deal larger.

8. According to the present Planning Commission's estimates, per capita income was 34 percent higher in West than in East Pakistan in 1964–65. My estimate shows the per capita income in the West as 45 percent higher for that year (see Table 4.3). Neither the Planning Commission's estimates of disparity nor my own takes into account the difference in the purchasing power of the rupee in the two regions. Ghafur (1967) has estimated the purchasing power to be 10 to 15 percent higher in the West than in the East; that is, things are even worse than they seem.

9. Very recently there has been an attempt in the Planning Commission and in the East Pakistan Planning Department to develop a more sophisticated approach to project analysis.

2. Foreign Exchange, Capital, and the Setting of Priorities

1. It should be pointed out that the modern surplus labor model is very much in the tradition of the classical models of Smith, Ricardo, and Marx. Surplus labor is Marx's "reserve army" under a new flag.

2. This version of the surplus labor argument portrays the industrial sector as adjusting the quantity of labor to the fixed wage. An alternative view is that, given the quantity of capital available in the industrial sector at any one time and given fixed proportions in industrial production functions, the quantity of labor required by the industrial sector will be determined. The wage would then be adjusted to bring forth that quantity of labor. The structural unemployment argument is explained by Eckaus (1955).

3. The controversy between Sen (1967a, 1967b) and Schultz (1967) regarding Schultz's interpretation (1964) of the 1918–19 Indian influenza epidemic brings out these points.

4. Even if the family-planning program is successful, it cannot be expected to effect a decline in the labor supply for at least fifteen years. In fact, the short run effect of the family-planning program may be a larger labor force, since women will be released from the burdens of pregnancy and child rearing.

5. An argument could be made that labor requirements should be taken into account as benefits, since unemployment is such a serious social problem in a labor surplus economy. The plans of both Pakistan and India imply that such an approach would be desirable; however, it has not been done in this study. Weisskopf (1966), in developing a similar model for the Indian economy, raises this issue, but he also does not construct his model to take into account the employment benefits of alternative programs.

6. The technical developments in the production of jute substitutes has, according to Reddaway (1962), kept the world jute market static. Reddaway's conclusion for India is probably valid for Pakistan as well: there is little likelihood of a large expansion of jute sales. In the case of cotton textiles, trade barriers and competition from other underdeveloped countries, which are trying to build their own economies on textiles, limit the opportunities for export expansion.

7. Another constraint to export expansion is port capacity. The port capacity constraint would, in the same way as the marketing constraint, be partially commodity specific and partially a general constraint.

8. The model formulated in Chapter 3 is based on the supposition that funds are channeled through the government. So long as the domestic savings constraint is a limit to growth in the model, foreign funds are used to supplement domestic savings (see Section 3.9).

9. In this study there is no consideration of choice among alternative techniques of production of a single product. Except in the foodgrains sectors, the only choice in each sector is the choice of source of supply: production, import from the other region, or import from abroad. In foodgrain sectors a choice between techniques is not considered, but the model does determine the degree of intensity of operation of the modern techniques (see Section 3.10).

10. The capital and foreign exchange intensity of a production activity is not completely determined by the source of supply choices in other sectors. First, different sectors require different noncompetitive imports. Second, there are certain important items, that is, services, that must be produced domestically and that are used differently by different sectors.

11. An isoconsumption line derived from the linear programming model of Chapter 3 would consist of many flat facets, rather than being continuous like the curve in Figure 2.1.

12. By "balanced" is meant expansion or contraction of the already operating production and trade activities.

13. Since convexity is assumed, the unbalanced expansion which takes place with both types of movement along the consumption frontier necessarily carries with it a rise in the marginal cost of further expansion. (In the region in which consumption is declining, the marginal cost of expansion falls.) This is reflected in that the consumption frontier is concave with respect to the origin.

3. A Multisectoral Regional Planning Model for the Pakistan Economy

1. While it would be interesting to determine the 1964–65 to 1974–75 time paths of variables, it does not seem essential to do so in order to deal with the problems posed in this study. To undertake a dynamic model—such as those of Eckaus and Parikh (1968); Bruno, Fraenkel, and Dougherty (1968); or Manne and Weisskopf (1968)—would involve first of all a tremendous computational cost. However, the issue is not only a computational one. A dynamic model requires many assumptions not needed in a comparative-static framework. The dynamic model requires explicit specification of the time path of exogenously determined variables and parameters. Results are usually quite sensitive to these specifications, and their empirical foundation may be quite weak.

2. Any error resulting from the exclusion of cottage activity will be small to the extent that the primary resources absorbed by the expansion of cottage industry are offset by the resources generated by that expansion.

3. Since population change is exogenous to the model, the welfare function may alternatively be written as the unweighted sum of total consumption in the two regions, $W = c^e + c^w$.

4. This is a result of working in purchasers' prices.

5. While these balances must hold as identities, it is not necessary for the economy to use its entire savings ability or foreign exchange earning ability (see Section 3.10).

6. It should be pointed out that the Khan-MacEwan sector classification was developed for the sort of exercise being undertaken here. It was the result of discussions with many persons in the Planning Commission and Regional Planning Departments and in the Pakistan Institute of Development Economics. An attempt was made to arrive at a sector classification that would present as few barriers as possible to the users of the tables.

7. It is this dual role, of course, which lies at the base of the Harrod-Domar model phenomenon.

8. The stock-flow conversion factor has an important interpretation in the dual problem. It can be viewed as the rate of return on capital (see Section 4.2).

9. That this is so can be easily derived from the commodity balance equations. Base year investments by sector of origin are shown in Tables A.3 and A.4.

10. This is a more serious simplification of reality than the assumption of proportionality between current inputs and outputs. It is one thing to argue that making a product requires certain inputs regardless of how it is made, and quite another to argue that the product will be made in only one way.

11. The holding of stocks for speculative purposes is not included here, since it is essentially a short-run, unstable phenomenon. Neither is the need for a wages fund considered. This might be of some importance in agricultural sectors, however (see Sen 1964).

12. It might be argued that it would be just as satisfactory to include a stock charge to import activities as well as to producing activities. This is undesirable because part of the stock required for this purpose would be charged against the producer and part

charged against the user. It seems better to allocate the entire charge to the user. Also, lack of direct estimates of inventories of imported items rules out the procedure.

13. There is, of course, some controversy over whether or not a linear relationship is appropriate. It is often argued that inventories should increase only in proportion to the square root of sales. See Baumol (1961), for example. Sen (1964), however, has shown that the square root rule is a rather special case, and the linear assumption is no less plausible.

14. Estimation of noncompetitive import coefficients and import costs is discussed in MacEwan (1968). It should be emphasized that the estimation of the noncompetitive import coefficients involved considerable subjective judgment. Errors, however, should not greatly affect the general results. More serious is the very weak basis of the import cost estimates. When the importance of these estimates to the results of the study is considered, it should probably be concluded that herein lies the weakest empirical link in the study.

15. This certainly seems an improvement over the sometimes used alternative of precisely specifying exports and thereby eliminating a choice.

16. Some qualification is necessary, at least in the case of East Pakistan. Conversations with agronomists in East Pakistan revealed that the new seed varieties are not unequivocally superior to the indigenous varieties. The main problem is that the new varieties require a longer growing season. In some areas where two crops may be obtained with traditional varieties, only one crop can be obtained with the new ones. Since multiple cropping is so important in East Pakistan, that factor cannot be overlooked. It is not unlikely that new varieties will be developed that have both a high yield and a short growing season. Nonetheless, the long growing season of the new varieties is one of the reasons a generally lower level of success of new techniques has been projected for the East.

17. This is not to imply that peasant farmers will not make economic decisions. For Pakistan (see Falcon 1964) as for elsewhere, there is strong evidence to the contrary. Nonetheless, proper economic decisions with regard to new techniques require an understanding of them and a knowledge of the possibilities they represent. Even in countries where the level of education of the agricultural labor force is relatively high, there is a high payoff to special efforts aimed at spreading information about new techniques (see Griliches 1957).

18. Numerous technical reports and projection reports based on the technical reports are available containing data which may be used to define production functions for modern cultivation in each of the foodgrain crops. Of most use have been the following documents: Alim et al. (1966); Chandler (1966); Abbasi et al. (1966); Qureshi and Narvaez (1967); Qureshi and Narvaez (1966); Pacheco (1966); and Laird (1966). These reports were supplemented, as explained in MacEwan (1968), by data from Khan and MacEwan (1967a, 1967b). The data in these reports, however, are not of the form or quality that will allow sophisticated statistical estimation; only in one case is data presented on the results of an experiment where more than one input was systematically varied. Furthermore, the data in these reports are primarily experimental data, and different results would exist in the field. It is necessary, therefore, to pull together these data in a rather subjective manner in order to obtain production functions. Accord-

190

ingly, the significance of any results that are sensitive to the specific parameters should be discounted. Nonetheless, the production functions used here are probably reasonable descriptions of the possibilities represented by the new technology, and the general implications are meaningful.

19. Seed, bullock power, dung, and the base level of capital allow this.

20. Nothing has been said of working capital requirements, that is, requirements of inputs to agriculture, and they are not shown in the tables. Working capital requirements for each type of input are determined in accord with the method of Section 3.7.

21. Because the supply of land is fixed.

22. In the *Third Five-Year Plan* (Pakistan 1965a), the projected agricultural growth rate for the period 1965–1970 is 5.0 percent and for the period 1965–1985 is 5.6 percent. The upper limit of 5 percent used here for the nonfoodgrain agriculture sectors would seem consistent with the plan.

23. In the case of the basic metals industries, this constraint is extended to insure that import substitution comes from production within the region (see discussion of "Absolute Import Substitution").

24. It must be pointed out that to work only with increments somewhat simplifies computation.

25. That situation was due to certain import liberalization in that year.

26. In East and West Pakistan, 1964–65 imports of basic metals were Rs660 million and Rs1,105 million (at purchasers' prices), respectively. Therefore, the import substitution activities in the model have relatively low limits and only give an idea of what is desirable.

27. The justification of this procedure is parallel to that used in specifying noncompetitive trade.

4. Solution, Dual, and Reference Point

1. While the maximand of the linear programming model is, in fact, unidimensional, some other planning goals are included in the model as constraints. Most important is the specification of investment which insures satisfactory postplan period growth. The level of foreign capital inflow and of government consumption expenditures could also be viewed as planning goals. The choice of instruments will meet those absolutely specified goals as well as maximizing the increment to consumption.

2. No attempt is made here to rigorously derive the properties of the primal solution and the dual solution. For more rigorous analysis of this sort of problem, see Dorfman, Samuelson, and Solow (1958); Arrow (1954).

3. There are numerous other variables of the model which have not been mentioned here: investment, working capital, sectoral consumption, noncompetitive imports. The values of all these other variables, however, can be directly determined once choices have been made regarding production, competitive trade, exports, aggregate consumption, and the flow of funds. Explicit consideration of those other variables and their solution values does not add to an understanding of the industrial priority issues.

4. It should be recalled, however, that an industry may produce only for export, the other demands for its product being met by imports. Also, while an industry may be

of very high priority, its expansion may be limited through a close tie to an agricultural sector. While its production costs would be low, its supply price would be high and exporting would not take place. These kinds of cases require some qualification of the general statement made above regarding the relationship between export programs and priorities.

5. When this interpretation is employed, one of the resource costs is the cost of capital with the stock-flow conversion factor acting as the price or rate of return on capital.

6. The equilibrium obtained, however, while being Pareto optimal, is not equivalent to a competitive equilibrium. In a model which simulated competitive behavior (see Evans 1968, for example) tariffs would be defined as costs of production rather than as contributions to savings. A different result would accordingly be obtained.

7. Ideally, the sectoral studies would feed back to the multisectoral study, and so on (see Dantzig 1963 and Chenery and Clark 1959).

8. For any feasible solution to a linear programming problem it is possible to compute the change in the objective function that would result from raising the value of any activity by one unit and adjusting other activities to maintain feasibility. The change in the objective function is referred to as the simplex criterion. If the simplex criterion of an activity is positive, then that activity should be included in the solution. (For an activity already in the solution, the simplex criterion will be zero.) When an optimal solution is obtained, the simplex criteria for all excluded activities will be negative. That is, when an optimal solution is obtained the simplex criterion of an excluded activity is the reduction in the objective function—the cost—that would be incurred were that activity included in the solution.

9. The difference in estimates for 1964–65 is the source of some or the other differences between the terminal year implied by the solution and the plan. Most notable are the differences for exports, imports, and inflow of foreign funds. Plan base-year estimates of these variables were larger than the estimates used here. Since the plan increment to foreign funds inflow and the plan assumption regarding export growth were used in the basic solution, the solution necessarily yields smaller export and import increments.

10. Somewhat contrary results have been obtained by Khan (1967a) and Stern (1968). A comparison of their results with those obtained here will be given more attention in Chapter 7.

11. Some tea supply is imported but only as a supplement to the domestic production. While agricultural resources cannot be shifted among sectors, they can be shifted among products in the other agricultural sector (6). This will be seen to have some significance.

12. The expansion of these sectors is limited by demand rather than by cost factors because expansion ceases in the middle of a "step" and all demand possibilities are exhausted by domestic supply.

13. No special program is considered for East Pakistan wheat. As a result, West Pakistan wheat is much cheaper, and no expansion of wheat production in East Pakistan takes place. Further, West Pakistan wheat completely replaces foreign supply for the East.

14. That the rapid growth of these sectors has a strong impact upon the solution is seen in the very high shadow prices for their outputs (see Table 4.8). The very low rate of growth of the other construction sector should not go unmentioned. It seems likely that some error has been made either in specifying the base year level of operation of this sector or in specifying demand for its products. Therefore, little faith should be placed in the output figure for this sector. The effect upon industrial priorities does not seem to be great, however (see Appendix B).

15. Presenting shadow prices in terms of aggregate consumption simply involves a proportional transformation of the actual dual variables of the model. I think they are easier to read and interpret in the form in which they are presented here. This procedure will be followed throughout the study.

16. The question may arise about the reasons why the model does not operate to shift resources between the two regions to make the shadow price of each resource the same in both regions. It must be recalled that capital and foreign exchange cannot be independently shifted between the two regions; a transfer of one of these resources carries with it a transfer of the other. This is the case because, as explained in Chapter 2, capital and foreign exchange are not really independent resources: the basic resource which the model can shift between the two regions is the supply of funds, which consequently has only one shadow price for the nation.

17. Of course, it is the relationship between interregional trade costs and the production cost differential for these sectors which prevents trade. Nonetheless, the lower shadow price of capital in the West contributes to keeping the differential low (see pages 103–104).

18. Tea and other agriculture are exceptions. They have higher prices in the East because of the special production and import limits.

19. Fertilizer and electricity would be good examples of industries where the disequilibrium is a result of conscious policy.

20. While the shadow prices obtained from a solution to the model might be useful to planners in their sectoral and project analyses, these shadow prices would not be appropriate as signals to a competitively operating market. As pointed out, the dual does not simulate the operation of a competitive system, since tariffs enter the model as benefits rather than as costs. The cost of high-tariff imports is consequently low, sometimes even negative. Were the low shadow prices used in the market, the high tariffs could not be collected.

5. Resource Availabilities and Industrial Priorities

1. It should be recalled that the savings rate on value added in the tobacco products sector is 50 percent plus 50 percent of the savings rate on value added in other non-agricultural sectors (See Section 3.9).

2. It should be emphasized that this is a reflection of real phenomena and is not simply a result of the absolute limits on agricultural growth in the model. In the real economy the higher costs might be incurred by greater intensity of cultivation rather than by using foreign exchange directly. Nonetheless, the costs of agricultural goods would rise, and industrial priorities would be affected in the same way.

3. East Pakistan cotton textiles (11) are active in all solutions. No East to West trade, however, in cotton textiles is allowed due to product-mix considerations. Therefore, when West Pakistan does not produce cotton textiles, it imports them from abroad.

4. It should be added that production in these sectors has high noncompetitive import requirements and that the tariff rates on imports of these products are very high.

5. Actually, East continues to obtain a share of its paper supply from the West. Because of product-mix considerations, it must obtain most of its paper either from its own production or from abroad (see Section 3.11).

6. The switch away from agricultural exports is much more important in the West than in the East. Aside from a slight decline in exports of jute, the increase in the number of exporting sectors in East Pakistan is accounted for by a switch from a large export of other textiles to small exports from several other manufacturing sectors.

7. It is, however, interesting to note that the change in the growth rate is not proportional to the change in the savings rate as it would be in a simple one-sector model. The growth requires a shift toward domestic production of more capital intensive goods; hence, the aggregate capital-output ratio is not independent of the rate of growth.

8. Since there are no sector specific growth limits on nonfoodgrain agricultural exports, it was necessary to place some limit on jute exports in the East when the over-all limit was reduced to 6.5 percent to prevent other exports from being eliminated. In this low export growth solution, the foreign exchange earnings of jute and jute textiles in East Pakistan were not allowed to exceed the proportion of earnings for the region they constituted in the basic solution (85 percent).

9. When the 1974–75 level of foreign funds inflow is different from that of 1964–65, the adjustment is implicitly assumed to be spread over the entire intervening period in a roughly exponential manner.

10. The decline in foreign funds productivity that occurs at the beginning of the curve shown in Figure 5.1 occurs because the limit to cotton production in West Pakistan becomes binding at that point. However, since cotton exports may be replaced by other agriculture exports, there is little secondary impact upon funds productivity.

11. It would seem that aid would have a greater effect as the savings constraint becomes more important, since the availability of savings is affected both directly and indirectly by additional aid.

12. There is also a difference in the regional allocation of consumption which follows from the difference in capital and foreign exchange productivity. In solution 15/25 the incremental disparity ratio is 1.11 and in solution 8.5 it is 1.07. That is consistent with the observation that West Pakistan consumption is relatively more capital intensive.

13. The larger increment to consumption is combined with the smaller increment to income because of the difference in the savings rate.

14. In all of the groupings noncompetitive importing and production for noncompetitive regional export are ignored.

15. There are two special cases in group I and one in group V that require comment. Edible oils production is limited in the West by being tied to the cotton sector, and supplemental edible oils are imported from both abroad and the East. Therefore, the

simplex criteria of the import activities are zero and cannot be used to rank the sector. The cost of cutting the production of the sector back by one unit is, however, easily obtained, since it is equivalent to the shadow price of the constraint limiting the sector's output. For the jute textiles industry in the East, there is no alternative source of supply. The alternative to producing jute textiles is a higher availability of raw jute. The cost of cutting back jute textiles production can be computed from the shadow price on the sector specific limit on its foreign exchange earning, and it may thereby be compared with the other group I sectors. In group V, East Pakistan's leather sector produces in the basic solution to meet noncompetitive regional export requirements, and the simplex criteria of the production activity cannot be used for ranking. This sector was ranked against the other group V sectors in East Pakistan on the basis of the shadow prices of the constraints on their foreign exchange earning in the solution, in which the export growth rate was taken as 8.5 percent. In that solution, all of the group V sectors in East Pakistan produced in order to export, making this comparison possible.

16. See Appendix C for more on these and other qualifications.

17. Metal products and wood, cork, and furniture also deliver some capital goods, but in general their products are intermediate goods and consumption goods.

18. However, it does not follow automatically that the reduction in aid will have a greater impact on the scarcity of foreign exchange than on the scarcity of capital.

19. Other low priority sectors have some production in the basic solution—for noncompetitive regional export, for example—and their marginal cost of expanding production is not so easily determined.

20. The Khan-MacEwan average capital-output ratios were used in this study, but only as a basis for estimating incremental coefficients.

21. Failing to use incremental cost data is not a serious drawback in those two studies, since neither is directly concerned with long-term planning problems.

22. Tims ranks according to the benefits per unit of foreign exchange cost required in expansion. The benefits for different sectors were aggregated using the weighting of the Stern (1967) and Rasul (1966) input-output tables which were the basis of the Tims study.

23. Of course, the conclusions which can be drawn about such a diverse sector as other chemicals are very limited.

24. However, even a wide error in the cost estimates would not justify foreign imports of fertilizer (see Appendix B for further discussion of the sensitivity of the results to cost estimation errors).

6. Agricultural Change and Industrial Planning

1. See Section 3.10 for a description of the production functions for modern cultivation. The Pakistan program seems to fit the prescription of Schultz (1964), who argues that a key to transforming agriculture is the creation of circumstances that will induce the use of modern inputs.

2. This classification of technical change can be viewed as roughly analogous to a Hicksian approach.

3. Several solutions could be obtained in a relatively short period of time using the parametric programming option of the basic linear programming program.

4. It should be recalled that no interregional trade in rice is allowed. To specify the model otherwise might have resulted in unrealistic trade in rice even at high levels of adoption of the new techniques. Furthermore, East Pakistan does not traditionally obtain rice from the West, but from Burma. Nonetheless, it would be an improvement in the model to allow some interregional trade in rice at the low levels of adoption of the new techniques.

5. Strong support for the neutrality of changes which directly save (or earn) foreign exchange can be inferred from the results obtained in section 5.2 above. It was found there that raising the limits to foreign exchange earning had very little effect on the relative scarcity of capital and foreign exchange, precisely because the foreign exchange earning effect was counterbalanced by the savings generation effect.

6. That is, were the level of success within about 25 percent of the level of success assumed in the basic solution, the results would not be seriously affected.

7. Interregional and Intersectoral Allocation

1. In spite of the concern with regional aspects of the plan, however, none of the formal planning models developed in the preparation of the Third Plan were formulated as regional models. See Tims (1968).

2. See Table 4.1 and Khan and Bergan (1966). Unofficial estimates differ widely about the degree of disparity in particular years, but all confirm the trend. See M. Anisur Rahman (1967) and Haq (1963).

3. These comparisons are made by M. Anisur Rahman (1967). It seems that only one index of development would show East Pakistan ahead: the 1960 Census (Pakistan 1961) showed a slightly higher level of literacy in the East.

4. Thus, the failure of East Pakistan to develop as rapidly as the West does not present a case like that of Southern Italy (see Chenery 1962) where a large inflow of government funds failed to stimulate development. A resource distribution policy as the one apparently followed by the Pakistan government might be justified as the appropriate means to attain most rapid national growth (see the argument offered by Hirschman 1959, regarding the need for unequal regional development). However, the Pakistan government certainly claims to be following a policy designed to bring about regional parity.

One other "resource" that is distributed very unequally between the two regions is political power. In 1960, out of a total of 2779 first-class officers in various central services, 87 percent were West Pakistanis (see Rahman 1967).

5. Prior to the creation of Pakistan, trade between the two regions of India which are now Pakistan was almost nil. In the early 1950s regional trade constituted about 15 percent of total imports, and in the mid 1960s regional trade had risen to almost 30 percent of total imports. However, in 1964–65 about two-thirds of interregional trade was agricultural goods and textiles (see Appendix A). Rahman (1963) and Islam (1963) provide analyses of the development of the trade ties between the two regions of Pakistan.

6. With the limits on production of agricultural products, expansion of the East necessarily requires import substitution for goods based on agricultural inputs. Edible oils must be obtained from abroad rather than from the West because there are special constraints limiting their production in the West. Within the range of the solutions considered, the same problem does not become so significant in the West.

7. The simplex criteria in Table 5.14 show that among importing industries these two industries would be the highest candidates for import substitution.

8. In 1964–65 rice and wheat constituted 40 percent of East Pakistan's consumption bundle while those commodities accounted for only 17 percent of consumption in West Pakistan. Even with the assumption of low incremental income elasticities, foodgrain consumption in the East will undoubtedly continue to be much larger than in the West for some time to come (see Tables 3.2 and 3.3 for the data).

9. That is, the rates of savings on value added in agriculture were set at 12 percent in the East and 15 percent in the West, and the rates of savings on value added in other sectors were set at 22 and 25 percent, respectively.

10. Khan, it should be remembered, deals only with the Third Plan period. The reduction in rice production costs will certainly be more important in the Fourth Plan period.

11. Stern used a two-sector optimizing model because he was concerned with long-run dynamic phenomena. He was forced to give up the sectoral in favor of the temporal distinctions.

8. Development Alternatives and Development Policy

1. The reader is advised that while this chapter does serve partially as "summary and conclusions," primary attention is given to issues of national policy. The interdependence between regional policy and comparative advantage is discussed in Chapter 7.

2. It is possible to divide the manufacturing industries into more categories on the basis of the alternative solutions (see Section 5.5). Nonetheless, this broad classification into three groups brings out the most important distinctions.

3. At the level of aggregation at which this study has been undertaken, the classification of sectors into capital goods, consumption goods, and intermediate goods is of questionable validity simply because many sectors include two or all three types of goods. Metal products, cotton textiles, and machinery are examples. One way to deal with this problem in discussing growth issues would be to use a set of input-output accounts to determine what part of each sector's output goes to intermediate, consumption, and investment uses (see Winston and MacEwan 1966).

4. Manne was dealing with a much more detailed specification of the capital goods sectors than has been employed here. He was therefore able to determine which particular parts of the capital goods sectors should and should not be developed. While his exercise again shows that to generalize about the comparative advantage of the capital goods sectors could be misleading, he does find a generally favorable outlook for those industries in Mexico.

197

5. In addition to demonstrating that economies of scale do not necessarily prohibit the development of certain industries in a poor country, Westphal's study brings out the point that economies of scale are important outside of the capital goods sectors—note his consideration of the petrochemicals industry. It is not difficult to think of several intermediate goods—fertilizer, paper, jute textiles, chemicals—and some consumption goods—sugar, cotton textiles—for which economies of scale are important.

6. Other limitations or qualifications of the approach are pointed out in Appendix C.

7. A study of Indian planning undertaken by Weisskopf (1967) provides an exception. Weisskopf distinguishes some 150 sectors.

8. That is, two sets of calculations were made. In the first, all benefits and costs of the production and foreign import activity for each sector were evaluated at the shadow prices obtained in the model. Whichever of those activities was included in the optimal solution necessarily had zero net benefit, whereas the other necessarily had negative net benefit. In the second calculation, the direct capital and foreign exchange costs were evaluated at model shadow prices; all other costs and benefits were evaluated at base-year prices. In choosing the industries to include in this exercise, an attempt was made to pick a few relatively interesting industries of various types, the costs and benefits of which were not complicated by special constraints.

References

Abbasi, Rasul B. M. et al. 1966. "Annual Progress Report on Accelerated Rice Research Program, West Pakistan, 1966." Government of West Pakistan, Lahore, Planning Cell, Agricultural Department (December 1966).

Alamgir, M. 1968. "The Domestic Prices of Imported Commodities in Pakistan: A Further Study." *Pakistan Development Review* (Spring 1968).

Alim, A., H. Zaman, and L. Johnson. (1966). "Progress Report on: Accelerated Rice Research Program of East Pakistan, January–August 1966." Tejgaon, Dacca, East Pakistan, Accelerated Rice Research Program, Agricultural Research Institute (September 24, 1966).

Arrow, K. J. 1954. "Import Substitution in Leontief Models." *Econometrica* (October 1954).

Bank of Israel. 1960. *Annual Report 1959.* Jerusalem.

Baumol, W. J. 1961. *Economic Theory and Operations Analysis.* Englewood Cliffs, New Jersey: Prentice-Hall.

Bose, S. R. 1968. "Trend of Real Income of the Rural Poor in East Pakistan, 1949–66: An Indirect Estimate." Karachi: Pakistan Institute of Development Economics Research Report Series, no. 68 (July 1968).

Bruno, M. 1966. "A Programming Model for Israel." In I. Adelman and E. Thorbecke, eds., *The Theory and Design of Economic Development.* Baltimore: The Johns Hopkins Press.

Bruno, M., M. Frankel and C. Dougherty. 1969. "Dynamic Input-Output, Trade and Development." In A. P. Carter and A. Brody, eds., *Application of Input-Output Analysis.* Amsterdam: North-Holland Publishing Co.

Bruton, H. J. and S. R. Bose. 1963. *The Pakistan Export Bonus Scheme.* Karachi: Pakistan Institute of Development Economics, Monographs in the Economics of Development, no. 11.

Chakravarty, S. and L. Lefeber. 1965. "An Optimizing Planning Model." *Economic Weekly* (February 1965).

Chandler, R. F. 1966. "Progress Report on: The Accelerated Rice Research Program of East Pakistan in Cooperation with the International Rice Research Institute." Karachi: Ford Foundation (February 12).

Chenery, H. B. 1962. "Development Policies for Southern Italy." *Quarterly Journal of Economics* (November 1962).

——— 1965. "Comparative Advantage and Development Policy." In *Surveys of Economic Theory, Growth and Development,* vol. II. New York: St. Martin's Press.

Chenery, H. B. and K. Kretschmer. 1956. "Resource Allocation for Economic Development." *Econometrica* (October 1956).

Chenery, H. B. and P. G. Clark. 1959. *Interindustry Economics.* London: John Wiley and Sons, Inc.

Chenery, H. B. and M. Bruno. 1962. "Development Alternatives in an Open Economy: The Case of Israel." *Economic Journal* (March 1962).

Chenery, H. B. and A. MacEwan. 1966. "Optimal Patterns of Growth and Aid: The Case of Pakistan." In I. Adelman and E. Thorbecke, eds., *The Theory and Design of Economic Development.* Baltimore: The Johns Hopkins Press.

Chenery, H. B. and A. M. Strout. 1966. "Foreign Assistance and Economic Development." *American Economic Review* (September 1966).

Clark, P. B. 1966. "A Study of Optimal Import Substitution Strategies for Nigeria." Paper presented to the Econometrica Society Meetings (December 1966).

Dantzig, G. B. 1963. *Linear Programming and Extensions.* Princeton, New Jersey: Princeton University Press.

Dorfman, R., P. A. Samuelson, and R. M. Solow. 1958. *Linear Programming and Economic Analysis.* New York: McGraw-Hill.

Eckaus, R. S. 1955. "The Factor Proportions Problem in Underdeveloped Areas." *American Economic Review* (September 1955).

Eckaus, R. S. and K. S. Parikh. 1968. *Planning for Growth: Multisectoral, Intertemporal Models Applied to India.* Cambridge, Mass.: Massachusetts Institute of Technology.

Evans, H. D. 1968. "A General Equilibrium Analysis of Protection: The Effects of Protection in Australia." Ph.D. dissertation, Harvard University.

Falcon, W. P. 1964. "Farmer Response to Price in a Subsistence Economy: The Case of West Pakistan." *American Economic Review* (May 1964).

Falcon, W. P. and C. H. Gotsch. 1968. "Lessons in Agricultural Development: Pakistan." In G. F. Papenek, ed., *Development Policy: Theory and Practice.* Cambridge, Mass.: Harvard University Press.

Fei, J. C. H. and G. Ranis. 1964. *Development of the Labor Surplus Economy.* Homewood, Illinois: Richard D. Irwin, Inc.

Ghafur, A. 1967. "A Comparison of the Interregional Purchasing Power of Industrial Wages in Pakistan." *Pakistan Development Review* (Winter 1967).

Glassburner, B. 1965. "The Balance of Payments and External Resources in Pakistan's Third Five-Year Plan. *Pakistan Development Review* (Spring 1965).

Griliches, Z. 1967. "Hybrid Corn: The Economics of Technological Change." *Econometrica* (October 1967).

Haq, M. 1963. *The Strategy of Economic Planning: A Case Study of Pakistan.* Karachi: Oxford University Press.

Haque, M. 1967. "Working Capital Requirements in Pakistan Manufacturing Industries." Karachi: Pakistan Institute of Development Economics, unpublished.

Hirschman, A. O. 1959. *The Strategy of Economic Development.* New Haven, Connecticut: Yale University Press.

Houthakker, H. S. 1957. "An International Comparison of Household Expenditure Patterns, Commemorating the Centenary of Engel's Law." *Econometrica* (October 1957).

Islam, N. 1963. "Some Aspects of Interwing Trade and Terms of Trade in Pakistan." *Pakistan Development Review* (Spring 1963).

Khan, A. R. 1963. "Import Substitution, Export Expansion and Consumption Liberalization: A Preliminary Report." *Pakistan Development Review* (Summer 1963).

—— 1967a. "A Multi-Sector Programming Model for Regional Planning in Pakistan." *Pakistan Development Review* (Spring 1967a).

—— 1967b. "What has been Happening to Real Wages in Pakistan?" *Pakistan Development Review* (Autumn 1967b).

Khan, A. R. and A. MacEwan. 1967a. "Regional Current Input-Output Tables for the East and West Pakistan Economies 1962–63." Pakistan Institute of Development Economics Research Report Series, no. 63 (December 1967).

—— 1967b. "A Multisectoral Analysis of Capital Requirements for Development Planning in Pakistan." *Pakistan Development Review* (Winter 1967).

Khan, T. M. and A. Bergan. 1966. "Measurement of Structural Changes in the Pakistan Economy: A Review of National Income Estimates, 1949–50 to 1963–64." *Pakistan Development Review* (Summer 1966).

Kindleberger, C. P. 1958. *Economic Development*. New York: McGraw-Hill.

Laird, R. J. 1966. "Report No. 3: Soil Fertility and Water Management." Government of West Pakistan, Lahore, Planning Cell, Agricultural Department (October 30, 1966).

Lewis, S. R. and R. Soligo. 1965. "Growth and Structural Change in Pakistan's Manufacturing Industry, 1954–1964." *Pakistan Development Review* (Spring 1965).

Lewis, S. R. and S. E. Guisinger. 1966. "Measuring Protection in a Developing Country: The Case of Pakistan." Project for Quantitative Research in Economic Development, Memorandum no. 20. Cambridge, Mass.: Harvard University.

Lewis, S. R. and S. M. Hussain. 1967. *Relative Price Changes and Industrialization in Pakistan, 1951–1964*. Monographs in the Economics of Development, no. 16. Karachi: Pakistan Institute of Development Economics.

Lewis, W. A. 1954. "Economic Development with Unlimited Supplies of Labor." *Manchester School* (May 1954).

Leontief, W. W. 1953. "Dynamic Analysis." In W. W. Leontief et al., *Studies in the Structure of the American Economy*. New York: Oxford University Press.

Manne, A. S. 1963. "Key Sectors in the Mexican Economy, 1960–70." In A. S. Manne and H. M. Markowitz, eds., *Studies in Process Analysis*. New York: John Wiley and Sons.

—— 1966. "Key Sectors in the Mexican Economy, 1962–72." In I. Adelman and E. Thorbecke, eds., *The Theory and Design of Economic Development*. Baltimore: The Johns Hopkins Press.

——, ed. 1967. *Investments for Capacity Expansion: Size, Location and Time Phasing*. London: George Allen and Unwin, Ltd.

Manne, A. S. and T. E. Weisskopf. 1969. "A Dynamic Multisectoral Model for India, 1967–75." In A. P. Carter and A. Brody, eds., *Application of Input-Output Analysis*. Amsterdam: North-Holland Publishing Co.

Marglin, S. A. 1967. *Public Investment Criteria: Benefit-Cost Analysis for Planned Growth*. London: George Allen and Unwin, Ltd.

Mason, E. S. 1966. *Economic Development in India and Pakistan*. Cambridge, Mass.: Center for International Affairs, Harvard University.

Meir, G. M. and R. E. Baldwin. 1957. *Economic Development*. New York: John Wiley and Sons, Inc.

Mellor, J. W. 1966. *The Economics of Agricultural Development*. Ithaca, New York: Cornell University Press.

Naqvi, S. N. H. 1966. "The Allocative Bias of Pakistan's Commercial Policy: 1953 to 1963." *Pakistan Development Review* (Winter 1966).

References

Narvaez, I. and O. Aresvik. 1966. "Projections for Wheat Yields, Wheat Production and Main Required Inputs in Order to Reach Self-Sufficiency from 1968 Onward." Government of West Pakistan, Lahore, Agricultural Department (November 11, 1966).

Pacheco, F. 1966. "Accelerated Crop Improvement Report No. 5 Plant Protection: Recommendations for Improving the Effectiveness of Plant Protection Research and Field Application in West Pakistan." Government of West Pakistan, Lahore, Planning Cell, Agricultural Department (October 30, 1966).

Pakistan. 1951. *Census of Pakistan 1951*. Office of the Census Commissioner, Karachi.

—— 1961. *Census of Pakistan 1961*. Office of the Census Commissioner, Karachi.

—— 1965a. *The Third Five-Year Plan (1965–1970)*. Planning Commission, Karachi.

—— 1965b. *Report of the Consistency Committee on the Third Five-Year Plan*. Planning Commission, Karachi.

—— 1966a. *Quarterly Survey of Current Economic Conditions 1963–64*. Central Statistical Office. Karachi.

—— 1966b. *Pakistan Statistical Yearbook 1964*. Central Statistical Office, Karachi.

—— 1966c. *New Index of Industrial Production*. Central Statistical Office, Karachi. Mimeographed.

—— 1966d. *Census of Manufacturing Industries in East Pakistan, 1962–63*. East Pakistan Bureau of Statistics, Dacca. Mimeographed.

—— 1966e. *Imports 1960–61 to 1964–65*. Industrial Development Bank of Pakistan, Karachi. Mimeographed.

—— 1966f. *Evaluation of the Second Five-Year Plan (1960–1965)*. Planning Commission, Karachi.

—— 1967a. *Monthly Statistical Bulletin*. Karachi, Central Statistical Office. 1967 and preceding years.

—— 1967b. *Evaluation of the First Year (1965–66) of the Third Five-Year Plan (1965–70)*. Planning Commission, Rawalpindi.

—— 1967c. *Pakistan Economic Survey 1966–67*. Ministry of Finance, Karachi.

—— 1967d. *Census of Manufacturing Industries in West Pakistan 1962–63*. West Pakistan Bureau of Statistics, Lahore, unpublished.

Pakistan Institute of Development Economics. 1967. *Population Projections for Pakistan, 1960–2000*. Karachi. Mimeographed.

Pal, M. 1964. "The Determinants of Domestic Prices of Imports." *Pakistan Development Review* (Winter 1964).

—— 1965. "Domestic Prices of Imports in Pakistan: Extensions of Empirical Findings." *Pakistan Development Review* (Winter 1965).

Papanek, G. F. 1967. *Pakistan's Development: Social Goals and Private Incentives*. Cambridge, Mass.: Harvard University Press.

Power, J. H. 1963. *"Industrialization in Pakistan: A Case of Frustrated Take-Off?" Pakistan Development Review* (Summer 1963).

Qureshi, S. A. and I. Narvaez. 1966. "Annual Technical Report on Accelerated Wheat Improvement Program, West Pakistan, 1965–66." Government of West Pakistan, Planning Cell, Agricultural Department (August 1966).

—— 1967. "Annual Technical Report: Accelerated Wheat Improvement Program,

West Pakistan, 1966–67." Government of West Pakistan, Lahore, Planning Cell, Agricultural Department (July 1967).

Rab, A. 1967. "Personal and Business Income Taxation in Pakistan." Ph.D. dissertation, Harvard University.

Radhu, G. M. 1964. "The Rate Structure of Indirect Taxes in Pakistan." *Pakistan Development Review* (Autumn 1964).

Rahman, M. Akhlaqur. 1963. *Partition, Integration, Economic Growth, and Interregional Trade: A Study of Interwing Trade in Pakistan: 1948–1959.* Karachi: Pakistan Institute of Development Economics Special Publications Series.

Rahman, M. Anisur. 1967. "East and West Pakistan: A Problem in the Political Economy of Planning." Economic Development Series, Report no. 59. Cambridge, Mass.: Center for International Affairs, Harvard University.

Rasul, G. 1966. West Pakistan Input-Output Table 1962–63. Typed. Karachi: Perspective Planning Section of the Pakistan Planning Commission (November 10, 1966).

Reddaway, W. B. 1962. *The Development of the Indian Economy.* Homewood, Illinois: Richard D. Irwin, Inc.

Sandee, J. A. 1960. *A Demonstration Planning Model for India.* New York: Asia Publishing House.

Schultz, T. W. 1964. *Transforming Traditional Agriculture.* New Haven: Yale University Press.

——— 1967. "Significance of India's 1918–19 Losses of Agricultural Labor: A Reply." *Economic Journal* (March 1967).

Sen, A. K. 1960. *Choice of Techniques.* Oxford: Basil Blackwell.

——— 1964. "Working Capital in the Indian Economy: A Conceptual Framework and Some Estimates." In P. N. Rosenstein-Rodan, ed., *Pricing Fiscal Policies.* Cambridge, Mass.: The M.I.T. Press.

——— 1966. "Peasants and Dualism with or without Surplus Labor." *Journal of Political Economy* (October 1966).

——— 1967a. "Surplus Labor in India: A Critique of Schultz's Statistical Test." *Economic Journal* (March 1967).

——— 1967b. "Surplus Labor in India: A Rejoinder." *Economic Journal* (March 1967).

Soligo, R. and J. J. Stern. 1955. "Tariff Protection, Import Substitution and Investment Efficiency." *Pakistan Development Review* (Summer 1965).

Stern, J. J. 1967. "Interindustry Relations in East Pakistan 1962–63." Pakistan Institute of Development Economics Research Report Series no. 62.

——— 1968. "Growth, Development and Regional Equity in Pakistan." Project for Quantitative Research in Economic Development, Economic Development Report no. 78, revised. Cambridge, Mass.: Harvard University (March 1968).

Stone, R. 1961. *Input-Output and National Accounts.* Paris: Organization for European Economic Cooperation.

Tendulkar, S. D. "Interaction between Domestic and Foreign Resources in Economic Growth: Some Experiments for India." Project for Quantitative Research for Economic Development, Economic Development Report no. 104. Cambridge, Mass.: Harvard University, July.

Tims, W. 1967. *Industrial Policy and Import Liabilities*. Rawalpindi: Pakistan Planning Commission.

———— 1968. *Analytical Techniques for Development Planning: A Case Study of Pakistan's Third Five-Year Plan*. Karachi: Pakistan Institute of Development Economics, Special Publications Series.

Tinbergen, J. 1956. *Economic Policy: Principles and Design*. Amsterdam: North-Holland Publishing Co.

———— 1958. *The Design of Development*. Baltimore: The Johns Hopkins Press.

Thomas, P. S. 1966. "Import Licensing and Import Liberalization in Pakistan." *Pakistan Development Review* (Winter 1966).

United States Treasury Department. 1964. *Depreciation Guidelines and Rules*. Publication no. 456, revised. Washington, D.C.: Government Printing Office.

Waterson, A. 1963. *Planning in Pakistan*. Baltimore: The Johns Hopkins University Press.

Weisskopf, T. E. 1967. "A Programming Model for Import Substitution in India." *Sankhya* (December 1967).

Westphal, L. E. 1968. "A Dynamic Multi-Sectoral Programming Model Featuring Economies of Scale." Ph.D. dissertation, Harvard University.

Winston, G. C. and A. MacEwan. 1966. "A Note on the Use Classification of Four Digit Industries or How to Call a Spade a Spade." *Pakistan Development Review* (Winter 1966).

Index